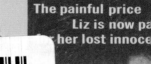

ELIZABETH TAYLOR

A Shining Legacy on Film

CINDY DE LA HOZ

Photographs from the
Joseph P. Cruz Collection

RUNNING PRESS
PHILADELPHIA • LONDON

To my girlfriends: I've been blessed with many great ones.
—CINDY DE LA HOZ

Books published by Running Press are available at special discounts for bulk
purchases in the United States by corporations, institutions, and other organizations.
For more information, please contact the Special Markets Department at the Perseus
Books Group, 2300 Chestnut Street, Suite 200, Philadelphia, PA 19103, or call (800)
810-4145, ext. 5000, or e-mail special.markets@perseusbooks.com.

ISBN 978-0-7624-4045-0
Library of Congress Control Number: 2012938583

E-book ISBN 978-0-7624-4517-2

9 8 7 6 5 4 3 2 1
Digit on the right indicates the number of this printing

Designed by Susan Van Horn
Edited by Jennifer Kasius
Typography: Donatora, Gotham Narrow, and Excelsior

Running Press Book Publishers
2300 Chestnut Street
Philadelphia, PA 19103-4371

Visit us on the web!
www.runningpress.com

contents

Introduction....9

ELIZABETH TAYLOR: *Her Life and Loves in Photos*....11

The Films of Elizabeth Taylor....25

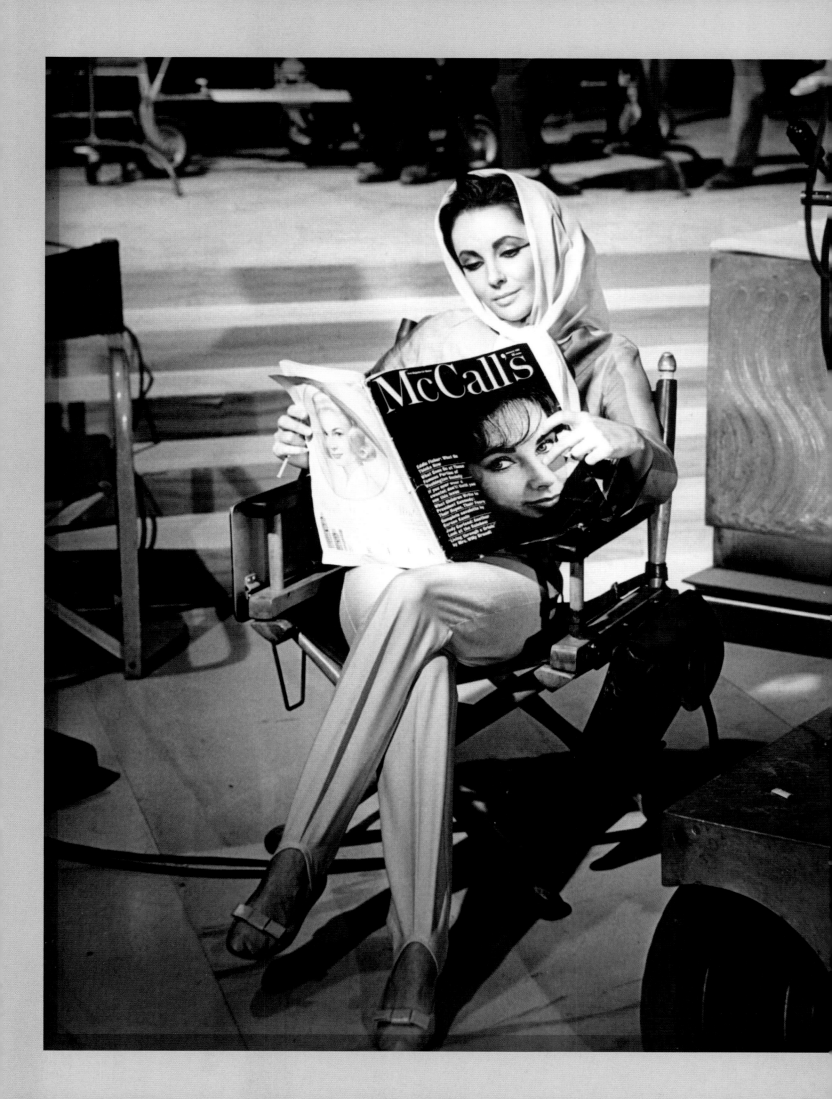

introduction

SHE WAS CALLED THE LAST OF THE GREAT HOLLYWOOD ICONS, but Elizabeth Taylor was also a defining member of that rarified class. For more than sixty years she fascinated the world by doing everything that her public did, only on a far grander scale. Everyone contends with sickness; she conquered so many near-death illnesses that she seemed indestructible. Most marry; Elizabeth wed eight times—once at Neverland, the fabled home of her good friend Michael Jackson. All women have their baubles; she had a king's ransom in jewelry, including the sixty-nine carat Taylor-Burton Diamond. People volunteer and make charitable donations; she raised hundreds of millions of dollars for AIDS research, in the course of a lifetime of humanitarian work. With sultry raven hair and expressive violet eyes, she also possessed otherworldly beauty.

All of these elements of a life lived at large were glittering fodder for the press but never obscured the fact of Elizabeth's extraordinary talent as a star of more than sixty films over the course of five decades. Greatest of all was her golden era, from the mid-1940s through the late '60s, which was

Elizabeth's work in movies started her on the road to stardom and was a mainstay throughout all but the last decade of her life.

filled with certifiable classics. Elizabeth's work in movies started her on the road to stardom and was a mainstay throughout all but the last decade of her life. In a transient business, her career lasted longer than most can ever hope, making it a uniquely fascinating study in cinematic history.

As with any person one watches grow up, we saw a definite evolution of Elizabeth both as an actress and a woman. It was all played out on the screen, from the fragility of her youth through the power of her later years. In her fifth movie, *National Velvet*, she became a child star. The ensuing years under contract to MGM saw her through an ingénue period capped by *Father of the Bride*, among a rapid succession of less memorable films in which the studio cast her. In the 1950s, critics and the general public were more awed by Elizabeth's beauty than by her acting. She was a singular standout in the blonde bombshell era of Marilyn Monroe, Jayne Mansfield, and Brigitte Bardot.

OPPOSITE: Elizabeth was just starting out when this photo was taken, and had much in store for her in the years to come. In 1992 she told *Life* magazine, "I've been lucky all my life. Everything was handed to me: looks, fame, wealth, honors, love. But I've paid for that luck with disasters. Terrible illnesses, destructive addiction, broken marriages."

A loan out to Paramount Pictures resulted in the first dramatic role in which she was taken seriously as an actress. There to make *A Place in the Sun*, she was inspired by her close friend and costar Montgomery Clift. Working with great actors always brought out the best in Elizabeth. Director George Stevens and costars Rock Hudson, James Dean, and Clift saw her through *Giant* and *Raintree County*, but the tragedy of her third husband Mike Todd's death in a plane crash in 1958 taught her to infuse her performances with her own raw emotions. This came through beginning with her sizzling work in *Cat on a Hot Tin Roof*. The fact that her role of Maggie ("the cat") was a character created by gifted playwright Tennessee Williams also worked in her favor, as it did in her next film, *Suddenly, Last Summer*. Elizabeth's performances in *Raintree County* and the two Williams-inspired movies earned well-deserved Academy Award nominations. She finally took home an Oscar for *BUtterfield 8*, though many—including Elizabeth—thought it was more out of sympathy for the fact that she had almost died of pneumonia at the start of filming *Cleopatra*.

Besides setting a precedent by clinching a $1 million salary for the movie, *Cleopatra* saw Elizabeth transition into the next phase of her life and career: the Richard Burton era. During this time they made many popular films together, she conquered every thespian's greatest challenge of Shakespeare in *The Taming of the Shrew*, and gave what is arguably the best performance of her career in *Who's Afraid of Virginia Woolf?*, for which she won her second Oscar. Untethered from her studio contract and able to choose her own roles, Elizabeth proved herself a daring actress. She later said, "I think ever since I was released by my penal servitude [at MGM] and was on my own making my own deals, I really started having fun."

Making her own choices in the '60s and '70s, Elizabeth played characters you either loved or hated. From a virago of a wife who sleeps with her husband's lover (*X, Y & Zee*) to a deranged woman on a mission to find the perfect man to kill her (*Identikit*), each role was deemed by critics either the best she had in years or cinematic suicide. Her daring was sometimes to her own detriment, but if a fan was disappointed by one movie it would soon be followed by another they did love. Although she was still beautiful, she never relied on her looks and was never afraid of a challenge. She said in 1973, "I like parts that aren't too easy for me, that aren't too close to me, because then it's acting, and you have to do more than read through it." After 1980 Elizabeth primarily turned to television, for work she found more interesting than the parts feature films offered to an aging screen goddess.

Through the decades Elizabeth grew from sweet-faced child star into a force of nature on the screen who could go toe-to-toe with any actor and commanded the viewer's attention. In her golden era, Elizabeth gave her fans a thrilling spectacle on the screen and brought to life a colorful array of characters. From tomboyish Velvet Brown to vain Amy March, blushing bride Kay Banks, love struck Angela Vickers, libidinous Gloria Wandrous, acid-tongued Martha, Maggie the cat, and Katharina the shrew, Elizabeth Taylor left the world a truly unique cinematic legacy. It serves as a brilliant and lasting record of what made her a celebrity in the first place. More luminous than other stars could ever hope to claim, the big screen was, undoubtedly, her place in the sun.

Elizabeth:

Her Life and Loves in Photos

Much of the private life of Elizabeth Taylor is discussed in succeeding texts,
as events occurred within the timeline of her film work. Presented here is a collection
of photos illuminating a selected overview of her offscreen world.

1935

1944

1950

1946

1950

TOP LEFT: Beautiful little Elizabeth Rosemond Taylor was born on February 27, 1932, in Hampstead, England, the second child of American parents who worked in London. Father and mother were Francis Taylor, an art dealer, and Sara Warmbrodt, a former actress. TOP MIDDLE: Elizabeth was signed to a long-term contract with MGM after her success in *National Velvet* in 1944. The honeymoon between her and studio head Louis B. Mayer (pictured here) ended quickly. She came to think of him as a tyrant and disliked the studio's control over her career, particularly her choice of roles. BOTTOM LEFT: Sara Taylor and her two children, Howard and Elizabeth, at home in California, where they moved from England in the wake of World War II. Elizabeth was always very close with her family—and they called her "Elizabeth." She said in 1961, "People who know me well call me Elizabeth. I dislike Liz. I guess it goes back to the days when my brother Howard called me Lizzie, or Lizzie the Cow, or Lizard." Sara tried to push both Howard and Elizabeth into show business. Howard wanted no part of it, but early on it was apparent that her lovely daughter was ideal for big screen close-ups. TOP RIGHT: Elizabeth was a graduate of MGM schooling in 1950, about the same time she got her first great adult roles, in *A Place in the Sun* and *Father of the Bride*. Just eighteen years old, she also became engaged to hotel heir Nicky Hilton that year. BOTTOM RIGHT: Her wedding to Hilton took place (with the help of police escort) at the Church of the Good Shepherd in Beverly Hills, May 6, 1950, amid a star-studded crowd of seven hundred. "Turn on the sirens. Let them know I'm coming!" she said on her way to the church.

1951

1952

1951

1955

TOP LEFT. Elizabeth matured fast. Fourteen films into her storied career she made *A Place in the Sun*. She won rave reviews for her performance, and attended the premiere with her best friend, actor Roddy McDowall, whom she met while making her first movie at MGM. BOTTOM LEFT: Elizabeth at her divorce proceedings from Hilton, following less than a year of marriage. She was devastated. Elizabeth was raised with the notion that when you loved someone you married, you didn't have an affair. Her firm belief in this led to eight marriages and seven divorces, none of which she took lightly; "Every divorce is like a little death," she said in 1996. TOP RIGHT: Elizabeth and British actor Michael Wilding were still engaged at the time this shot was taken in London. She met him during the making of *Ivanhoe* in England and they were wed on February 21, 1952. BOTTOM RIGHT: Elizabeth's marriage to Wilding was short-lived, but it provided her with her two sons, Michael and Christopher. Of the marriage Elizabeth said, "[We] had a lovely, easy life, very simple, very quiet. Two babies were born. We had friends. We didn't do much."

1957

TOP LEFT Film producer Mike Todd swept Elizabeth off her feet. They were married in Acapulco in 1957. **BOTTOM LEFT:** One legacy Todd left her was a start of her passion for jewelry. He regularly surprised her with expensive, gleaming gifts. **TOP RIGHT:** During her marriage to Todd, she was just starting to get roles in films that were important to her, such as *Raintree County*, and she blossomed under his larger-than-life personality. "I grew up for all America to see," Elizabeth said, "and I ached to become a real woman." **BOTTOM RIGHT:** Elizabeth and Todd were blessed with a daughter, Liza, born August 6, 1957.

1958

BOTTOM LEFT: Elizabeth's short but idyllic period with Todd ended with his death in a plane crash in March 1958. She attended the funeral in Chicago with her brother, Howard. **TOP:** Todd and Elizabeth were good friends with actress Debbie Reynolds and her husband, singer Eddie Fisher. Elizabeth's coupling with Fisher following Todd's death erupted in the Liz-Eddie-Debbie Scandal. She was called a home wrecker in the press, irate citizens picketed Fisher's shows in Las Vegas, and NBC opted to cancel his television show. **BOTTOM RIGHT:** In the midst of her despair over Todd's death, Elizabeth was making *Cat on a Hot Tin Roof*. The movie turned out to be one of her greatest. Splashed on the covers of magazines, she was one of the most famous women in the world and would remain so for the next five decades.

1959

1961

1961

1962

TOP LEFT: Elizabeth and Fisher were married in Las Vegas in May 1959. The same year she converted from the Christian Science faith to Judaism, not for either of her Jewish husbands, Mike Todd or Fisher, as is often thought, but because, in her words, "I needed, after Mike's death, some sort of very strong faith to keep me alive. Something to hang on to—and I didn't find it in Christian Science. And I wanted to be close to Mike. So I studied Judaism for a year after his death and then converted." **TOP MIDDLE:** Elizabeth and Eddie Fisher, after her return from London, 1961. **TOP RIGHT:** Fisher saw her through a near-death bout with double pneumonia in England, where she was to film *Cleopatra*. When she returned to Los Angeles on the mend they attended a Cedars-Sinai Hospital charity dinner, where this shot of the couple was taken. The ordeal she had been through endeared Elizabeth to the public once again—and many, including Elizabeth, felt cinched her the Academy Award win as Best Actress for *BUtterfield 8*. **BOTTOM:** The only love affair in Hollywood more notorious than that between Elizabeth and Eddie Fisher was the one between Elizabeth and Richard Burton when it first began, during the making of *Cleopatra* in 1962. They fell in love on the set and could not hide it, so soon the entire world knew. "I try not to live a lie," Elizabeth said, "I'm a human being, and I do make mistakes like all human beings. I can't be that hypocritical to protect my public." One of the great romances of the century was sealed with their marriage on March 15, 1964. They would later adopt a girl, Maria Burton.

1964

1970

1963

BOTTOM: Elizabeth and Burton were inseparable through all the years of their marriage. They made eleven films together, and when not working in tandem they were making appearances on the sets of each other's films. Here she joins a conference between Burton and director John Huston on the set of their film, *The Night of the Iguana*. **TOP LEFT:** A snapshot following Elizabeth and Burton's benefit performance of poetry readings at the Lunt-Fontanne Theatre in June 1964. **TOP RIGHT:** As a presenter at the Academy Awards in 1970. Prominently displayed on her décolletage is the sixty-nine carat Taylor-Burton Diamond. Burton bought the necklace for $1.1 million, saying, "I wanted that diamond because it is incomparably lovely. And it should be on the loveliest woman in the world."

TOP LEFT: The Burtons, the most famous couple in the world, appeared on *Here's Lucy* in 1970 with the most famous comedienne in the world, Lucille Ball. The crux of the show's story line was Elizabeth's thirty-three carat Krupp Diamond, given to her by Burton. **BOTTOM LEFT:** On the cover of a magazine at the time of her seventeen-year-old son Michael's marriage to his first wife, Beth Clutter, in 1970. Elizabeth maintained close relationships with all of her children throughout her life (as well as with several stepchildren and grandchildren). **TOP AND BOTTOM RIGHT:** Richard Burton and Elizabeth were divorced and then remarried in 1975. Their reunion in wedlock was officiated by Abrose Masalila of the Botswana civil court in Chobe National Game Park. She wore a dress that had been given to her by Burton's beloved late brother, Ifor. Their second marriage lasted just a few months. They never seemed able to explain why their marriage did not work. Elizabeth once said, "Maybe we have loved each other too much. I never believed such a thing was possible." Their relationship was undeniably passionate. Burton wrote in his diary in 1968: "I have been inordinately lucky all my life, but the greatest luck of all has been Elizabeth. She has turned me into a moral man but not a prig, she is a wildly exciting lover-mistress, she is shy and witty, she is nobody's fool, she is a brilliant actress, she is beautiful beyond the dreams of pornography, she can be arrogant and willful, she is clement and loving. . . . she is an ache in the stomach when I am away from her, and she loves me! And I'll love her till I die."

1976

1980

1981

TOP LEFT: Elizabeth's seventh marriage was to Republican politician and about-to-be senator for the state of Virginia, John Warner, with whom she is pictured at center. Along with them are Michael Wilding, Jr., her daughter Liza, his daughter Mary, her grandchild Naomi Wilding, and daughter-in-law Jo Wilding. **TOP RIGHT:** John Warner successfully campaigned and was elected senator of the state of Virginia. Elizabeth was a devoted politician's wife for a time, bringing her in contact with a new stratum of well-known names outside of Hollywood and the European jet set. Here in 1980, she meets then GOP presidential candidate Ronald Reagan and wife, Nancy, and Virginia governor John Dalton (second from left). **BOTTOM:** After decades of success on the screen, Elizabeth made a triumphant Broadway debut in *The Little Foxes* in 1981.

1983

1988

1988

1989

TOP LEFT: Playing tourist at the Great Wall of China with Mexican lawyer Victor Gonzalez Luna, to whom she became engaged in 1983. The romance ostensibly ended amid her despair following the death of Richard Burton in 1984. BOTTOM LEFT: Elizabeth's boyfriend in 1988, George Hamilton. TOP RIGHT: Sara Taylor lived to be ninety-nine years old, well cared for all the while through the aid of Elizabeth. She attended a tribute to her daughter at Lincoln in 1988. BOTTOM RIGHT: In addition to unqualified success in movies, theater, and humanitarian work, Elizabeth launched a line of best-selling fragrances, including Black Pearls, which debuted in 1996.

1990

c. 1994

1991

1997

TOP LEFT: Elizabeth met her last husband, Larry Fortensky, during a stay at the Betty Ford Center in 1988 and married him in 1991. TOP RIGHT: An Elizabeth Taylor AIDS Foundation benefit. The cause of fighting AIDS was one of the most important aspects of Elizabeth's entire life. BOTTOM LEFT: Larry Fortensky was Elizabeth's last husband. They divorced in 1996. BOTTOM RIGHT: Elizabeth and one of her best friends, Michael Jackson.

1999

1999

2002

TOP LEFT: As ever, decorated with an enviable adornment, the day she received the honor of being named Dame by Queen Elizabeth in 1999.
TOP RIGHT: Elizabeth was awarded an Academy Fellowship from the British Academy in 1999. **BOTTOM:** In 2002, Elizabeth achieved the highest recognition in the United States given to a performer, the Kennedy Center Honors, given for a lifetime of contributions to American culture. President George W. Bush and First Lady Laura Bush pose with Elizabeth and her fellow honorees: James Earl Jones, Chita Rivera, Paul Simon, and James Levine.

Elizabeth passed away on March 23, 2011 of congestive heart failure. In her room at Cedars-Sinai Hospital she was comfortable and peacefully surrounded by those most important to her: her children. After she had survived numerous grave illnesses, the world was shocked to lose Elizabeth Taylor. Her final service was held the following day at Forest Lawn Cemetery. She had left instructions that the service must begin fifteen minutes behind schedule, so she would "be late for the last bloody judgment," as Richard Burton used to tell her she would most certainly be. Even beyond the grave, after a lifetime of triumphant highs and heartbreaking lows, Elizabeth never lost her sense of humor.

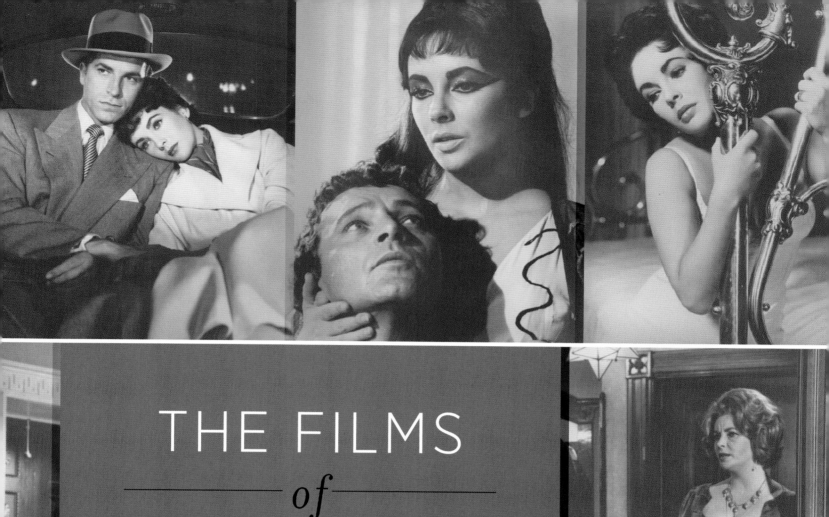

THE FILMS
of
ELIZABETH
TAYLOR

There's One Born Every Minute

UNIVERSAL PICTURES

CAST

Hugh Herbert ....*Lemuel P. Twine*

Peggy Moran ....*Helen Barbara Twine*

Tom Brown ....*Jimmy Hanagan*

Guy Kibbee ....*Lester Cadwalader, Sr.*

Catherine Doucet ....*Minerva Twine*

Edgar Kennedy ....*Mayor Carson*

Guy Schilling ......*Professor Quisenberry*

Elizabeth Taylor ....*Gloria Twine*

Charles Halton ....*Trumbull*

Carl "Alfalfa" Switzer..........*Junior Twine*

CREDITS

Ken Goldsmith *(producer)*; Harold Young *(director)*; Robert B. Hunt, Barbara Weisberg *(screenplay)*, based on story by Robert B. Hunt; John W. Boyle *(photography)*; H. J. Salter *(music)*; Jack Otterson, Martin Obzina *(art directors)*; R. A. Gausman *(set decorations)*; Bernard B. Brown, Charles Carroll *(sound)*; Maurice Wright *(editor)*; Vera West *(costumes)*

RELEASE DATE: June 26, 1942

RUN TIME: 60 minutes, black and white

RIGHT: As Gloria Twine

SUMMARY: Pudding maker Lemuel P. Twine is an unlikely candidate for mayor, backed by crooked local businessman Lester Cadwalader, who is the one really pulling the strings behind the mayoral race. Twine suddenly gains enormous popularity (and campaign funding) through the success of his patented pudding, which is packed with "essential" Vitamin Z. Cadwalader, now fearful of Twine's power, turns on him and embarks on a smear campaign to discredit Twine along with his pudding. But through the support of his family—and a ringing musical endorsement from the youngest Twines (Elizabeth Taylor and Carl Switzer)—the pudding king ends up victorious.

notes

ABOVE: Elizabeth played the bratty daughter of the Twine family (pictured here) in *There's One Born Every Minute*.

WHILE CROSSING OVER FROM ENGLAND, HOME TO AMERICA to escape the perils of Europe on the brink of war in 1939, Elizabeth and her mother, Sara, were treated onboard ship to a screening of the latest Shirley Temple film, *The Little Princess*. According to her mother, seeing the pint-sized princess of cinema in her first Technicolor feature, and in a story set in the England so recently lost to them, made a powerful impression on her little refugee daughter. The film's influence on Sara Taylor was greater still, fanning the flames of her own desire: For the former stage actress, seeing Elizabeth in a career in the performing arts seemed not to be a far-fetched dream. With a final destination of Los Angeles, where Elizabeth's father, Francis Taylor, was to run an art gallery owned by his brother, the Taylors were headed in the right direction to see their own little princess up on the big screen.

> *"The kid has nothing. Her eyes are too old. She doesn't have the face of a kid."*
>
> —UNIVERSAL STUDIOS CASTING DIRECTOR

> *Playing a smart-mouthed little girl, she clowned with Carl Switzer and sang a little campaign-song duet with him.*

Living in Pasadena and then Pacific Palisades put the Taylors in close proximity to the film community and, primarily through Francis's gallery at the Beverly Hills Hotel, Sara made some important friends—one being the fiancée of John Cheever Cowdin, the chairman of Universal Pictures. When she and Cowdin visited the Taylors, the movie mogul was impressed by little Elizabeth's poise and beauty, and through him she landed her first film contract at Universal.

At the age of nine, Elizabeth made her screen debut in *There's One Born Every Minute*. Politics met pudding in this zany low-budget comedy, which was originally called *Man or Mouse*. Playing a smart-mouthed little girl, she clowned with Carl Switzer (formerly of *Our Gang* fame as the beloved Alfalfa) and sang a little campaign-song duet with him. The comic number showed off the tuneful, if untrained, singing abilities that Elizabeth possessed as a child. Her voice certainly had volume, and Sara hoped it could develop to a degree that would boost her career. Universal even touted Elizabeth in the trades as a singer and dancer when she was first signed. She was no rival in that respect, however, for the studio's resident young singing superstar, Deanna Durbin, then at the height of her fame.

Though she displayed energy and charm in her first role, the executives at Universal saw no future for Elizabeth under their aegis. Years later she recalled that casting director Dan Kelly "just didn't like me." Famous last words from Universal: "The kid has nothing. Her eyes are too old. She doesn't have the face of a kid." She did not make another film for the studio for the duration of her year-long contract. At age nine, it was on to the next job for Elizabeth.

ABOVE FROM LEFT: With Catherine Doucet and Carl Switzer | With Carl "Alfalfa" Switzer, former star of the wildly popular *Our Gang* short **LEFT:** In England, Sara Taylor hoped to one day make a good marriage for her daughter; when the war drove the family back to America, specifically to California, she seemed destined for the movies.

Lassie Come Home

METRO-GOLDWYN-MAYER

CAST

Roddy McDowall .... *Joe Carraclough*

Donald Crisp .... *Sam Carraclough*

Dame May Whitty .... *Dally*

Edmund Gwenn .... *Rowlie*

Nigel Bruce .... *Duke of Rudling*

Elsa Lanchester .... *Mrs. Carraclough*

Elizabeth Taylor .... *Priscilla*

Ben Webster .... *Dan'l Fadden*

J. Patrick O'Malley .... *Hynes*

Alan Napier .... *Jock*

CREDITS

Samuel Marx *(producer)*; Fred M. Wilcox *(director)*; Hugo Butler *(screenplay)*, based on novel by Eric Knight; Leonard Smith *(photography)*; Daniele Amfitheatrof *(music)*; Cedric Gibbons, Paul Groesse *(art directors)*; Edwin B. Willis, Mildred Griffiths *(set decorations)*; Douglas Shearer *(sound)*; Ben Lewis *(editor)*; Jack Dawn *(makeup)*

RELEASE DATE: December, 1943

RUN TIME: 89 minutes, color

SUMMARY: The Carraclough family has fallen on hard times, forcing them to sell young Joe's beloved collie, Lassie. The dog is bought by the wealthy Duke of Rudling and is soothed by the affection of the duke's niece, Priscilla, but for Lassie there is no place like home. After being taken far away, the journey back to the Carracloughs is a treacherous one, and proves Lassie is one extraordinary animal who belongs at the side of Joe.

With Nigel Bruce, who portrayed Elizabeth's uncle in *Lassie Come Home*

notes

IN 1942 WORLD WAR II WAS RAGING AND PART-TIME AIR-RAID wardens were on duty even in Beverly Hills. Francis Taylor was one of them, Sam Marx was another. Marx's full-time job was as a producer at Metro-Goldwyn-Mayer. In the past he had worked on some of the studio's lower-budget productions, a highlight being *A Family Affair*, which spun off into the enormously popular *Hardy* family series starring Mickey Rooney. Francis told Marx all about his beautiful, talented daughter and showed him a picture of her. Being a movie producer, it was a situation Marx had been in many times before. He agreed that Francis's daughter was quite lovely but gently brushed him off.

Marx was currently at work on a screen adaptation of *Lassie Come Home*, based on the novel by Eric Knight. Set in England, the main characters included a boy, a dog, and a girl. Roddy McDowall would play the boy and a fledgling actress named Maria Flynn was set to play the girl, but the daily rushes showed that she and McDowall were not well matched because Flynn was a head taller than him. Marx needed a replacement for her in a hurry and asked the studio casting department to send over the girls that had been signed up for a recent film with an English setting, *Mrs. Miniver*. He also remembered Francis Taylor and asked him to send Elizabeth over to the studio. Marx later said that when Elizabeth arrived with her mother she was the obvious standout among the other girls. They made a screen test of her which remained memorable to Elizabeth because she was asked to act opposite a mop acting as a stand-in for Lassie. She photographed beautifully, she had the necessary English accent, and she was the perfect height for McDowall. The part was hers.

As charming as McDowall and Elizabeth were, it was the title character of *Lassie Come Home* who was the true star of the film. The fictional character of Lassie was made famous by a story by Eric Knight that ran in the *Saturday Evening Post*, and then was expanded into the novel *Lassie Come Home*, first published in 1940. MGM's 1943 film was the first time Lassie made it to the big screen. It was the beginning of a major franchise; thereafter Lassie has appeared on radio, films, television, and comic books, and continues to well into the twenty-first century. In *Lassie Come Home* the female collie was portrayed by a supremely talented male collie named Pal. Pal assumed the "stage name" of Lassie and played the character onscreen into the mid-'50s, when one of his sons began starring in the television series. It remained a family business; Lassie has always been portrayed by descendents of Pal.

Production began on *Lassie Come Home* in September 1942. Elizabeth immediately took to both Pal and Roddy McDowall. Like Elizabeth, McDowall was a refugee from war-weary England. Four years older than Elizabeth, he had already appeared in over twenty films, the most notable being the Best Picture of 1941, *How Green Was My Valley*. Speaking in 1974, costar Donald Crisp remembered McDowall and Elizabeth as "the nicest little kids you'd ever want to meet. They were always on time and worked like little professionals." The two became best friends on the set and remained so until his death in 1998.

REVIEWS

"Oftentimes, animal pictures make the unhappy mistake of attributing almost human rationalization to simple four-footed beasts. An outstanding virtue of this picture is that it does nothing of the sort. It treats the dog as an animal whose loyalty is all the more wondrous and appealing because it is simple and free of human wile."
—*The New York Times* (Bosley Crowther)

"Elizabeth Taylor, pretty little moppet, gives promise of fine things to come."
—*New York Daily Mirror* (Lee Mortimer)

Recalling his first impression of Elizabeth, McDowall said, "She was so rapturously beautiful a little girl that you couldn't believe it." Her looks, even as a child, caught people by surprise. After shooting her first scene in *Lassie Come Home*, cameraman Leonard Smith asked Elizabeth to remove her false eyelashes and was astonished to learn she was not wearing any. Shot in Technicolor, Elizabeth's dark hair and blue-violet eyes were striking. Her salary for the film was $150 less than her canine costar, but MGM recognized her star quality and signed Elizabeth to a one-year contract.

MGM in those days was the most prestigious studio in Hollywood. It boasted of having "more stars than there are in the heavens," and it spent lavishly on productions showcasing those stars, who then included Judy Garland, Lana Turner, James Stewart, Greer Garson, Spencer Tracy, Katharine Hepburn, Clark Gable, and Hedy Lamarr. At the time, it was a coup for Elizabeth to have landed at MGM of all studios, and she would be in good company.

> ## "She was so rapturously beautiful a little girl that you couldn't believe it."
>
> —RODDY MCDOWALL

ABOVE FROM LEFT: MGM studio portrait | Elizabeth was MGM's newest contract player in the fall of 1942.

Jane Eyre

TWENTIETH CENTURY FOX

CAST

Orson Welles .... *Edward Rochester*

Joan Fontaine .... *Jane Eyre*

Margaret O'Brien .... *Adele Varens*

Peggy Ann Garner .... *Jane Eyre*
(as a child)

John Sutton .... *Dr. Rivers*

Sara Allgood .... *Bessie*

Henry Daniell .... *Henry Brocklehurst*

Agnes Moorehead .... *Mrs. Reed*

Aubrey Mather .... *Colonel Dent*

Elizabeth Taylor .... *Helen*

CREDITS

William Goetz *(executive producer)*; Robert Stevenson *(director)*; Aldous Huxley, Robert Stevenson, John Houseman *(screenplay)*, based on novel by Charlotte Brontë; George Barnes *(photography)*; Bernard Herrmann *(music)*; William Pereira *(production designer)*; James Basevi, Wiard B. Ihnen *(art directors)*; Thomas Little, Ross Dowd *(set decorations)*; W. D. Flick, Roger Heman *(sound)*; Walter Thompson *(editor)*; Guy Pearce *(makeup)*

RELEASE DATE: April 7, 1944
RUN TIME: 97 minutes, black and white

RIGHT: With Peggy Ann Garner, Elizabeth created pivotal early drama in *Jane Eyre*.

SUMMARY: Traumatic years growing up in an orphanage form a meek, soft-spoken Jane Eyre into adulthood. Jane takes a position as governess at Thornfield Hall, the home of Edward Rochester, where she finds joy in Adele, her beautiful young charge. Jane also falls deeply in love with Mr. Rochester, whose tormented soul is both frightening and mystifying. Jane's gentle manner wins his love in return, but their future happiness may be impossible because of the mystery in the tower of Thornfield, where Mr. Rochester's wife, a raving lunatic, is kept locked away. The shocking revelations and ensuing drama test Jane's spirit and the power of her and Mr. Rochester's love.

notes

CHARLOTTE BRONTË'S CLASSIC NOVEL *JANE EYRE*, FIRST published in England in 1847, served as inspiration for many a film, stage production, and television series over the years. In 1943, the last Hollywood attempt at the story was from the poverty-row studio Monogram, starring Virginia Bruce and Colin Clive. Nine years had passed since that low-budget feature and Twentieth Century Fox planned on mounting the definitive Hollywood edition of the story, starring Academy Award-winning actress Joan Fontaine and the most controversial filmmaker in Hollywood: Orson Welles.

Welles was only two years removed from *Citizen Kane*, the landmark film that earned him as many enemies in the industry as it did admirers. His detractors notwithstanding, no one could deny the revolutionary cinematic talent he displayed in his debut film and its follow-up, *The Magnificent Ambersons*. Welles, top-billed above Jane herself, took the reigns behind the scenes of *Jane Eyre* to the point where he was offered a producer credit, which he turned down. The talent of director Robert Stevenson, who went on to have a long and successful career in films, was not to be dismissed, but in film circles in years to come Welles was widely the one credited with bringing the brooding, moody quality of Charlotte Brontë's novel to the screen. Welles was on a winning streak at the moment. Shortly after production he married the Love Goddess of Hollywood, Rita Hayworth.

The Gothic atmosphere of *Jane Eyre* was enhanced by Joan Fontaine, who reminded audiences of her great performance in Alfred Hitchcock's *Rebecca*. Three other girls made an impression in the movie: Peggy Ann Garner as the young Jane, Margaret O'Brien as the French-accented Adele, and eleven-year-old Elizabeth Taylor. MGM loaned Elizabeth out to Fox to play Helen, the impossibly lovely childhood friend of Jane. For the rest of her life Elizabeth was known to befriend and take to heart underdogs and those fighting inner demons. The role of Helen in *Jane Eyre* brought her compassionate nature to the screen. In her first scene she descends the staircase of an exquisitely lit set like a little angel of mercy bringing comfort to the tortured Jane. The tragic Helen, battling a persistent cough, dies of a severe cold, and Elizabeth would suffer with similar symptoms for the rest of her life, through numerous bouts of bronchitis and pneumonia.

Helen was a small but important role, yet Fox saw fit to exclude her from billing. Elizabeth said years later that she saw it on television with her children and was disappointed to see that in the truncated version she had been cut out of the film entirely.

REVIEW

"*Jane Eyre* is a picture photographed and directed with an eye to mood. Its settings are desolate and terrifying, with photography to match. Often the film is reminiscent of *Rebecca* and often of *Wuthering Heights*. It is a picture to please those who enjoy the desperate, melodramatic love stories of the sisters Brontë."

—**New York** *Sun* **(Eileen Creelman)**

TOP LEFT: With John Sutton. In Elizabeth's first onscreen death, her star quality shone through. **ABOVE:** She played a lovely little girl whose hair sits "in one mass of curls" to the dismay of the headmaster of Lowood Orphanage. The cruel headmaster promptly lops the offending hair off with scissors, to the horror of her friend Jane Eyre.

The White Cliffs of Dover

ABOVE: A tender moment between Elizabeth and Roddy McDowall in *The White Cliffs of Dover*. She once said, "Genuine friends are the rarest of all in Hollywood." For the rest of their lives Elizabeth and McDowall fit that bill for each other.

METRO-GOLDWYN-MAYER

CAST

Irene Dunne .... *Susan Dunn*

Alan Marshal .... *Sir John Ashwood*

Roddy McDowall .... *John Ashwood II (as a boy)*

Frank Morgan .... *Hiram Porter Dunn*

Van Johnson .... *Sam Bennett*

C. Aubrey Smith .... *Colonel Walter Forsythe*

Dame May Whitty .... *Nanny*

Peter Lawford .... *John Ashwood II (as a young man)*

John Warburton .... *Reggie Ashwood*

Elizabeth Taylor .... *Betsy Kenney (at age ten)*

CREDITS

Clarence Brown, Sidney Franklin *(producers)*; Clarence Brown *(director)*; Claudine West, Jan Lustig, George Froeschel *(screenplay)*, based on poem by Alice Duer Miller; Robert Nathan *(additional poetry)*; George Folsey *(photography)*; Herbert Stothart *(music)*; Cedric Gibbons, Randall Duell *(art directors)*; Edwin B. Willis, Jacques Mersereau *(set decorations)*; Douglas Shearer *(sound)*; Robert J. Kern *(editor)*; Irene, Gile Steele *(costumes)*; Jack Dawn *(makeup)*

RELEASE DATE: June 19, 1944

RUN TIME: 126 minutes, black and white

SUMMARY: In World War I–era England, American girl Susan Dunn falls in love and marries English nobleman John Ashwood. Their idyllic world is torn apart by the ravages of war and John is killed in action. Susan honors his memory by remaining in England to raise their son, John II. Two decades later, World War II calls John, Jr. to action. The courageous Susan does her part by becoming a nurse near the front. Her worst fears are realized when she finds herself caring for her own mortally wounded son.

notes

IN 1943 WORLD WAR II WAS STILL RAGING AND AT A RAPID rate Hollywood was producing films that celebrated, brought attention to, or otherwise paid homage to United States allies. Some were escapist fare set in exotic locales and some faced the war head-on and honored servicemen and women stateside and abroad. Films such as *Mrs. Miniver* (Best Picture of 1942) and *Tonight and Every Night* (a musical drama starring Rita Hayworth), saluted the British allies. *The White Cliffs of Dover* captured a similar need in the market, pure soap opera but with a heartfelt story that audiences wanted to hear in that era. The film showed a profit of more than $4 million and Louis B. Mayer was so proud of it that he named it MGM's official twentieth-anniversary film.

The White Cliffs of Dover was based on a poem of the same name by Alice Duer Miller. Actor Ronald Colman held the film rights, which he sold to director Clarence Brown. Brown, in turn, sold the rights to MGM, and himself as director in the bargain. Brown had been one of the top directors at the studio since the mid-1920s, when he began a collaboration with Greta Garbo that saw the actress through the peak of her stardom. He had also put a number of MGM's other top female stars through their paces on the screen, including Joan Crawford, Jean Harlow, and Norma Shearer.

On his latest film in the spring of 1943, Brown had another strong lead actress in Irene Dunne and continued his association with legendary ladies by directing Elizabeth Taylor in one of her first films. They were about to be allied in a landmark movie in her career, but for the present Elizabeth already seemed to shine under his leadership. Brown had cast Roddy McDowall as the young John Ashwood II, and he shared scenes with Elizabeth. Being close friends already gave them a natural chemistry that Brown was able to capture on camera. Elizabeth played a girl with a crush on McDowall; their characters grow up to be played by June Lockhart and Peter Lawford. In a film that could be classified as a three-hanky weepie, Elizabeth and McDowall's are among the most heartfelt and subtly sweet moments.

FROM TOP: Studio portrait of Elizabeth, c. 1943. The movie was filmed primarily between late May and September of that year. | A visit with brother Howard during the time she made *The White Cliffs of Dover*. Before Elizabeth, Sara Taylor tried to interest Howard in an acting career but he rebelled.

REVIEW

"That it is more episodic than dramatic is the fault of the script rather than the acting. With Irene Dunne giving an illuminating portrayal of an American woman who marries a Britisher, the film has emotional depth and significance. Since the other acting in the Sidney Franklin production is above reproach, it has all the fascination of an upper-bracket tear-jerker. But it skips so blithely through thirty years of ominous history that it wastes the power of its central theme."

—New York *Herald Tribune* (Howard Barnes)

National Velvet

METRO-GOLDWYN-MAYER

CAST

Mickey Rooney .... *Mike "Mi" Taylor*
Donald Crisp .... *Mr. Brown*
Elizabeth Taylor .... *Velvet Brown*
Anne Revere .... *Mrs. Brown*
Angela Lansbury .... *Edwina Brown*
Jackie Jenkins .... *Donald Brown*
Juanita Quigley .... *Malvolia Brown*
Arthur Treacher .... *race patron*
Reginald Owen .... *Farmer Ede*
Norma Varden .... *Miss Sims*

CREDITS

Pandro S. Berman (*producer*); Clarence Brown (*director*); Theodore Reeves, Helen Deutsch (*screenplay*), based on novel by Enid Bagnold; Leonard Smith (*photography*); Herbert Stothart (*music*); Cedric Gibbons, Urie McCleary (*art directors*); Edwin B. Willis, Mildred Griffiths (*set decorations*); Douglas Shearer (*sound*); Joseph Boyle (*assistant director*); Robert J. Kern (*editor*); Irene, Kay Dean, Valles (*costumes*); Jack Dawn (*makeup*)

RELEASE DATE: January 26, 1945
RUN TIME: 123 minutes, color

RIGHT: As Velvet Brown

SUMMARY: An accident that prevents Mi Taylor from continuing his career turns the ex-jockey into a shiftless wanderer. He turns up at the country home of the Brown family and there meets Velvet, a young girl determined to enter her horse, the Pie, in the Grand National Sweepstakes. Taming the Pie's wild ways and preparing him for the big race gives Mi new purpose in life. Velvet masquerades as a boy to ride the Pie in the big race herself. The journey to the finish line in the Grand Nationals is a bumpy and at times dangerous one, but Mi, Velvet, and the Pie prove to be a winning triumvirate.

notes

ABOVE: Jackie Jenkins, Mickey Rooney, and Elizabeth

ELIZABETH TAYLOR ONCE SAID, "WHEN I WAS A LITTLE KID I wanted to grow up and get married and have a house with a white picket fence and six children and one maid and lots of dogs, cats, horses, and cows." What she got in 1943 was a prized movie role, a studio contract, and mostly importantly for her at the time—that horse.

Enid Bagnold's 1935 novel *National Velvet* was Elizabeth's favorite as a child, so when she and her mother, Sara, learned that MGM was planning to adapt it for the big screen, they set out to make the starring role hers. The little heroine of Bagnold's story was a spirited one and perfectly suited Elizabeth, but producer Pandro Berman thought her physically too small. He considered casting an older teen in the part. As the story goes, eleven-year-old Elizabeth hit a fortuitously timed growth spurt that added might to her small frame and three inches to her height in just four months. Berman and director Clarence Brown were satisfied and Elizabeth happily took to the saddle for her first iconic screen characterization.

> *Enid Bagnold's 1935 novel* National Velvet *was Elizabeth's favorite as a child.*

Besides capturing the essence of Velvet Brown, Elizabeth was an ideal choice for the role because of her experience with horses. Her affinity for equines dated back to her childhood in England where, Sara Taylor said, "That's all she ever wanted to do—ride horses." Elizabeth had strong riding skills but she had never encountered a "total renegade" such as the animal that played the Pie onscreen. During filming it once lunged forward and threw Elizabeth to the ground. The

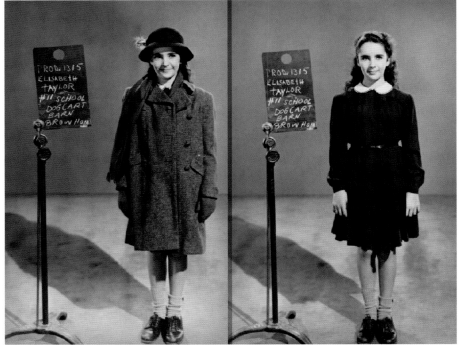

RIGHT: Test shots show costumes and hairstyles considered appropriate for the character of Velvet. **OPPOSITE FROM TOP LEFT:** With director Clarence Brown. The horse in the film was a birthday gift for Elizabeth, who said, "They gave him to me because no one else could ride him." | "I sometimes think I prefer animals to people. And I was lucky. My first leading men were dogs and horses." | Elizabeth, one of the studio's newest contract players, dines in the studio commissary. Actor Darryl Hickman sits beside her.

> *No one else could manage the horse, so the studio gave it to Elizabeth as a birthday gift.*

accident resulted in a spinal injury that exacerbated her preexisting scoliosis. Back pain would plague Elizabeth for the rest of her life and eventually put her in a wheelchair decades later, but for the present she mustered her strength and got back in the saddle, too devoted to the role to even think of giving it up. No one else could manage the horse, so the studio gave it to Elizabeth as a birthday gift.

National Velvet director Clarence Brown had a history of making great films with MGM screen icons, especially the ladies. His alliance with young Elizabeth in their second film venture added another stellar credit to his name. Sara Taylor was known to occasionally direct her young daughter with hand signals from off camera, but her presence did not diminish Brown's duties. He brought out an endearing, high-spirited performance from Elizabeth that showed all the charm of a girl frantic to please her mother (played to perfection onscreen by Anne Revere) and driven to achieve big dreams. Both aspects of the characterization were a mirror into Elizabeth's own world.

Mickey Rooney, Elizabeth, and Anne Revere. Elizabeth's rapport with her onscreen mother was vital in the film.

Besides Elizabeth, Brown had superstar Mickey Rooney in the cast of *National Velvet*. The lasting impression is that it is an Elizabeth Taylor movie, but her costar really drove the box office in the mid-1940s. The dynamic Rooney was at the peak of his career as costar of a series of lively musicals with Judy Garland, and as the leading player of the lucrative *Hardy* family films. Known as a larger-than-life personality, Rooney was generous in sharing the star spotlight with Elizabeth in *National Velvet*, and utterly impressed by her talents. He remembered her as a "marvelous" young professional who required only one or two takes when the cameras were rolling.

> *Known as a larger-than-life personality, Rooney was generous in sharing the star spotlight with Elizabeth in* National Velvet, *and utterly impressed by her talents.*

National Velvet was made between January and June 1944, and was in theaters by January of the following year. It was great family fodder that brought in over $4 million at the box office in 1945. The movie was also big at the Academy Awards in 1946. Anne Revere won the Oscar for Best Supporting Actress. The film also took home the award for Best Editing and earned nominations for Best Art Direction, Best Cinematography, and Best Director.

Though not nominated for any Oscars, Elizabeth was recognized as an essential part of the film's success too, meaning a new, long-term contract with MGM was in order. Signing the deal was the start of a tumultuous relationship with the studio, and specifically with her boss, Louis B. Mayer, whom Elizabeth called "an absolute dictator." They got off to a rocky start when Sara Taylor suggested Elizabeth take voice and dance lessons. Mayer did not mince words in telling Mrs. Taylor that he did not need her to tell him how to run his studio. Elizabeth,

"[Elizabeth Taylor] imparts a breath-less, utterly genuine charm to the character of Velvet, and takes top acting honors in an excellent cast."
—*Liberty*

"*National Velvet* should be a joy to all right-minded folks. For this fresh and delightful Metro picture, based on Enid Bagnold's novel of some years back, tells by far the most touching story of youngsters and of animals since Lassie was coming home. . . . Mr. Brown has also drawn some excellent performances from his cast, especially from little Elizabeth Taylor, who plays the role of the horse-loving girl. Her face is alive with youthful spirit, her voice has the softness of sweet song and her whole manner in this picture is one of refreshing grace."
—*The New York Times* (Bosley Crowther)

"Mr. Brown's direction may account for the quietness of Mr. Rooney's work. It is good work, anyway, an emotional part without any mugging. That beautiful child of *Lassie Come Home*, a dark-haired, blue-eyed girl named Elizabeth Taylor, plays the dreamy Velvet and makes her one of the screen's most lovable characters."
—New York *Sun* (Eileen Creelman)

appalled by Mayer's tone and language with her mother, stood up and told her boss, "You and your studio can both go to hell!" She walked out of his office expecting to be fired. Only she was not let go; already she was too intrinsically valuable to MGM for an argument with the boss to lead to her dismissal. Elizabeth was on her way to sixteen years at the studio that would produce a fair share of duds as well as some of the all-time classics of her career.

Velvet Brown masquerades as a young male jockey in order to race her beloved horse in the Grand Nationals.

Courage of Lassie

METRO-GOLDWYN-MAYER

CAST

Elizabeth Taylor .... *Kathie Merrick*

Frank Morgan .... *Harry MacBain*

Tom Drake .... *Sergeant Smitty*

Selena Royle .... *Mrs. Merrick*

Harry Davenport .... *Judge Payson*

George Cleveland .... *old man*

Catherine Frances McLeod .... *Alice Merrick*

Morris Ankrum .... *Farmer Crews*

Mitchell Lewis .... *Gil Elson*

Jane Green .... *Mrs. Elson*

CREDITS

Robert Sisk *(producer)*; Fred M. Wilcox *(director)*; Lionel Houser *(screenplay)*; Leonard Smith *(photography)*; Scott Bradley, Bronislau Kaper *(music)*; Cedric Gibbons, Paul Youngblood *(art directors)*; Edwin B. Willis, Paul Huldschinsky *(set decorations)*; Douglas Shearer *(sound)*; Conrad A. Nervig *(editor)*; Irene *(costumes)*

RELEASE DATE: November 8, 1946

RUN TIME: 92 minutes, color

RIGHT: Kathie has Bill trained as a sheepdog.

SUMMARY: A resourceful collie, born and bred in the wilderness, is accidentally shot. Young Kathie Merrick nurses the dog, which she calls Bill, back to health. Trained as a sheepdog, Bill becomes a useful addition to the family farm until an accident lands him far away from the Merricks and amidst warfare in the line of enemy fire. His instinctive cunning and courage lead him to save a platoon but the war takes a toll on Bill. He eventually makes his way back home but the vicious streak the war has given him leads to serious trouble—until Kathie and kindly neighbor Harry McBain reenter Bill's life.

REVIEWS

"The principal human actors are excellent in their simple roles. Elizabeth Taylor is refreshingly natural as Lassie's devoted owner. . . . But it is Lassie's, or Bill's, picture. And, despite some improbabilities in the plot, it is his 'acting' and the polychromatic settings which are the chief delights of the offering."

—New York *Herald Tribune* (A. W.)

"Anyone who doesn't like a dog picture, especially one starring Lassie, is an unqualified cad. . . . The plot of *Courage of Lassie* is not likely to give you pause. Neither is the acting by the bipeds. Lassie walks off with all the honors, which is as it should be."

—*The New York Times* (Bosley Crowther)

"I hope the ASPCA can't get me for being unkind to animal pictures when I warn other fans that it is unreal and slightly tedious. There is a great deal of scenic beauty in the Technicolor production and parts of the story are delightful and some of it touching. . . . Elizabeth Taylor, very beautiful and charmingly sincere, has the leading role as Bill's devoted mistress."

—New York *Daily News* (Wanda Hale)

CLOCKWISE FROM TOP: Elizabeth and Lassie study their script on location at Lake Chelan, Washington. | Preproduction work on *Courage of Lassie* got underway in November 1944. This test shot shows Elizabeth on the set of the Merrick family barn.

AFTER ELIZABETH'S GREAT TRIUMPH IN *NATIONAL VELVET*, her career took an unusual turn in that MGM did not immediately rush another film into theaters to capitalize on her success. She was Hollywood's latest and greatest child star, but MGM could not decide what to do with this supposedly juvenile actress who was growing up by leaps and bounds. There was not an obvious place in movies for a girl of twelve or thirteen, whose face already possessed a mature beauty. She could not sing or dance, and musicals were the studio's bread and butter.

As a result, an entire year and a half passed before Elizabeth's newfound fan base got to see her again. Ultimately, MGM solved their Elizabethan dilemma, echoing *National Velvet* by giving her another costar from the animal kingdom. It was a dog this time, but no ordinary pup—this was Lassie once again. Now in his third film, Pal, under the stage name of Lassie, received above-the-title billing. Elizabeth was listed second and her former *There's One Born Every Minute* costar, Carl Switzer, ranked considerably lower.

The film was originally called *Hold High the Torch* and later *Blue Skies*, before it was decided that any film starring Lassie needed to have his name in the title. Interestingly, in the movie they decided to call him Bill. Be it Pal, Lassie, or Bill though, Elizabeth adored the dog and they were inseparable throughout filming, which took them on location to picturesque Lake Chelan, Washington. A friend who watched her grow up under the firm hand of a studio and a mother anxious to make Elizabeth a star observed her passion for animals and said, "I often wondered about this, and then I realized that the animals were the only ones around her who couldn't tell her where to go, what to do, what to say."

Elizabeth's great affinity for animals was already well known. Part of her time between films was spent writing and illustrating the book *Nibbles and Me*. In it, Elizabeth provided lively anecdotes about her prized pet chipmunk, which was a fixture on the set of many of her early films. Nibbles was even planned to make a guest appearance in the woodland scenes of *Courage of Lassie*, but the housebroken chipmunk just seemed out of place in nature and its scenes did not make the final cut.

Elizabeth's own appearance in the Technicolor film was quite striking. Her entrance in a bare-midriff top and shorts, coupled with her rapidly maturing face and physique, made her appear older than she does throughout the rest of the film. While Lassie got far more screen time, Elizabeth made a memorable impression.

FROM TOP: Elizabeth's love of animals became famous at an early age, especially after she published *Nibbles and Me,* a story about her pet chipmunk. | Elizabeth's saucy charm and striking looks shown through from the time she was in her early teens.

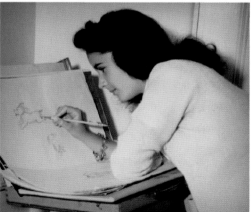

These shots show new MGM star Elizabeth about the time she made *Courage of Lassie*. Such photos attempted to show fans that she was just an ordinary girl between films—which she was. Playing with her animals, sewing, taking school lessons (with actress Shirley Johns), and creating art, were but a few of the activities that occupied her time between movies.

Life with Father

WARNER BROS.

CAST

William Powell .... *Clarence Day, Sr.*
Irene Dunne .... *Vinnie Day*
Elizabeth Taylor .... *Mary Skinner*
Edmund Gwenn .... *Reverend Dr. Lloyd*
Zasu Pitts .... *Cora Cartwright*
Jimmy Lydon .... *Clarence Day, Jr.*
Emma Dunn .... *Margaret*
Moroni Olsen .... *Dr. Humphries*
Elisabeth Risdon .... *Mrs. Whitehead*
Derek Scott .... *Harlan Day*

CREDITS

Robert Buckner *(producer)*; Michael Curtiz *(director)*; Donald Ogden Stewart *(screenplay)*, based on memoir by Clarence Day and play by Howard Lindsay; Russel Crouse; Peverell Marley, William V. Skall *(photography)*; Leo F. Forbstein *(musical director)*; Max Steiner *(music)*; Robert Haas *(art director)*; James Hopkins *(set decorations)*; C. A. Riggs *(sound)*; Robert Vreeland *(assistant director)*; George Amy *(editor)*; Milo Anderson *(costumes)*; Perc Westmore *(makeup)*

RELEASE DATE: September 13, 1947
RUN TIME: 118 minutes, color

OPPOSITE, FROM TOP: Out-of-towner Mary Skinner enjoys luncheon with the Days. William Powell played the patriarch of the family and gave one of the best performances of his career. Playwright Howard Lindsay had originated the part on Broadway. | Jimmy Lydon finds his first crush in dreamy young Elizabeth. | Opposite Jimmy Lydon, Elizabeth played an amorous adolescent, but in this scene she cannot compete with the power Lydon thinks his hand-me-down pants have. He simply is in no mood for romance when wearing his father's trousers.

SUMMARY: In nineteenth-century New York, the Day household is run with an iron fist and a heart of gold by financier Clarence Day. The real power behind the scenes though is Vinnie, a loving wife whose major ambition is to see Clarence baptized so that he may be saved and rejoin the God-fearing members of the family in the hereafter. The story follows the ever-charming everyday happenings of Clarence, Vinnie, and their four children: including an errant money-making venture selling patent medicine and burgeoning puppy love between eldest son Clarence, Jr., and visiting neighbor Mary Skinner.

ABOVE: Her bangs from the film suddenly disappeared, but the unique look of Elizabeth's eyebrows in *Life with Father* make photos of the period unique among her early career shots.

notes

THE RUSSEL CROUSE/HOWARD LINDSAY PLAY *LIFE WITH FATHER*, based on the memoirs of Clarence Day, was a show business legend that had an astonishing run of eight years and 3,224 performances. Up until *Fiddler on the Roof* in 1972, it was the longest-running nonmusical play ever put on the Broadway stage. Transferring its success to the big screen was a natural next step in the life of the story, which first came to the attention of the pubic as a humorous and touching series of articles based on the experiences of Clarence Day and his family in 1880s New York.

After paying half a million dollars for the screen rights, Warner Bros. put the film into production on April 11, 1946. The play was so revered that the studio gave Russel Crouse, Howard Lindsay, and Day's widow, Vinnie, approval over all phases of production. Former silent-screen star Mary Pickford was rumored to be making a comeback in the film, but director Michael Curtiz instead gave the role of Vinnie to Irene Dunne, whom Mrs. Day so approved of that she lent Dunne some of her clothes, in turn lending unique authenticity to the proceedings. The venerable William Powell starred as Clarence Day, a role in which the actor earned his third Academy Award nomination as Best Actor.

Third-billed Elizabeth Taylor was cast as Mary Skinner, a part that had been portrayed on stage by Alfred Hitchcock's *Shadow of a Doubt* star Teresa Wright. Jimmy Lydon was her tentative love interest. Lydon was smitten with her off-screen as well. He later said Elizabeth was a pleasure to work with but that it was also rather difficult to play opposite her because "You just didn't believe anybody could be that beautiful."

REVIEWS

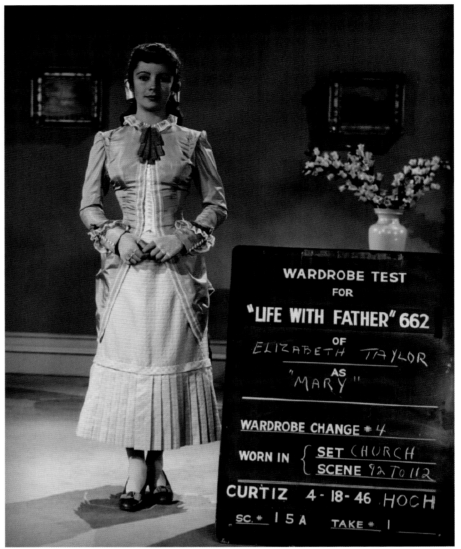

ABOVE FROM LEFT: Warner Bros. publicity shot of Elizabeth | A test shot for *Life with Father*

Elizabeth appeared in the film through a loan out arranged with MGM. Once she was on Warner Bros. territory, Perc Westmore, of the famed Hollywood makeup dynasty, saw fit to experiment with Elizabeth's appearance. Fans can recognize any photo of her taken at the time or in connection with *Life with Father* because of the unique way in which her eyebrows are thinned out and shaped. The moment she returned to her home lot, the plucking halted as the MGM makeup crew waited for her eyebrows to grow back into the fuller form that better suited her face.

The play *Life with Father* closed at the Alvin Theatre on July 12, 1947. Just a month later, the film adaptation of the Broadway staple had its New York premiere. Its homespun warmth and humor was reminiscent of hits of the era such as *Meet Me in St. Louis*. *Life with Father* proved to be a success in any shape from a series of articles, to a play, and on to film*. The movie brought in more than $5 million at the box office.

*The only format that did not seem to work for the *Father* franchise was television. A short-lived series ran from 1953–55.

Cynthia

METRO-GOLDWYN-MAYER

CAST

Elizabeth Taylor .... *Cynthia Bishop*

George Murphy .... *Larry Bishop*

S. Z. Sakall .... *Professor Rosenkrantz*

Mary Astor .... *Louise Bishop*

Gene Lockhart .... *Dr. Fred I. Jannings*

Spring Byington .... *Carrie Jannings*

Jimmy Lydon .... *Ricky Latham*

Scotty Beckett .... *Will Parker*

Carol Brannon .... *Fredonia Jannings*

Anna Q. Nilsson .... *Miss Brady*

CREDITS

Edwin H. Knopf *(producer)*; Robert Z. Leonard *(director)*; Harold Buchman, Charles Kaufman, Buster Keaton *(screenplay)*, based on play by Viña Delmar; Charles Schoenbaum *(photography)*; Johnny Green *(musical director)*; Bronislau Kaper *(music)*; Cedric Gibbons, Edward Carfagno *(art directors)*; Edwin B. Willis, Paul Chamberlain *(set decorations)*; Douglas Shearer *(sound)*; Irvine Warburton *(editor)*; Irene *(costumes)*; Jack Dawn *(makeup)*

RELEASE DATE: August 29, 1947

RUN TIME: 98 minutes, black and white

SUMMARY: Cynthia Bishop is a beautiful bird in a gilded cage, under the constant vigil of her parents, Larry and Louise, who worry after their daughter's delicate health to the point of stifling her everyday teen-aged existence. The Bishop marriage is also in need of doctoring. Through Cynthia's maturing individuality, baby steps open up a whole new world for her. Cynthia discovers a passion for singing under the tutelage of kindly Professor Rosenkrantz; handsome young Ricky Latham provides love interest; the upcoming school prom promises to be an unforgettable night; and her personal development brings renewed strength to her parents' marriage.

CLOCKWISE FROM TOP: Re-creating the first kiss with Lydon, for the benefit of the still photographer. | Ready for her first onscreen kiss, with James Lydon | Puppy love with Lydon

REVIEWS

"Do you like candy—gooey candy—such as these nickel (or six-cent) nut-fruit bars? If so, you probably will like *Cynthia*, . . . Played by Elizabeth Taylor in a dewy-eyed, fluttery style, little Cynthia will chew her way softly, like a moth, into susceptible hearts. And Jimmy Lydon, playing her boyfriend, will completely knock the props from under all those sentimental people who have got their ideas of teen-age boys from Alcott books."

**—*The New York Times*
(Bosley Crowther)**

"Able acting and a few moments of emotional intensity do not keep *Cynthia* from being a fragmentary screen drama. . . . Miss Taylor does a brilliant job in the title role. In vivid contrast to Hollywood's general conception of the bobby-soxer, she plays an unwilling invalid with grave charm. The scenes in which she has her first taste of the rich full life are interpreted with subtle authority."

**—New York *Herald Tribune*
(Howard Barnes)**

CYNTHIA WAS THE FIRST REAL SHOWCASE FOR ELIZABETH Taylor as a burgeoning leading lady. No one seemed to mind that it was based on an unsuccessful play by Viña Delmar titled *The Rich, Full Life*, which had run on Broadway for only twenty-seven performances, starring Virginia Weidler. Once a child star at MGM most famous for playing Katharine Hepburn's little sister in *The Philadelphia Story*, Weidler retired from show business shortly after the play closed.

Since the show had been a flop there was no need for the film to carry on either its name or its plagued history, so the title changed and Elizabeth was cast in the lead role. The release of *Life with Father* was held back to coincide with the stage edition's closing on Broadway. As a result, *Cynthia* opened in movie houses first, but it actually went into production six weeks after the completion of *Life with Father*, on October 8, 1946. Elizabeth was given the chance to stretch her wings as never before playing Cynthia, a sickly but spirited fifteen-year-old. She was to perform a song (dubbed) and experience her first onscreen kiss. The fortunate man on the receiving end was James Lydon, a particularly good choice to put Elizabeth at ease for her first kiss as she had just gotten to know him during the making of *Life with Father* at Warner Bros. So much attention surrounded this cinematic smooch, the first of many to come, that for a time MGM considered changing the film's title to *First Kiss*.

Given all the attention to her growing up before the eyes of the public, Elizabeth was anxious to make herself appear older. Her figure had already taken on a womanly form, but she learned early on to emphasize her shape with good posture, and to give her face maturity by becoming an expert at makeup tricks taught to her by studio professionals. Lydon later attested she was still a kid at heart who brought animals to the studio everyday. On the set of *Cynthia* her favorite was a pet squirrel that director Robert Z. Leonard banished from the set because it made too much noise during filming. The squirrel was just a minor distraction from business as usual. *Cynthia* came in on time and under budget, and Elizabeth won praise from critics for putting her best foot forward in her first solo starring role.

ABOVE: Elizabeth began to land her first magazine covers in this period, including a very early Italian front page. **OPPOSITE:** As Cynthia Bishop

THIS PAGE, CLOCKWISE FROM TOP LEFT: At the premiere of *Cynthia*, with George Murphy, who played her father | Candid of Elizabeth while vacationing in England | Elizabeth's pet squirrel was a troublemaker on the set and was eventually banned by director Robert Z. Leonard. | Primping her own hair

ABOVE: A jaunt to jolly old England with her mother in 1946. BELOW FROM LEFT: Barbequing with her father, Francis Taylor | With fellow MGM kids Jane Powell, Margaret O'Brien, and Claude Jarman, Jr.

A Date with Judy

METRO-GOLDWYN-MAYER

CAST

Wallace Beery .... *Melvin R. Foster*

Jane Powell .... *Judy Foster*

Elizabeth Taylor .... *Carol Pringle*

Carmen Miranda .... *Rosita Cochellas*

Xavier Cugat ....*himself*

Robert Stack .... *Stephen Andrews*

Scotty Beckett................... *Ogden Pringle*

Selena Royle............................*Dora Foster*

Leon Ames.....................*Lucien T. Pringle*

Clinton Sundberg........................*Jameson*

CREDITS

Joe Pasternak *(producer)*; Richard Thorpe *(director)*; Dorothy Kingsley, Dorothy Cooper *(screenplay)*, based on character created by Aleen Leslie; Robert Surtees *(photography)*; Georgie Stoll *(musical director)*; Stanley Donen *(dance director)*; Cedric Gibbons, Paul Groesse *(art directors)*; Edwin B. Willis, Richard A. Pefferle *(set decorations)*; Hugh Boswell *(production manager)*; Douglas Shearer *(sound)*; Harold F. Kress *(editor)*; Helen Rose *(costumes)*; Sydney Guilaroff *(hairstylist)*; Jack Dawn *(makeup)*

RELEASE DATE: July 29, 1948

RUN TIME: 113 minutes, color

SUMMARY:

Judy Foster and Carol Pringle are best friends with one too many things in common: Each has a crush on the same handsome, older man: Stephen Andrews, who has an eye for Carol. The circumstances are further complicated by the fact of Oogie Pringle, Carol's brother and Judy's boyfriend. This complicated foursome is not the only romantic web in need of untangling. Judy's father, Melvin, is hoping to surprise wife Dora by taking rumba lessons from the exotic Rosita Cochellas, but the amount of time Melvin spends with Rosita only leads everyone to believe that they are having an affair. By fade-out, all romantically crossed wires are happily sorted out to a happy conclusion.

RIGHT: As Carol Pringle **OPPOSITE:** Shots from this photo session at Malibu were used to publicize *A Date with Judy*. Roddy McDowall, seen in some of the images, was not in the film.

"The outlandishly colorful world which youngsters create for themselves has often made good motion-picture material, but in this case the goings-on have neither much humor nor much adolescent dignity. . . . The big surprise in *A Date with Judy* is Elizabeth Taylor as the petulant, dark-eyed banker's daughter. The erstwhile child star of *National Velvet* and other films has been touched by Metro's magic wand and turned into a real, 14-carat, 100-proof siren with a whole new career opening in front of her." —New York *Herald Tribune* (Otis L. Guernsey, Jr.)

"One of its more amusing songs, 'Strictly on the Corny Side,' just about epitomizes *A Date with Judy*. . . . Hollywood has developed an extensive and rigid set of conventions for its unceasing stream of comedies of adolescence, and *Judy* adheres carefully to all of them. But within the limits of this familiar pattern, the picture is pleasantly entertaining. The young people in the cast, Elizabeth Taylor, Jane Powell, and Scotty Beckett, are attractive to the eye and ear." —*The New York Times* (Thomas F. Brady)

THE TECHNICOLOR MUSICAL *A DATE WITH JUDY* **OSTENSIBLY** served as a vehicle to highlight the talents of singing star Jane Powell, the protégé of MGM producer Joe Pasternak. But the movie also turned out to be a showcase for a number of other players in the cast. Most notably there was the usually acerbic Wallace Beery playing against type as Jane's father, Carmen Miranda as the outrageous Latin star who gives him rumba lessons, and Elizabeth Taylor as the glamorous teen who just cannot help being the center of male attention. These personalities helped the film musical cash in at the box office to the tune of $3.7 million. *A Date with Judy*, which originated as a popular radio series, also saw life as a short-lived television show of the early 1950s.

The film went into production on December 15, 1947, and was completed on January 27, 1948. During that time Elizabeth and Jane Powell became fast friends. Powell admired her for the rest of her life. In a 1981 interview, Powell said, "[Elizabeth's] not afraid to say exactly what she feels. She's not afraid to show it all. I think the public respects Elizabeth for her honesty. You can't fool them for too long." The movie featured a large ensemble cast—an MGM specialty during the studio era, when long-term contracts ensured that the services of a reliable stable of stars and character actors were always on call. Given the youth-oriented subject matter of *A Date with Judy*, with the exception of Beery it was not a company of longtime MGM stalwarts but a group of fresh young faces romping through the proceedings.

Powell, Elizabeth, costar Robert Stack, and friends Roddy McDowall, Marshall Thompson, Peter Lawford, and Margaret O'Brien, were all young MGM contract stars at the time who, to some degree more than others, were raised by the studio. It formed a familial bond between them all that Elizabeth cherished. Working in movies at such a young age did not allow her to have a normal childhood by any stretch of the imagination. The young actors were educated on set between takes and at MGM's Little Red School House, as much as time permitted given their hectic schedules. No one took the lesson plans too seriously, and no matter what subjects they were learning, the actors were expected to retain little beyond their lines.

For Elizabeth, Powell, McDowall, and others, a life of being groomed for stardom was all they knew. Elizabeth said, "MGM taught me how to be a star . . . and I have never really known how to be anything else." On a still darker note, she shared in 1966 that "I was bred and raised like a fine thoroughbred horse. . . . Stars, to their manipulators, are not human beings but investments." The feelings of resentment and of being manipulated by the

> *"I think the public respects Elizabeth for her honesty. You can't fool them for long."*
> —JANE POWELL

studio would grow in years to come, but in 1948 Elizabeth just did what was expected of her, and forever after appreciated and maintained the friendships formed around the studio and in films such as *A Date with Judy.*

Julia Misbehaves

METRO-GOLDWYN-MAYER

CAST

Greer Garson.........................*Julia Packett*

Walter Pidgeon .... *William Sylvester Packett*

Peter Lawford....................*Ritchie Lorgan*

Elizabeth Taylor .... *Susan Packett*

Cesar Romero .... *Fred Ghenoccio*

Lucile Watson.......................*Mrs. Packett*

Nigel Bruce........*Col. Bruce Willowbrook*

Mary Boland....................*Mrs. Gheneccio*

Reginald Owen................ *Benny Hawkins*

Henry Stephenson....... *Lord Pennystone*

CREDITS

Everett Riskin *(producer)*; Jack Conway *(director)*; Monckton Hoffe, Gina Kaus *(screenplay)*, based on novel *The Nutmeg Tree* by Margery Sharp; Joseph Ruttenberg *(photography)*; Adolph Deutsch *(music)*; Stanley Donen *(dance director)*; Cedric Gibbons, Daniel B. Cathcart *(art directors)*; Edwin B. Willis, Jack D. Moore *(set decorations)*; Douglas Shearer *(sound)*; John Dunning *(editor)*; Irene *(costumes)*; Sydney Guilaroff *(hairstylist)*; Jack Dawn *(makeup)*

RELEASE DATE: August 8, 1948

RUN TIME: 99 minutes, black and white

RIGHT: With Peter Lawford, a crush at the time. They became fast friends. **OPPOSITE, FROM TOP:** As Susan Packett | Greer Garson, Lawford, and Elizabeth. Julia is back in town for her daughter's wedding but wonders if Susan might do better heading down the aisle with Ritchie (Lawford).

SUMMARY: After splitting from her husband Walter, showgirl Julia Packett decided to leave their daughter, Susan, in the care of his affluent, respectable family. While working in a music hall twenty years later, she receives an invitation to Susan's wedding in Paris and is determined to attend. Once in France Julia reestablishes her relationship with Susan and affects a change in partners for her when Julia sees Susan may be in love with another man—this is but one among many ways in which the stodgy William Packett's staid existence is turned upside down by Julia in the days leading up to Susan's wedding. Still, he must admit he finds her zaniness endlessly endearing, and may like her to stay forever.

"*Julia Misbehaves* is a mighty undignified lady—and a might funny one. A riot of screwball slapstick that never takes itself seriously for a single moment, film is geared for grosses as hearty as its laughs. Greer Garson unbends in this one and the ballyhoo exploiting that unbending shapes it for big returns." —*Variety* ("Brog")

"It is hard to conceive of [Greer Garson] attempting anything more impulsive or crude than the slapstick, bedroom-farce romance, which is what this explosion is. A little bit of frivolity—yes, that would be all right. And a little less emphasis on the sentiment would be quite welcome, too. But when the dignified lady starts scrambling about on the heads of a troupe of acrobatic tumblers as Lou Costello might do; when she goes down gurgling into a lake in a leaky rowboat and then ends up wrapped in a tablecloth, she's out of her element. . . . Maybe Miss Garson's wild adorers will think it the giddiest sort of lark, but it looks to this anxious observer like a fall on her beautiful face."

—*The New York Times* (Bosley Crowther)

ABOVE, FROM LEFT: A hairstyle test | Elizabeth was growing up fast before the eyes of movie audiences.

> *By leaps and bounds Elizabeth was maturing into a breathtaking woman.*

SOME SEVENTY YEARS AFTER THE PEAK OF HER FAME GREER Garson is often overlooked or even forgotten, but in the 1940s she was a critically acclaimed, Oscar-winning actress as well as one of the top box-office stars in all of Hollywood. In 1945 she was the leading lady in Quigley's annual list of top-ten stars who attracted the movie-going public, and films in which she starred opposite Walter Pidgeon, such as *Mrs. Miniver*, were among the most popular. By 1948 though, her name had fallen off the top-ten list and she had experienced back-to-back flops. MGM decided to give typically dramatic leads Garson and Pidgeon a change of pace with the comedy *Julia Misbehaves*.

The movie began life in the form of a book by Margery Sharp called *The Nutmeg Tree*, which went on to play on Broadway as *Lady in Waiting* during the spring of 1940 starring Gladys George. In the film, fans used to the dignified,

heroic image of Garson exemplified by *Mrs. Miniver* now encountered her playing an irrepressible dance-hall performer cum high-flying aerialist, trying to get back in the good graces of her estranged husband and their child. Elizabeth portrayed Garson's daughter, a girl blossoming into womanhood and encountering love for the first time. The love interest in this case was Peter Lawford. Elizabeth formed a real-life crush on the actor, but he was a sophisticated twenty-four at the time and immune to charms of his sixteen-year-old costar. He enjoyed their time working together though, and they became lifelong friends.

Though not quite ripe enough for Lawford, Elizabeth's childhood youth was fading at a rapid rate, as noted by reviewers of *Julia Misbehaves*. By leaps and bounds she was maturing into a breathtaking woman. Lawford gave Elizabeth her second onscreen kiss. Contrasting the baby-faced Jimmy Lydon, who gave Elizabeth her first cinematic smooch, playing opposite the urbane Lawford made her appear truly all grown up. Lawford and Elizabeth made an attractive pair and added spice to the proceedings of *Julia Misbehaves*, but it remained a mild offering in spite of being blessed with a top-notch cast and receiving ample press as a change of pace for Garson. The film did nothing to either harm or enhance Greer Garson's career, but it proved to be most significant to the star on a personal level. On the set of *Julia Misbehaves* Peter Lawford introduced her to his friend, E. E. "Buddy" Fogelson, who became her third husband and to whom she would remain married until his death in 1987.

ABOVE, FROM LEFT: Inspecting a bust of herself offscreen during *Julia Misbehaves* | Playing backstage with star Walter Pidgeon **BELOW:** A portrait of the happy young couple. Elizabeth and Lawford lent their youthful charm to the film.

Little Women

METRO-GOLDWYN-MAYER

CAST

June Allyson	Jo
Peter Lawford	Laurie
Margaret O'Brien	Beth
Elizabeth Taylor	Amy
Janet Leigh	Meg
Rosanno Brazzi	Professor Bhaer
Mary Astor	Marmee
Lucile Watson	Aunt March
C. Aubrey Smith	Mr. Laurence
Elizabeth Patterson	Hannah

CREDITS

Mervyn LeRoy *(producer/director)*; Sarah Y. Mason, Andrew Solt, Victor Heerman *(screenplay)*, based on novel by Louisa May Alcott; Robert Planck, Charles Schoenbaum *(photography)*; Adolph Deutsch *(music)*; Cedric Gibbons, Paul Groesse *(art directors)*; Edwin B. Willis, Jack D. Moore *(set decorations)*; Douglas Shearer *(sound)*; Ralph E. Winters *(editor)*; Walter Plunkett *(costumes)*; Sydney Guilaroff *(hairstylist)*; Jack Dawn *(makeup)*

RELEASE DATE: April, 1949
RUN TIME: 122 minutes, color

RIGHT: Dressed up as Amy March

SUMMARY: In Civil War–era New England, the March sisters, Jo, Meg, Amy, and Beth, along with their mother, cope with life without their father. While he is away at war, they face numerous tribulations and circumstances that are at turns heartwarming and heart-wrenching. The independent Jo departs home to find herself; Meg takes the more conventional route of marrying a charming neighbor; Amy matures from vanity to selflessness through the gentle spirit of sickly sister Beth. Amy also finds love with Jo's former romantic interest, Laurie; Jo, in turn, finds a kindred spirit in her loyal friend from New York, Professor Bhaer. Through it all, the March sisters remain devoted to each other and grow from little women to adulthood.

FROM TOP: A lobby card for *Little Women* | Reprimanded for her amusing caricature of the teacher, Amy is a spirited March sister.

"Cinematized in Technicolor by Metro-Goldwyn-Mayer with great affections, charm, and elegant appointments, acted by a cast of admirable players. . . . *Little Women* is an excursion into authentic Americana. It is as gay as a Christmas card, as wondrous as childhood's happiest dream."
—*New York Journal of Commerce* (Russell Rhodes)

"In short, in the first part of this picture, Metro has managed to contain a pretty agreeable assortment of period fun and sentiment. Jo is the bold, dynamic leader; Meg is the sweet, ambitious lass; Amy is the vixen and Beth is the soulful baby sis. And, of course, the neighbor, Laurie, is the lad of whom maidens softly dream. You should find them all appealing—provided you have a sweet tooth. But the latter part of the picture, in which clouds of trouble descend and the fictions of girlish disposition take artificial command, has got away from the scriptwriters. . . . As Amy, Elizabeth Taylor is appropriately full of artifice."
—*The New York Times* (Bosley Crowther)

notes

LOUISA MAY ALCOTT'S *LITTLE WOMEN, OR MARGARET, JO, Elizabeth, and Amy* (full original title) was first published in two volumes released in 1868 and 1869 and became an instant classic. An American favorite, it was not long after movies first came into being that the first screen adaptations of *Little Women* began to appear. By the time MGM took a crack at it, a critically acclaimed cinematic edition of the story had come from RKO in 1933, produced by David O. Selznick and starring Katharine Hepburn. In 1946, Selznick himself began mounting a new production of *Little Women*, planning to have his wife, Jennifer Jones, along with Rhonda Fleming, Shirley Temple, and Anne Revere among the cast. Ultimately Selznick abandoned the project and MGM took up the reins in 1948 for what was to be the most elegantly charming, if not the most universally respected, version of *Little Women*.

The four March sisters would be played by two of the studio's top moneymakers, June Allyson and Margaret O'Brien, and two of their up-and-coming stars, Elizabeth Taylor and Janet Leigh. Elizabeth was to portray the beautiful, vain, but big-hearted Amy. It is fitting that it was a role she inherited from her future famous onscreen mother of *Father of the Bride*, Joan Bennett, who played Amy in the 1933 edition. The touch of pretentiousness and blond wig notwithstanding, among the March sisters it was the character of Amy that suited Elizabeth best. As a result she gave one of the finest performances of her early career.

> *The touch of pretentiousness and blond wig notwithstanding, among the March sisters it was the character of Amy that suited Elizabeth best.*

FROM TOP: Test shots of Elizabeth as Amy March | A Danish magazine cover depicting Elizabeth and Peter Lawford in *Little Women*

ABOVE: MGM publicity of up-and-coming "little women": Janet Leigh, Elizabeth, Jane Powell, and Ann Blyth BELOW, FROM LEFT: Elizabeth and screen sister Janet Leigh | Five years apart in age makes a difference to teenagers. Costar Margaret O'Brien appreciated that Elizabeth played with her.

ABOVE, FROM LEFT: Famously brunette Elizabeth was still a brunette while filming *Little Women*. This portrait is from that period. Her blondness onscreen came by courtesy of a wig. | Oscar time with best friend Roddy McDowall. That evening *Little Women* was nominated for two Academy Awards and won one. BELOW: In costume for *Little Women,* Elizabeth visits Frank Sinatra and Gene Kelly on the set of their film, *Take Me Out to the Ballgame*.

Director Mervyn LeRoy admired her during the making of *Little Women* in 1948 as well as decades later, when he said, "Elizabeth has always had a lot of warmth and heart. The public has always been able to recognize that quality in her—and has responded with adulation." As usual, Elizabeth got along well with her costars, too. She was reunited with Peter Lawford, who again was the man with whom her character would end up in a romantic twist of fate. Eleven-year-old Margaret O'Brien, who played Beth, enjoyed her time in Elizabeth's company, later commenting, "Here was a little girl who was very nice and not at all pretentious. She wasn't snooty. She would jump rope and play with me." Elizabeth may have been given to airs as Amy onscreen, but she was far more down to earth off the screen.

Production on MGM's *Little Women* wrapped in September 1948 and the film hit theaters in April 1949. It took in $3.6 million at the box office and brought home an Academy Award for Best Art Direction.

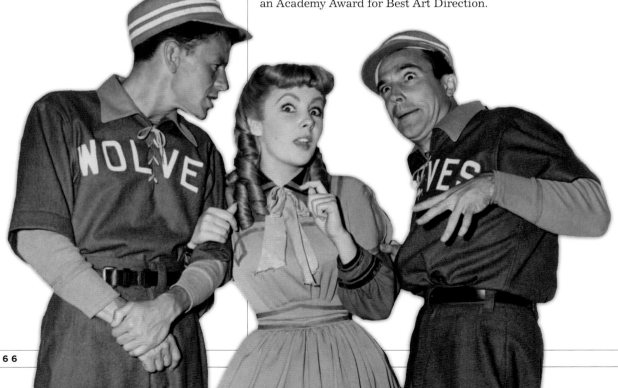

At turns dramatic and euphoric,
a photo shoot at Elizabeth's home
during the making of *Little Women*

Conspirator

METRO-GOLDWYN-MAYER

CAST

Robert Taylor ..... *Major Michael Curragh*

Elizabeth Taylor .... *Melinda Greyton*

Robert Flemyng .... *Captain Hugh Ladholme*

Harold Warrender .... *Colonel Hammerbrook*

Honor Blackman .... *Joyce*

Marjorie Fielding .... *Aunt Jessica*

Thora Hird .... *Broaders*

Wilfred Hyde-White ..... *Lord Pennistone*

Marie Ney .... *Lady Pennistone*

Jack Allen .... *Raglan*

CREDITS

Arthur Hornblow, Jr. *(producer)*; Victor Saville *(director)*; Sally Benson, Gerard Fairlie *(screenplay)*, based on novel by Humphrey Slater; F. A. Young *(photography)*; John Wooldridge *(music)*; Alfred Junge *(art director)*; Dora Wright *(production manager)*; A. W. Watkins, Sash Fisher *(sound)*; Frank Clarke *(editor)*

RELEASE DATE: July 29, 1949 (U.K.); March 24, 1950 (U.S.)

RUN TIME: 87 minutes, black and white

RIGHT: Taylor and Taylor, together for the first time in *Conspirator*

SUMMARY: While visiting a friend in London, Melinda Greyton enters into a whirlwind romance with a high-ranking officer in the British Army, Major Michael Curragh. Not long after they marry, Michael's secretiveness and mysterious absences mount to an alarming degree, but Melinda has no inkling that her new husband is actually a communist spy reporting secrets of British Intelligence to the Soviets. He cannot keep the secret from his wife for long. Melinda discovers his covert identity and his Soviet commanders order Michael to kill his wife because she knows too much. Melinda becomes haunted not only by the secrets she has discovered, but by the fact that Michael may be trying to murder her.

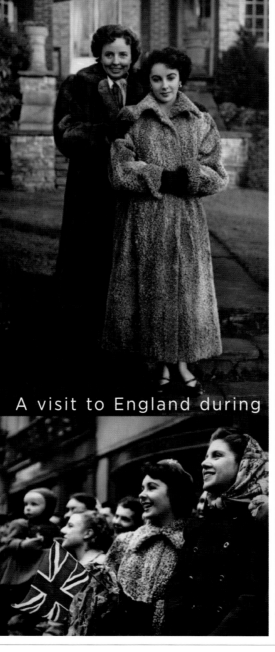

A visit to England during the making of *Conspirator*.

LEFT: Among these photos Elizabeth is seen shopping with her mother; recording a radio show; proudly holding a British flag; at a premiere with Robert Taylor; and on London Bridge wearing Glenn Davis's football sweater.

ABOVE, FROM LEFT: The wedding—with Harold Warrender, Robert Taylor, Honor Blackman, and Robert Flemyng | Robert Taylor plays a "model" officer; Elizabeth soon learns the truth. **BELOW:** Elizabeth and one-time flame Bill Pawley, Jr.

"THE MAN SHE LOVED WAS A TRAITOR, SWORN TO KILL HER," so said the tagline of *Conspirator*, a definite change of pace for Elizabeth that played into the hysteria in Hollywood gaining momentum at the time: finding communist spies skulking behind every soundstage.

Elizabeth had already had her first kiss, romance, and marriage on the big screen, but playing Melinda Greyton was her first truly grown-up, dramatic role opposite a male star of the first order, Robert Taylor. She was seventeen and he was twenty years her senior, a fact which MGM pointedly subdued by establishing within moments of their onscreen meeting that the character Elizabeth played was eighteen and Taylor's character was thirty-one. Thereafter Elizabeth's youth was utilized to show how blindly joyous or, at times, how out of her depth and inexperienced the girl she played in the film was when faced with life-changing facts about the man she married.

> *As in all her films of this period, it was abundantly clear that the public grew to love Elizabeth more with each appearance.*

The two Taylors were sent on location to film *Conspirator* in London from November 1948 to February 1949. Elizabeth enjoyed returning "home" to England for the visit and took photo shoots—with and without her mother Sara—all around town. The finished work was not among Elizabeth's favorites, but there is much to recommend the film, not the least of which is her engaging performance, or genuinely suspenseful moments created amid lush MGM accoutrements by wolf-in-sheep's-clothing Robert Taylor.

As in all her films of this period, it was abundantly clear that the public grew to love Elizabeth more with each appearance. In acknowledgment of this, she began to be rushed into one film after another. All the while, the stirrings of her resentment toward being controlled both by the studio and her mother began to grow. She later said, "During the early part of my growing up period and through my first two marriages, I was searching for a purpose to my daily routine." Elizabeth made a bid for independence by dating some of the most eligible bachelors of the era, including American football star Glenn Davis and William Pawley, Jr., the son of a wealthy aviation entrepreneur whom she met while vacationing with her mother in Miami. These were the first of many amours for Elizabeth that fascinated her fans.

A fitting for *Conspirator*, with MGM costume designer Helen Rose

Full view of an Elizabeth Taylor photo shoot

Rare portraits of Elizabeth in her *Conspirator* period

The Big Hangover

METRO-GOLDWYN-MAYER

CAST

Van Johnson........................ *David Muldon*

Elizabeth Taylor .... *Mary Belney*

Percy Waram......................... *John Belney*

Fay Holden......................... *Martha Belney*

Leon Ames............................... *Carl Bellcap*

Edgar Buchanan.... *Uncle Fred Mahoney*

Selena Royle...................... *Kate Mahoney*

Gene Lockhart .... *Charles Parkford*

Rosemary DeCamp............ *Claire Bellcap*

Philip Ahn... *Dr. Lee*

CREDITS

Norman Krasna *(producer/director/screenplay)*; George Folsey *(photography)*; Adolphe Deutsch *(music)*; Cedric Gibbons, Paul Groesse *(art directors)*; Edwin B. Willis, Henry Grace *(set decorations)*; Douglas Shearer *(sound)*; Frederick Y. Smith *(editor)*; Helen Rose *(costumes)*; Jack Dawn *(makeup)*

RELEASE DATE: May 26, 1950
RUN TIME: 82 minutes, black and white

RIGHT: Elizabeth and Van Johnson **OPPOSITE:** Elizabeth, Johnson, and their canine pal in *The Big Hangover*

SUMMARY: Ex-serviceman David Muldon returned home from war with a most unique battle scar. Nearly drowning in a wine cellar resulted in his developing an allergy that renders him roaring drunk at the mere scent of spirits. This threatens the bright future ahead of David at a top law firm, until he links up with the boss's daughter, Mary Belney. They fall in love and Mary takes charge of keeping David out of trouble and keeping his problem under wraps. David is a fine lawyer with his star in the ascendant, but he discovers a discriminatory policy at the firm that calls into question his moral convictions of equality. Should he stay or should he go becomes the new dilemma for David and Mary.

REVIEWS

"Norman Krasna, as a writer-director-producer, has done a good job on his one-man show. Granted it's a slight story, he's decked it out in some amusing and tender situations, with sprightly, adult dialog and an expert cast of farceurs in support of the two romantic leads. Film gets a little too cute at times, and has a few dull stretches, but neither happens often enough to be serious. . . . Miss Taylor is warm and appealing as the amateur psychiatrist . . ." —*Variety* ("Brog")

"Van Johnson gives a rather agreeable, if at times somewhat forced, performance . . . the boss's lovely daughter [is] most engagingly represented by Elizabeth Taylor. Generally speaking the performances are nicely keyed . . . *The Big Hangover*, although it runs an uneven course; still is good for some laughs and is deserving of attention." —*The New York Times* (Thomas M. Pryor)

notes

RIGHT: In this candid shot Elizabeth wears the All-Star football sweater of the boyfriend who preoccupied her mind at the time, Glenn Davis.

NORMAN KRASNA WAS A ONE-MAN ARMY AS WRITER, PRODUCER, and director of *The Big Hangover*, on the surface a light comedy about a man allergic to alcohol, but with dark undertones that addressed social issues of the day in a thoughtful if mild manner. It stretched to bear a comic resemblance to *The Lost Weekend*, the 1945 Best Picture Oscar winning film that was even referenced in the movie. Krasna had won an Academy Award in 1943 for his screenplay for *Princess O'Rourke* and had many other stellar comedy credits to his name, including *Wife vs. Secretary*, *Bachelor Mother*, and *The Devil and Miss Jones*, but his latest effort in 1950 was not among his finest.*

> *This was a time of uncertainty for Elizabeth in which she seriously pondered whether or not she wanted to remain in films.*

Shortly after her return from England for the filming of *Conspirator*, MGM cast Elizabeth in *The Big Hangover* opposite one of the most popular stars of the day, Van Johnson. Elizabeth herself admitted that she basically just went through the motions of her performance in *The Big Hangover*. Her heart was simply not in it: Both heart and mind were fixed on West Point football star and Heisman Trophy winner Glenn Davis. The relationship had gotten serious at the same time she felt her career was eroding.

Elizabeth had come to feel used and mistreated by the studio for making her appear in any variety and class of film whether she wanted to or not; *The Big Hangover* being a shining example of a project she did not want. If she objected her contract could be suspended and she would find herself without income. This was a time of uncertainty for Elizabeth in which she seriously pondered whether or not she wanted to remain in films. Glenn Davis wanted her to become Mrs. Davis, but the romance fizzled out, giving Elizabeth renewed dedication to her work. Her next movie was among the best of her career.

*Acclaimed Krasna films in years to come included *White Christmas*, *The Ambassador's Daughter*, and *Indiscreet*.

A Place in the Sun

PARAMOUNT PICTURES

CAST

Montgomery Clift.........*George Eastman*

Elizabeth Taylor ....*Angela Vickers*

Shelley Winters ....*Alice Tripp*

Anne Revere ....*Hannah Eastman*

Keefe Brasselle ....*Earl Eastman*

Fred Clark ....*Bellows*

Raymond Burr..............*R. Frank Marlowe*

Herbert Heyes...............*Charles Eastman*

Shepperd Strudwick ....*Anthony Vickers*

Frieda Inescort.............*Mrs. Ann Vickers*

CREDITS

George Stevens *(producer/director)*; Michael Wilson, Harry Brown *(screenplay)*, based on the novel *An American Tragedy* by Theodore Dreiser and play by Patrick Kearney; William C. Mellor *(photography)*; Franz Waxman *(music)*; Hans Dreier, Walter Tyler *(art directors)*; Emile Kuri *(set decorations)*; Gene Merritt, Gene Garvin *(sound)*; Ivan Moffat *(associate producer)*; Fred Guiol, C. C. Coleman, Jr. *(assistant directors)*; William Hornbeck *(editor)*; Edith Head *(costumes)*; Wally Westmore *(makeup)*

RELEASE DATE: August 15, 1951

RUN TIME: 122 minutes, black and white

RIGHT: Elizabeth as Angela Vickers. She was rich, beautiful, and unwittingly stole a pregnant woman's boyfriend, yet Elizabeth's performance and Stevens's treatment of the material managed to make Angela truly lovable.

SUMMARY: George Eastman takes a position in a swimsuit factory run by his distant uncle Charles Eastman. There he meets an assembly worker named Alice and they begin dating. Through ambition and diligence, George proves himself in the company and gets promoted. He also gains acceptance into the social life of his rich uncle Charles. In that rarified scene George meets and falls in love with the winsome Angela Vickers. Just as life turns idyllic, Alice reveals she is pregnant. Alone in the world, she insists George marry her. George cares for Alice but is torn because of his love for Angela. After Alice later drowns in George's presence, he is put on trial for murder. Angela stands by him. Regardless of the outcome, he must grapple with his conscience to decide whether or not he did all he could to save Alice in her final moments.

ABOVE: Frieda Inescort is at the head of the table. To the left of her is Clift and next to him, Elizabeth. *A Place in the Sun* was Paramount's "prestige" picture of the year. It took home six Oscars and $3.5 million at the box office.

REVIEWS

"Sticks pretty close to the values of a story that has become an American classic. In the main, the success of *A Place in the Sun* is probably attributable to George Stevens, who produced and directed it with workmanlike, powerful restraint and without tricks of sociological harangue. He has drawn excellent performances from Montgomery Clift, who is thoroughly believable as the young man; Elizabeth Taylor, who is remarkably well cast as the daughter of a wealthy social clan, and Shelley Winters, who is particularly moving."
—**New York *Herald Tribune*** (G. A.)

"Montgomery Clift, Shelley Winters, and Elizabeth Taylor give wonderfully shaded and poignant performances. For Miss Taylor, at least, the histrionics are of a quality so far beyond anything she has done previously, that Stevens' skilled hands on the reins must be credited with a minor miracle."   —***Variety*** ("Herb")

"Elizabeth Taylor's delineation of the rich and beauteous Angela is the top effort of her career. It is a shaded, tender performance and one in which her passionate and genuine romance avoids the pathos common to young love as it sometimes comes to the screen. . . . Mr. Stevens, his associates, and cast, have fashioned a work of distinction and conviction. And, though its theme is somber, it is beautiful and compassionate in its present state. It is, most of all, a rich and rewarding experience and a film drama of which its makers and Hollywood can be proud."

—***The New York Times*** (A. H. Weiler)

ABOVE: Elizabeth was Clift's companion to the premiere of his film *The Heiress*, which opened shortly after they began filming *A Place in the Sun*.

RIGHT: A costume fitting with designer Edith Head BELOW: Elizabeth and Clift. He had been a stage actor, like other fresh Hollywood faces of the day, such as Shelley Winters and Marlon Brando. Brando's *A Streetcar Named Desire* came out just a month after *A Place in the Sun*. Brando, Winters, and Clift astounded critics, audiences, and costars with their intense style of acting. OPPOSITE: With Montgomery Clift. Elizabeth later said, "I watched how much time he spent thinking about his character, studying, experimenting, and that became the key to the kind of acting I do—if you call what I do acting."

notes

> For Elizabeth, who had begun to feel disenchanted with movies and acting, Montgomery Clift was a revelation.

THEODORE DREISER'S *AN AMERICAN TRAGEDY*, PUBLISHED in 1925, was inspired by actual events and a murder trial that took place in Herkimer, New York, between 1906 and 1908. The human drama of the novel made it an instant classic that Paramount Pictures first adapted for the big screen in 1930. Released under the same title as the novel, the film was directed by Josef von Sternberg and starred Phillips Holmes, Sylvia Sidney, and Frances Dee. Dreiser was so incensed with Sternberg's final cut that he filed a lawsuit against Paramount in an effort to halt the film from being released. In court Dreiser testified, "It has been said that *An American Tragedy* has succeeded in presenting the life of a real human being and has made clear the motives that actuated him. I would not have put my name or devoted my efforts to telling merely a murder story. And yet, that is what the defendant (Paramount) has portrayed." Dreiser lost the court battle and Sternberg's film hit theaters in 1931. Most critics of the day agreed with the novelist's assessment.

Dreiser passed away before he ever got to see Paramount again attempt to capture the spirit of *An American Tragedy* under the aegis of director George Stevens. He understood the delicacy and power of Dreiser's story: "Any narrow interpretation is false. . . . In the story the people driven, and those who drive, seem close to us because what happens could easily have been our problem." Stevens assembled a remarkable cast headed by Montgomery Clift and Elizabeth Taylor (whose services came courtesy of a loan-out deal with MGM). For the third lead role of Alice, Stevens tested many actresses, including Hollywood's ultimate child star Shirley Temple, but it was Shelley Winters who got the part. Both Clift and Winters came from the New York stage, as did a group of other new faces in Hollywood who were then gaining much deserved praise for the white-hot style of acting they popularized in this period: the Method approach of full immersion into a role.

Elizabeth and Montgomery Clift were as devoted to each other as friends offscreen as they were romantically onscreen.

One of the most famous kisses ever filmed. Director George Stevens made it a magic cinematic moment by shooting in a tight close-up.

For Elizabeth, who had begun to feel disenchanted with movies and acting, Montgomery Clift was a revelation. She developed a mad crush on him that went nowhere as Clift's sexual orientation did not permit it. His personal anguish and instability touched Elizabeth's deeply empathetic spirit and maternal nature; they became the most devoted of friends. Besides loving him as a friend, Elizabeth was totally overwhelmed by Clift on a professional level. She had never been close to anyone like him: "I was agog. This genius young actor—and for the first time I took acting seriously and realized it wasn't a game. It was a craft." Perhaps due to their close personal bond, Elizabeth and Clift's screen chemistry was luscious, and fittingly they shared one of the most famous kisses ever committed to film. Shot in extreme close-up during a party scene, the world of the movie seemed to stop as their faces filled the screen.

> *Perhaps due to their close personal bond, Elizabeth and Clift's screen chemistry was luscious, and fittingly they shared one of the most famous kisses ever committed to film.*

Externally Elizabeth had long since matured on the screen, but *A Place in the Sun* marked her transition into maturity as an actress. Clift inspired her to stretch herself, "instead of walking through [films] as I had been doing." Elizabeth was an actress who fed off the energy and talent of her costars. Over the years she developed her own brilliance for the camera, but a great performance by an actor starring opposite her improved her own work to a stunning degree, particularly early in her career. She received her best reviews to date for *A Place in the Sun*.

The film went into production in October 1949, but Paramount held the release for a year and a half after its completion because *Sunset Boulevard* was planned as the studio's preeminent release of 1950, and they did not want *A Place in the Sun* to compete with it either at the box office or in the year's Academy Award race. The film made it to theaters in late summer of 1951. Though Stevens could boast of such outstanding credits as *Swing Time*, *Woman of the Year*, *The Talk of the Town*, *The More the Merrier*, and *I Remember Mama*, he called *A Place in the Sun* "the best thing I've ever done."

The movie took home six Oscars: Best Score, Best Director, Best Adapted Screenplay, Best Cinematography, Best Costume Design, and Best Editing. It also earned nominations for Best Picture, Best Actor, and Best Actress (Winters). It was named among the "100 Greatest Movies of All Time" by the American Film Institute, and the National Film Registry selected it for preservation in the Library of Congress in 1991, naming *A Place in the Sun* a "culturally, historically, and aesthetically significant" film.

ABOVE: The movie's tagline read: "A love story of today's youth . . . filling the screen with ecstasy as they seek a place in the sun!"

Father of the Bride

METRO-GOLDWYN-MAYER

CAST

Spencer Tracy .... *Stanley Banks*

Joan Bennett .... *Ellie Banks*

Elizabeth Taylor .... *Kay Banks*

Don Taylor .... *Buckley Dunstan*

Billie Burke .... *Doris Dunstan*

Leo G. Carroll .... *Mr. Massoula*

Moroni Olsen .... *Herbert Dunstan*

Melville Cooper .... *Mr. Tringle*

Taylor Holmes .... *Warner*

Paul Harvey .... *Reverend A. I. Galsworthy*

Frank Orth .... *Joe*

Russ Tamblyn .... *Tommy Banks*

CREDITS

Pandro S. Berman *(producer)*; Vincente Minnelli *(director)*; Frances Goodrich, Albert Hackett *(screenplay)*, based on novel by Edward Streeter; John Alton *(photography)*; Adolph Deutsch *(music)*; Cedric Gibbons, Leonid Vasian *(art directors)*; Edwin B. Willis, Keogh Gleason *(set decorations)*; Douglas Shearer *(sound)*; Ferris Webster *(editor)*; Walter Plunkett, Helen Rose *(costumes)*; Sydney Guilaroff *(hairstylist)*; Jack Dawn *(makeup)*

RELEASE DATE: June 16, 1950

RUN TIME: 92 minutes, black and white

SUMMARY: Stanley Banks's world is turned on its head when his daughter Kay announces her engagement to boyfriend Buckley Dunstan. A myriad of questions arise at once. Is the boy good enough for Kay? A man-to-man talk is necessary. Will Kay get over her last-minute jitters? Only after an unforgettable father-daughter talk. Are his parents accepting of martinis? Apparently anytime except at engagement parties. Is their home big enough for the reception? Well, just put all the furniture into storage. As wedding plans get underway, Stanley meets each disaster, unpleasant encounter, and money-draining suggestion with equal parts frustration and terror but always with a soft spot for his ever-loving daughter, Kay.

OPPOSITE: Kay and "Pops" ABOVE: The bride in all her glory, fashioned by Helen Rose

REVIEWS

"It's the second strong comedy in a row for Spencer Tracy, doing the title role, and he socks it. There's also the timely casting of Elizabeth Taylor as the bride (a title she just assumed in real life) to help stir wicket interest, and Joan Bennett completes the star trio with an elegant performance as the mother."

—*Variety* ("Brog")

"Elizabeth Taylor's good looks aid her in creating the illusion that in each successive scene the audience, like the father, is suddenly seeing her for the first time. . . . *Father of the Bride* is something like a good party. The occasion is well ordered, the people charming, the lapses not serious, and the end achieved before the conviviality is exhausted."

—New York *Herald Tribune* (Otis L. Guernsey, Jr.)

"The film, while it packs all the modern tribal matrimonial rite that was richly contained in the original [Streeter novel], also possesses all the warmth and poignancy and understanding that makes the Streeter treatise much beloved. . . . *Father of the Bride* is a honey of a picture of American family life."

—*The New York Times* (Bosley Crowther)

notes

ABOVE, FROM TOP: A costume sketch for Elizabeth by designer Helen Rose | Primping in her dressing room before going in front of the cameras RIGHT: Reading on the set, what else? Edward Streeter's *Father of the Bride*.

OPPOSITE TOP: The blushing bride with her groom, onscreen (Don Taylor) and in real life (Nicky Hilton). Hilton, of the famed hotel chain, was the great uncle of "celebutantes" Paris and Nicky. BOTTOM, FROM LEFT: Elizabeth gets a visit from studio head Louis B. Mayer (left). Mayer could not have been more pleased to have Elizabeth's own marriage to tie in with publicity for the film. | A charity fashion show at the studio during the making of *Father of the Bride*

THERE WAS NO MORE APPROPRIATE CASTING FOR ELIZABETH in 1950 than in *Father of the Bride*. In 1949 she had become engaged to Bill Pawley, Jr., but during the making of *A Place in the Sun* the romance had about run its course. In October of that year she met hotel heir Conrad "Nicky" Hilton, Jr. at a nightclub and they began dating. Elizabeth grew up with the strong conviction that when two people fall in love they seal it with marriage. Her romance with Hilton escalated rapidly and by February 1950 they became engaged. *Father of the Bride* had gone into production just a few weeks earlier and this most fortuitous timing allowed MGM to put the film on a schedule that would have it premiere just two days after her actual wedding to Hilton, and in general release a month later.

The film, based on a popular novel by Edward Streeter, was a comedy of the highest order. Frances Goodrich and Albert Hackett's script, coupled with Minnelli's sensitive handling of the material, created an authentically comical succession of events that were honest and poked fun at the hoopla surrounding marriage ceremonies without ever diminishing the state of marriage itself. Spencer Tracy, in one of the first comedies of his long career, was nothing short of brilliant in the title role, appropriately frustrated, baffled, harried, and put-upon, but all the while loving and genuinely funny. Elizabeth was at her best in their scenes

together, both sincere in the more serious moments and getting mileage out of inherently comedic scenes with her straight-faced line readings. Elizabeth and Tracy's rapport on the screen carried over from the friendship that quickly formed between them offscreen. From this time on, important events in Elizabeth's life always elicited a note of congratulations from Tracy signed "Love Pops."

OPPOSITE: On the set with her "Pops," Spencer Tracy. They became great friends during filming. **ABOVE:** Portrait of an eighteen-year-old bride-to-be, onscreen and off

Elizabeth's marriage to Nicky Hilton took place on May 6, 1950, at the Church of the Good Shepherd in Beverly Hills. She arrived amid screeching police sirens to a church filled with hundreds of guests, among them celebrity friends she had made at MGM, including Tracy, Lana Turner, and Fred Astaire. It was a dream ceremony for the press and MGM. *Father of the Bride* was so well-executed that it did not need the ballyhoo of Elizabeth's wedding to help it along at the box office, but it certainly did not hurt. After its release the film became the most profitable comedy in MGM history at that time. Tracy earned an Academy Award nomination as Best Actor for his performance. The film was also nominated for Best Picture and Best Screenplay.

> *Elizabeth and Tracy's rapport on the screen carried over from the friendship that quickly formed between them offscreen.*

Quo Vadis

RIGHT: Costume test shot of Elizabeth as Lygia. The role was played in the film by Deborah Kerr.

SUMMARY:

Roman soldier Marcus Vinicius returns home from years of war and meets Lygia, an early Christian woman whose religious beliefs prevent her from returning Marcus's love. The spurned Marcus then arranges to buy her as his slave, but she flees and returns to her people, fellow Christians. Meanwhile, Emperor Nero's twisted mind compels him to set Rome aflame. When he ultimately blames the destruction of the city on the Christians, followers of the new religion are rounded up and thrown into an arena to fight for their lives amid wild beasts of prey. Marcus, still in love with Lygia, makes it his mission to save her life.

REVIEW

"Here, in this mammoth exhibition, upon which they say that M-G-M has spent close to $7,000,000 and which runs for just shy of three hours, is combined a perfection of spectacle and of hippodrome display with a luxuriance of made-to-order romance in a measure not previously seen. Here is a staggering combination of cinema brilliance and sheer banality, of visual excitement and verbal boredom, of historical pretentiousness and sex. We have a suspicion that this picture was not made for the overly sensitive or discriminate. It was made, we suspect, for those who like grandeur and noise—and no punctuation."

—*The New York Times* (**Bosley Crowther**)

notes

WHILE IN ROME IN THE SUMMER OF 1950, ON HER FIVE-MONTH honeymoon across Europe with Nicky Hilton, the newlyweds visited the set of *Quo Vadis* and Elizabeth agreed to participate in the filming as an extra, just for fun. Her uncredited (and indiscernible) cameo in the film was as a Christian slave girl in the arena.

Henryk Sienkiewicz's *Quo Vadis* had been adapted for the screen numerous times in the past. MGM's version was of the breed of epic, supercolossal historical films Hollywood made in abundance in the early 1950s, as an answer to the home entertainment provided to formerly devoted moviegoers by television. MGM spent $7.6 million on the production, an expense that proved justified when it took in nearly twice that amount at the box office. Elizabeth made costume tests for the lead female role of Lygia, but she was already well occupied with both work and a new husband and ultimately took part only as an extra. Lygia was played by Deborah Kerr.

Father's Little Dividend

METRO-GOLDWYN-MAYER

CAST

Spencer Tracy .... *Stanley Banks*

Joan Bennett .... *Ellie Banks*

Elizabeth Taylor .... *Kay Dunstan*

Don Taylor .... *Buckley Dunstan*

Billie Burke .... *Doris Dunstan*

Moroni Olsen .... *Herbert Dunstan*

Richard Rober .... *police sergeant*

Marietta Canty .... *Delilah*

Russ Tamblyn .... *Tommy Banks*

Tom Irish .... *Ben Banks*

Hayden Rorke .... *Dr. Andrew Nordell*

Paul Harvey .... *Reverend Galsworthy*

CREDITS

Pandro S. Berman *(producer)*; Vincente Minnelli *(director)*; Frances Goodrich, Albert Hackett *(screenplay)*, based on characters created by Edward Streeter; John Alton *(photography)*; Albert Sendrey *(music)*; Georgie Stoll *(music conductor)*; Cedric Gibbons, Leonid Vasian *(art directors)*; Edwin B. Willis, Keogh Gleason *(set decorations)*; Douglas Shearer *(sound)*; Ferris Webster *(editor)*; Helen Rose *(costumes)*; Sydney Guilaroff *(hairstylist)*; William Tuttle *(makeup)*

RELEASE DATE: April 27, 1951

RUN TIME: 82 minutes, black and white

RIGHT: The young Dunstans with Grandma and Grandpa Banks, clockwise: Elizabeth, Don Taylor, Joan Bennett, Spencer Tracy, and baby Donald Clark

SUMMARY: Stanley Banks has recovered from daughter Kay's wedding, the boys are settled in school, and with no financial woes to cast a shadow upon him and wife Ellie, life is good. Then Kay drops the big news: She and Buckley are going to have a baby. Buckley's parents and Ellie are ecstatic, but Stanley is unsure becoming a grandfather is worthy of such overblown enthusiasm. He is confounded throughout many of the events to come, from arguments over baby names, to the manner of childbirth, to the hysteria surrounding the birth itself. Then when the young man finally arrives, he develops an instant, mystifying aversion to Stanley—but it's nothing a little quality time with his young namesake can't solve.

"Things couldn't be better than they are in this sequel to the movie version of John Streeter's *Father of the Bride*. . . . All the players are just right in the roles to which they have become accustomed, but once again Spencer Tracy wraps the picture up with a grand comedy performance as an innocent bystander turned babysitter."

—**New York** *Herald Tribune*
(Otis L. Guernsey, Jr.)

"The glib script by Albert Hackett and Frances Goodrich, based on the characters created by Edward Streeter, misses none of the situations that make for laughs among those about to become grandparents or parents for the first time. Real-life situations have just the broad touch needed to sharpen comedic flavor, and the entire cast goes about the duties with obvious enjoyment." —*Variety* ("Brog")

"All the way through the picture Mr. Tracy does a wonderful job of displaying the agonized reactions of a father and a badly baffled man. In him is again superbly mirrored a real American type—slightly prettified and idealized, we'll grant you, but never sugared or overdone. And the same goes entirely for Joan Bennett as the charmingly eccentric wife, for Elizabeth Taylor as the expectant mother and for Billie Burke and Moroni Olsen as the other in-laws. Don Taylor does even better as the tormented husband of the girl, and in him one sees the definite glimmers of another distracted father twenty years hence."

—*The New York Times*
(Bosley Crowther)

FROM TOP: Doting "grandmother" Joan Bennett with Elizabeth, Don Taylor, and Donald Clark | On Pops's lap. Tracy and his longtime partner on the screen and in life, Katharine Hepburn, were two of Elizabeth's favorite actors, and inspired her to work at her craft.

Between takes of
Father's Little Dividend

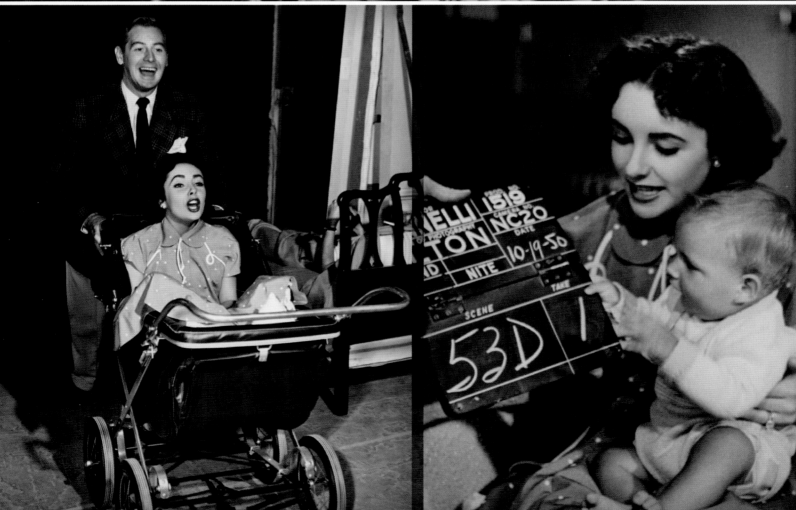

notes

IF *FATHER OF THE BRIDE* WAS SO APTLY TIMED IN THE LIFE of Elizabeth Taylor, its successor, *Father's Little Dividend*, was the complete opposite. Buckley and Kay Dunstan and Nicky and Elizabeth Hilton may have reached the altar at the same time, but the Dunstans had beaten them to the nursery. Immediately after their wedding, Elizabeth and Hilton departed on a honeymoon lasting five months, spent primarily in casinos across Europe. This epic honeymoon comprised most of their 203-day marriage. Reports back from Europe alluded to Hilton's drinking problem and possible domestic violence. It has been written over the years that Elizabeth became pregnant on the trip and suffered a miscarriage caused by Hilton's physical abuse. Whatever the precise circumstances between them may have been, the marriage was evidently over by the time they returned from Europe.

Elizabeth had filmed *Father of the Bride* in the blush of love. As *Father's Little Dividend* went into production in October 1950, Elizabeth's marriage was falling apart and she was in an entirely converse state of mind. No matter what was happening in her personal life though, she maintained her professionalism on the set. Director Vincente Minnelli later said he was struck by how, in spite of the breakup of her first marriage, Elizabeth remained a pleasure to work with: "I was delighted. I found her so responsible, intelligent, and professional."

Elizabeth and Spencer Tracy continued their mutual admiration society as well. She later said, "He was one of the people I learned from. He had a stillness, a quietness about him that spoke more than volumes, and it just was mesmerizing. He could play any role and he just drew you in." Tracy repeated his successful interpretation of Stanley Banks. In fact, the team behind *Father's Little Dividend*, the same that had crafted *Father of the Bride*, remained at the top of their game and produced that rarest of rare gems in Hollywood: a

In spite of the breakup of her first marriage, Elizabeth remained a pleasure to work with.

sequel that did not diminish but indeed measured up to its predecessor.

By the time *Father's Little Dividend* was in theaters, Elizabeth was no longer married. She filed for divorce from Nicky Hilton on December 22, 1950. She did not take a penny from her wealthy ex-husband. Elizabeth was now a single woman again—and there was no shortage of suitors beating a path to her door.

OPPOSITE, CLOCKWISE FROM TOP: Snack time with her onscreen husband, Don Taylor | Elizabeth plays with baby Donald Clark. | Clowning with Don Taylor. This baby-themed sequel to *Father of the Bride* earned $3.1 million in domestic film rentals. **ABOVE, FROM TOP:** Dutch magazine cover of Elizabeth and baby | *Screenland* cover from her *Father's Little Dividend* period

Callaway Went Thataway

METRO-GOLDWYN-MAYER

CAST

Fred MacMurray	Mike Frye
Dorothy McGuire	Deborah Patterson
Howard Keel	Stretch Barnes/ Smoky Callaway
Jesse White	Georgie Markham
Fay Roope	Tom Lorrison
Natalie Schafer	Martha Lorrison
Douglas Kennedy	drunk
Elisabeth Fraser	Marie
Johnny Indrisano	Johnny Terrento
Stan Freberg	Marvin
Elizabeth Taylor	herself

CREDITS

Melvin Frank, Norman Panama (producers/directors/screenplay); Ray June (photography); Marlon Skiles (music); Cedric Gibbons, Eddie Imazu (art directors); Edwin B. Willis, Hugh Hunt (set decorations); Douglas Shearer (sound); Irvine Warburton (editor); Helen Rose, Gile Steele (costumes); Sydney Guilaroff (hairstylist); William Tuttle (makeup)

RELEASE DATE: November 15, 1951

RUN TIME: 81 minutes, black and white

RIGHT: The real Elizabeth Taylor greets the bogus Smoky Callaway. She appeared in this scene with Dorothy McGuire, Fred MacMurray, and Howard Keel.

SUMMARY: Advertising wizards Mike Frye and Deborah Patterson come up with a very profitable plan of putting the old movies of Western star Smoky Callaway on television, à la the latter-day fame of *Hopalong Cassidy*. Kids discovering Smoky for the first time clamor for a personal appearance. It falls to Mike and Deborah to produce him, but the former star has taken to booze since his glory days and is nowhere to be found. Mike and Deborah then produce a look-alike, Stretch Barnes. But the plan goes awry when the real Smoky rears his head, and an epic battle ensues between him and Stretch, as Smoky insists on just deserts from his resurrected fame.

notes

CALLAWAY WENT THATAWAY, **THOUGH A SCREWBALL COMEDY,** is an interesting look into the early days of television, concerning the resurrected fame of old stars when their films were rerun on television for the first time. In this case it was a series of old Westerns so popular with boys of the era. Also of interest is Howard Keel playing a dual role, and the spectacle of the extended fight scene he has with himself. Elizabeth made a cameo appearance as herself in the movie, as did other familiar MGM faces, including Esther Williams and Clark Gable.

REVIEW

"That old team of Hollywood sharpshooters, Norman Panama and Melvin Frank, whose writing, directing, and producing are now being done for M-G-M, has leveled the sights of satire upon a sitting duck in *Callaway Went Thataway*. . . . The target at which they are sniping with cheerful but deadly aim is the typical cowboy idol of the television fans, and they are riddling their vulnerable victim with juicily splattering slugs. But when the boys get through with their spoofing and the slug-juice has been wiped away, it is not the victim so much as his exploiters who are pocked with embarrassing holes." —*The New York Times* (Bosley Crowther)

Love Is Better Than Ever

METRO-GOLDWYN-MAYER

CAST

Larry Parks................................*Jud Parker*

Elizabeth Taylor........*Anastacia "Stacie"
Macaboy*

Josephine Hutchinson.......*Mrs. Macaboy*

Tom Tully.................................*Mr. Macaboy*

Ann Doran.................................*Mrs. Levoy*

Elinor Donahue.........*Pattie Marie Levoy*

Kathleen Freeman..............*Mrs. Kahrney*

Doreen McCann.........*Albertina Kahrney*

Alex Gerry..*Hamlet*

Dick Wessel..*Smittie*

CREDITS

William H. Wright *(producer)*; Stanley
Donen *(director)*; Ruth Brooks Flippen
(screenplay); Harold Rosson *(photography)*; Lennie Hayton *(music)*; Cedric
Gibbons, Gabriel Scognamillo *(art directors)*; Edwin B. Willis, Keough Gleason
(set decorations); Douglas Shearer
(sound); George Boemler *(editor)*; Helen
Rose *(costumes)*; Sydney Guilaroff *(hairstylist)*; William Tuttle *(makeup)*

RELEASE DATE: February 23, 1952
RUN TIME: 81 minutes, black and white

CLOCKWISE, FROM TOP: Girl chases boy in *Love Is
Better Than Ever*. | Jud and Stacie ponder the end
of their time together in New York. | A temporary
fight before final fade-out, with Parks

SUMMARY: Dance instructor Stacie Macaboy attends a dance
convention in New York to learn the latest trends to bring back to her school.
Instead, her time in New York is monopolized by talent agent Jud Parker. By the
end of their whirlwind week together Stacie is in love, but Jud is merely out for
a good time. Stacie returns to her small-town dance school with a broken heart,
no new routines, and is the target of gossip surrounding how she spent her time
in New York. Stacie uses the mild scandal as a means of bringing Jud to her,
convincing him to pretend to be engaged so she can gain back her unsullied
reputation. Jud eventually realizes he would prefer that their staged engagement end in a real wedding instead of a breakup.

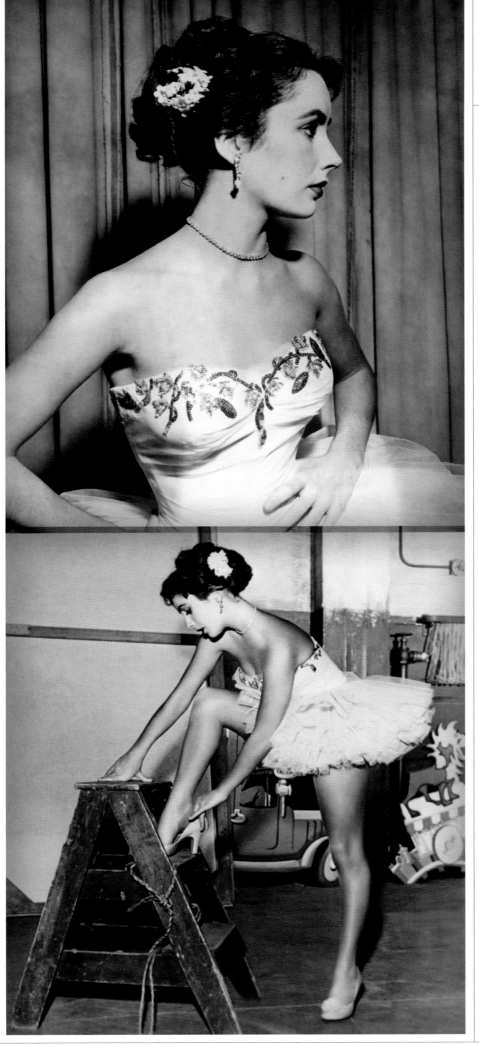

"A reasonable amount of lightly paced fun is concocted to sustain it for the over 80-minute course. Larry Parks and Elizabeth Taylor team and each adds to the amusement offered in the Ruth Brooks Flippen original script. . . . Dialog is glib, with plenty of flip phrasing, and pacing is excellent. Donen's guidance is generally good."

—*Variety* ("Brog")

"The presence of the new and muchly pictured Mrs. Michael Wilding (Elizabeth Taylor) in the cast of *Love Is Better Than Ever* is the only remotely valid reason that this reviewer can see for spending an hour and twenty minutes looking at this film. And then it is only valid if you don't pay much attention to what she does—excepting so far as it brings her within your visual range. For the ornamental beauty of Mrs. Wilding in a variety of dancing costumes is considerably counter-balanced by the trivia she has to play." —*The New York Times* (Bosley Crowther)

FROM TOP: Hairstyle test of Elizabeth as Stacie Macaboy | Elizabeth's brief costumes as a dance-school instructor provided ample opportunity to show off her legs. **OPPOSITE, FROM TOP:** A Swiss movie magazine cover, with Parks | 1951 magazine cover. Fans wanted to know which man she might be phoning after her split from Nicky Hilton. | With Larry Parks, whose presence in the film almost prevented its release

notes

LOVE IS BETTER THAN EVER WAS MADE IN LATE 1950 AND early 1951, but its release was withheld by MGM for more than a year due to the scandal surrounding Larry Parks after he admitted before the House Un-American Activities Committee (HUAC) that he had been a member of the Communist Party. It was the height of the Red Scare, when HUAC was conducting extensive investigations into any possible infiltration of communists in the film industry who could potentially impose un-American views upon an unsuspecting public in their films. Many careers were destroyed by the investigations.

One among the casualties was Parks, who rose to the upper echelons of stardom briefly in 1946, when he starred as Al Jolson in *The Jolson Story*, a role which earned him an Academy Award nomination. By the time *Love Is Better Than Ever* was completed his reputation was tarnished to such a degree that MGM considered the film unfit for release. An Elizabeth Taylor film was not to languish too long, however, so *Love Is Better Than Ever* quietly tiptoed into theaters in February 1952. It opened to poor notices and did nothing to help Parks's flagging career; but neither did it do any harm to Elizabeth's, as audiences were by now intrigued by everything she did.

Interest in Elizabeth's private life was soaring after her breakup with Nicky Hilton. Fans were anxious to see whom she would link up with next. The man turned out to be *Love Is Better Than Ever* director Stanley Donen. Donen had just finished directing Fred Astaire in *Royal Wedding*. His career was on the rise through his collaborations with Gene Kelly, who even made a cameo appearance in *Love Is Better Than Ever*. They had made *On the Town* a year earlier and Donen's next directorial effort would be the classic *Singin' in the Rain*.

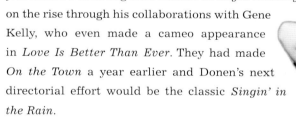

Love Is Better Than Ever may have been comparatively insignificant in Donen's repertoire of the period, but for the director it was momentous because he fell head over heels in love with Elizabeth during production. He said at the time, "She was the most beautiful woman on earth." Elizabeth became serious about him too, but her mother Sara did not like him. Donen used aspects of his experiences with Elizabeth's mother in the film, including the messages and missed calls from her mother while the couple was out on a date. According to Donen, he and Elizabeth were engaged at the time she left for England to make *Ivanhoe*, and it came as a shock to him back in Hollywood to receive the news that she had married Michael Wilding. Donen's love for Elizabeth comes across in *Love Is Better Than Ever* through a succession of lingering close-ups on her throughout, making the film a time capsule commemorating their past romance, though not one of the finer credits of either of their artistic careers.

> ## "She was the most beautiful woman on earth."
>
> —STANLEY DONEN

Ivanhoe

METRO-GOLDWYN-MAYER

CAST

Robert Taylor .... *Ivanhoe*

Elizabeth Taylor .... *Rebecca*

Joan Fontaine .... *Rowena*

George Sanders .... *De Bois-Guilbert*

Emlyn Williams .... *Wamba*

Robert Douglas .... *Sir Hugh de Bracy*

Finlay Currie .... *Cedric*

Felix Aylmer .... *Isaac*

Francis DeWolff .... *Front de Boeuf*

Norman Wooland .... *King Richard*

CREDITS

Pandro S. Berman *(producer)*; Richard Thorpe *(director)*; Noel Langley *(screenplay)*; Aeneas MacKenzie *(adaptation)*, based on story by Sir Walter Scott; F. A. Young *(photography)*; Miklós Rózsa *(music)*; Alfred Junge *(art director)*; A. W. Watkins *(sound)*; Frank Clarke *(editor)*; Roger Furse *(costumes)*; Joan Johnstone *(hairstylist)*; Charles Parker *(makeup)*

RELEASE DATE: February 20, 1953
RUN TIME: 106 minutes, color

RIGHT: Taylor and Taylor, the reunited pair of *Conspirator*

SUMMARY: Ivanhoe returns from battle in the Crusades to find England ruled by the wicked Norman Prince John, while King Richard the Lionhearted is imprisoned in Austria. Ivanhoe's mission is to raise ransom funds and see Prince John deposed, but his favoring King Richard is not a popular position among Saxons in England, including the lovely Lady Rowena and his own father, Cedric. Meanwhile, anti-Semitism reigns among the Normans and Ivanhoe's friendship with the wealthy Jew Isaac and his daughter Rebecca brings dishonor upon him and ultimately leads Rebecca to be tried as a suspected witch. After exciting jousting tournaments and epic adventures, and even a cameo by Robin Hood, Ivanhoe and King Richard triumph over evil.

REVIEWS

"The beauty of *Ivanhoe* is that there is little pretention in it, and no vulgarity disguised as grandeur. It is simple, fast, and entertaining, a romantic daydream in action."

—New York *Herald Tribune* (Otis L. Guernsey, Jr.)

"[A] brilliantly colored tapestry of drama and spectacle . . . They have emphasized such episodes in the novel as the beating of Isaac and the trial of Rebecca as a witch to high-light the sobering implications of the universal injustice of social bigotry. In this aspect of the drama, a remarkable forcefulness is achieved and the pic-ture brings off a serious lesson in fair-

ness and tolerance not customary in spectacle films. Credit for this may be given to Elizabeth Taylor, in the role of Rebecca, and Felix Aylmer, as Isaac, as well as to the men who made the film. For both of these able performers handle with grace and eloquence the frank and faceted characters of the rejected Jews." —*The New York Times* (Bosley Crowther)

notes

As Rebecca, a persecuted Jewish woman in 1192 England

MGM CAST AND CREW PACKED UP AND MOVED THEIR CINEMATIC accoutrements to Elstree Studios in June 1951 to begin production on *Ivanhoe*, which London newspapers reported to be "the largest-scale film in point of sets and cast ever to be made in England." Novels, stories, and poems by Sir Walter Scott had been committed to film many times. Most popular for transition to film were his novels *The Bride of Lammermoor* and *Rob Roy*, and the poem "Lochinvar." *Ivanhoe*, Scott's epic novel of 1819, had reached the screen twice before, in long-forgotten editions made in the U.S. and Britain, both in 1913.

Producer Pandro Berman had been keen to take on *Ivanhoe* since the 1930s, but it was not until after World War II, when much filming by the Hollywood studios was being done in England again, that Berman began preparations to put the film into production. The producer wanted to create as authentic a picture of late twelfth-century England as possible, and therefore had art directors, costume designers, and historical experts on the period researching for years before he felt ready to begin principal photography.

OPPOSITE, CLOCKWISE FROM TOP LEFT: With George Sanders, who played the double-crossing De Bois-Guilbert | As the lovely Jewish maiden Rebecca | A visit to the set by Elizabeth's friend Peter Lawford | A rare portrait of Elizabeth in the *Ivanhoe* period

Elizabeth's *Conspirator* costar, Robert Taylor, fresh from his great success in the historical epic *Quo Vadis*, was cast in the title role. Elizabeth would play the beautiful Jewess, Rebecca, a part that almost went to Robert Taylor's *Quo Vadis* costar, Deborah Kerr, when Elizabeth briefly threatened to drop out of the production. Other lead roles went to Joan Fontaine, George Sanders, and Emlyn Williams. Filming primarily outdoors between July and September 1951 often required very early morning hours, overtime, and work on weekends as needed to take advantage of good weather.

Any hardships connected to filming were more than tolerable for Elizabeth, who was in high spirits as she was falling in love again with a new man she met in England, Michael Wilding. Wilding was a respected British actor, star of the prestigious 1942 U.K. production *In Which We Serve*. In Hollywood he starred for Alfred Hitchcock in *Under Capricorn* and *Stage Fright*. Wilding possessed great charm but was not the kind of man Elizabeth would come to love and admire most. "I need a strong man," she once said, "Some women need to dominate, others need to be dominated. I'm one of the last kind." But Wilding was older and cultured where Elizabeth was young and educated only by MGM, and she appreciated that she could grow and learn from him up to a certain point. Wilding met Elizabeth at the time his fourteen-year marriage to Kay Young was ending. The Wildings divorced in December 1951 and two months later, Elizabeth and Michael Wilding were wed.

As for *Ivanhoe*, the film that brought her to England and Wilding, it premiered in London in June 1952, in New York in July, and then opened across other European markets throughout the rest of the year. It grossed $6.2 million in domestic film rentals, earning distinction as MGM's top moneymaker of the year. At the Academy Awards *Ivanhoe* earned nominations for Best Picture, Best Music, and Best Color Cinematography.

> "*Some women need to dominate, others need to be dominated. I'm one of the last kind.*"
>
> —ELIZABETH TAYLOR

TOP, FROM LEFT: Modeling the back of her gown for the film's premiere | The premiere of *Ivanhoe*, on the arm of new husband Michael Wilding | At a movie premiere in London during the making of *Ivanhoe* **ABOVE:** A publicity shot from the *Ivanhoe* period

The Girl Who Had Everything

METRO-GOLDWYN-MAYER

CAST

Elizabeth Taylor	*Jean Latimer*
Fernando Lamas	*Victor Y. Raimondi*
William Powell	*Steve Latimer*
Gig Young	*Vance Court*
James Whitmore	*Charles "Chico" Menlow*
Robert Burton	*John Ashmond*
William Walker	*Julian*
George Brand	*Senator*
Frank Dae	*Old Man Kinkaid*
Elmer Peterson	*himself*

CREDITS

Armand Deutsch *(producer)*; Richard Thorpe *(director)*; Art Cohn *(screenplay)*, based on novel *A Free Soul* by Adela Rogers St. Johns; Paul Vogel *(photography)*; André Previn *(music)*; Cedric Gibbons, Randall Duell *(art directors)*; Edwin B. Willis, Jack D. Moore *(set decorations)*; Douglas Shearer *(sound)*; Sid Sidman *(assistant director)*; Ben Lewis *(editor)*; Helen Rose *(costumes)*; Sydney Guilaroff *(hairstylist)*; William Tuttle *(makeup)*

RELEASE DATE: March 27, 1953

RUN TIME: 69 minutes, black and white

ABOVE RIGHT: High tension with William Powell and Fernando Lamas

SUMMARY: Steve Latimer is a hot-shot attorney defending Victor Raimondi, a well-known racketeer. Steve is willing to put forth his best efforts to save the criminal from jail time, but it is an entirely different matter when Victor begins dating his daughter, Jean. As a single father, Steve brought her up with a loving but *laissez faire* attitude that has resulted in a relationship with Jean more resembling friendship than father-daughter rapport. Jean discards her dependable boyfriend Vance Court, and will not take Steve's advice to stay away from the dangerous Victor. In time she learns for herself that Victor has a terrifying violent streak, but not before becoming his fiancée, and dodging gunfire and the authorities.

REVIEWS

"Talents of William Powell, Elizabeth Taylor, and Fernando Lamas are more or less wasted in the talky, implausible plot, and the dramatics seem dated, even though such modern touches as telecasts of U.S. crime investigation hearings are used." —*Variety* ("Brog")

"Miss Taylor is her usual beautiful self, gracing the screen in formals, bathing suits and sports clothes."
—*Motion Picture Herald*

CLOCKWISE FROM TOP LEFT: Elizabeth waits as a scene is set up for *The Girl Who Had Everything*. | Selecting her breakfast pastry on the set | Elizabeth was an expert at touching up her own makeup for the camera. | Behind the scenes with costar Powell and husband Michael Wilding **OPPOSITE, FROM LEFT:** A Finnish magazine cover of the period featuring Elizabeth | Costume test of Elizabeth in the role of Jean Latimer

notes

THE GIRL WHO HAD EVERYTHING HAD THE MAKINGS OF A fine film. It was a remake of a Norma Shearer/Lionel Barrymore/Clark Gable movie called *A Free Soul*. Made in the pre-Code era, before Hollywood's morals watchdogs enforced strict censorship on the screen, the sizzling drama had earned Barrymore an Oscar and nominations for Shearer and director Clarence Brown. It was based on a novel by groundbreaking journalist Adela Rogers St. Johns. Add to the above the star power of Elizabeth in 1953, the charm of the screen's newest Latin lover, Fernando Lamas, and the reverence earned by William Powell, and it would all give movie audiences high expectations. For all its potential it turned out to be a programmer for MGM, badly diluted from the excitement of *A Free Soul* by stricter censorship mandates in place more than twenty years after the release of the original film. Granted, a B movie for MGM was apt to be mistaken for an A film at other studios, but *The New York Times* did not even bother to review *The Girl Who Had Everything*.

MGM director Richard Thorpe, who had worked with Elizabeth in England a year earlier on the epic *Ivanhoe*, was workmanlike at the helm. Elizabeth had been married to Michael Wilding for five months when the film went into production and as an inside joke her husband appeared as an extra. Wilding's career had thrived in England more than in America. MGM put him under contract and he was soon playing Joan Crawford's love interest in *Torch Song*.

Elizabeth may have been happy in her home life at the moment, but without a strong director, leading man, or mentor regularly on the set to inspire her, she lacked the zeal for her work that marked recent experiences with films such as *A Place in the Sun* and *Father of the Bride*. She later said, "Much of my life, I've hated acting. I was doing the most awful films—walking around like Dracula's ghost in glamorized B movies. . . . It was either that or be suspended by MGM, and I needed the money."

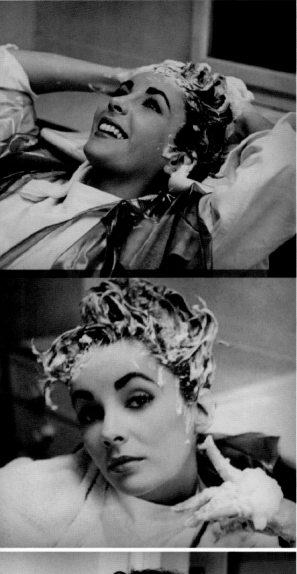

Primping behind the scenes.

Elizabeth debuted a new, shorter cut in this film.

Elizabeth was indeed glamorous as ever in *The Girl Who Had Everything*, and sporting a flattering new short hairstyle. Leading man Fernando Lamas cut a striking figure himself. He was fairly new to Hollywood and then renowned for his brief romance with Lana Turner. For costar William Powell, the beloved star of the *Thin Man* series and dozens of other acclaimed films over the past twenty years for MGM, *The Girl Who Had Everything* marked the end of his career at the studio. He would make only two more films before his official retirement.

Rhapsody

METRO-GOLDWYN-MAYER

CAST

Elizabeth Taylor .... *Louise Durant*
Vittorio Gassman .... *Paul Bronte*
John Ericson .... *James Guest*
Louis Calhern .... *Nicholas Durant*
Michael Chekhov ...... *Professor Schuman*
Barbara Bates .... *Effie Cahill*
Richard Hageman .... *Bruno Fürst*
Richard Lupino .... *Otto Krafft*
Celia Lovsky .... *Frau Sigerlist*
Stuart Whitman .... *Dove*

CREDITS

Laurence Weingarten (*producer*); Charles Vidor (*director*); Fay Kanin, Michael Kanin (*screenplay*); Ruth Goetz, Augustus Goetz (*adaptation*), based on novel *Maurice Guest* by Henry Handel Richardson; Robert Planck (*photography*); Johnny Green (*musical director*); Bronislau Kaper (*musical adaptation*); Cedric Gibbons, Paul Groesse (*art directors*); Edwin B. Willis, Hugh Hunt (*set decorations*); Douglas Shearer (*sound*); John Dunning (*editor*); Helen Rose (*costumes*); Sydney Guilaroff (*hairstylist*); William Tuttle (*makeup*)

RELEASE DATE: April 16, 1954
RUN TIME: 115 minutes, color

RIGHT: With passionate pianist James Guest, played by John Ericson

SUMMARY: Beautiful Louise Durant has been spoiled by her father's wealth all her life and is used to getting what she wants. What she wants most is a violinist named Paul Bronte. His single-minded devotion to music leads Louise into the waiting arms of pianist James Guest. The pianist's all-consuming love for Louise threatens to destroy his career and his personal well-being. Louise, meanwhile, cannot stop thinking about Paul, who has become a concert violinist. James turns increasingly to drink for comfort. When he needs her most though, Louise comes to James's aid to give him the strength to go on with his music. She is then left to make up her mind which man is most deserving of her love.

REVIEWS

"The point of the whole story is to show off Miss Taylor wearing attractive gowns, sobbing in loneliness, or radiant at a concert. It is a ravishing show of feminine charm, in vivid color, but in it director Charles Vidor has evoked hardly a single honest gesture or expression. It looks as though Miss Taylor's charm had struck everyone senseless, leaving nothing but this charm for the movie to go on."

—New York *Herald Tribune*
(Otis L. Guernsey, Jr.)

"Miss Taylor never looked lovelier than she does in this high-minded film, which is all wrapped up in music on the starry-eyed classical plane. Her wind-blown black hair frames her features like an ebony aureole, and her large eyes and red lips glisten warmly in the close-ups on the softly lighted screen. A wardrobe befitting an heiress is provided by M-G-M—which is not to the least out of order, for an heiress is what she plays. Any gent who would go for music with this radiant—and rich—Miss Taylor at hand is not a red-blooded American. Or else he's soft in the head."

—*The New York Times* (Bosley Crowther)

RIGHT: Rare candid shots of Elizabeth during the making of *Rhapsody* **OPPOSITE, CLOCK-WISE FROM TOP LEFT:** Is it truly impossible to have music *and* Louise? She is torn between two dedicated musicians in *Rhapsody*. | James Guest chooses Louise over the piano. | A Swedish magazine cover of the period

notes

THOUGH SHE WAS NOT IMPRESSED WITH THE FILM ROLES
MGM was doling out to her since *Father's Little Dividend*, up to and including
her latest assignment, prior to making *Rhapsody* in 1953, Elizabeth signed a
new contract with the studio that upgraded her salary to $5,000 a week. It was
money the Wildings could well use, now more than ever. Between *The Girl Who
Had Everything* and *Rhapsody*, Elizabeth gave birth to their first child, Michael,
born on January 7, 1953. Though only twenty-one years old, she had wanted
children desperately for years. Therefore, regardless of the script or lack of
excitement for her role, Michael's birth made *Rhapsody* a happy memory for her.

Elizabeth's costars were newcomers John Ericson and Vittorio Gassman. It was
only Ericson's second feature film, and Italian import Gassman's fourth in America,
leaving all marquee value in the film to rest on Elizabeth's shoulders. Based on the
novel *Maurice Guest* by Henry Handel Richardson, Michael and Fay Kanin's script
was a soap opera glossed up in the grandest MGM manner. The story, which had
Elizabeth mooning over a violinist to the tune of classical music over the course of
two hours, seemed to crawl to a finish,
and the fact that any man would choose
a violin over the ravishing Elizabeth
left audiences and critics mystified. Yet
none could deny the sheer beauty of the
production, particularly when director Charles Vidor's camera closed in on
Elizabeth's face.

> *Regardless of the script or lack of excitement
> for her role, Michael's birth made* Rhapsody
> *a happy memory for Elizabeth.*

Helen Rose designed Elizabeth's exquisite wardrobe for *Rhapsody*, in the eighth film collaboration between star and designer. Like many other MGM leading ladies, Elizabeth loved working with Rose. The designer was an expert for films and female stars because she had the gift of being able to rein in her own artistic sensibilities and ambitions and instead let the star shine in clothes appropriate for the individual, the character, and the setting. "When I had someone as beautiful as Elizabeth Taylor," Rose later said, "I had to be very careful not to overdress her. It's like a beautiful jewel. My job was to keep Elizabeth Taylor looking like Elizabeth Taylor."

> *"My job was to keep Elizabeth Taylor looking like Elizabeth Taylor."*
>
> —HELEN ROSE

Working in the studio era, with craftsmen and stars all under long-term contracts, Elizabeth got to form close bonds with many of the people behind the scenes who worked with her from film to film, year after year. Hairstylists, makeup artists, and wardrobe woman were among Elizabeth's favorite people at the studio, not the studio brass. Louis B. Mayer had left MGM in 1951, but there had been no love lost between her and the revered production chief. For all her glamour, Elizabeth was a down-to-earth person. Helen Rose later commented that Elizabeth was very generous and kinder to the crew on her films than to the studio executives who pulled the strings of her career.

ABOVE, FROM LEFT: Rose's designs never overpowered Elizabeth, but complemented her beauty. | Gowned by Helen Rose, between takes

Elephant Walk

PARAMOUNT PICTURES

CAST

Elizabeth Taylor .... *Ruth Wiley*
Dana Andrews........................ *Dick Carver*
Peter Finch .... *John Wiley*
Abraham Sofaer .... *Appuhamy*
Abner Biberman........................ *Dr. Pereira*
Noel Drayton.................. *planter Atkinson*
Rosalind Ivan............................ *Mrs. Lakin*
Barry Bernard .... *planter Strawson*
Philip Tonge.............. *planter John Ralph*
Edward Ashley................ *planter Gordon Gregory*
Madhyma Lanka
Nritya Mandala Dancers ....*dancers*

CREDITS

Irving Asher *(producer)*; William Dieterle *(director)*; John Lee Mahin *(screenplay)*, based on novel by Robert Standish; Loyal Griggs *(photography)*; Franz Waxman *(music)*; Ram Gopal *(choreography)*; Hal Pereira, Joseph MacMillan Johnson *(art directors)*; Sam Comer, Grace Gregory *(set decorations)*; Gene Merritt, John Cope *(sound)*; Alvin Ganzer *(second unit director)*; Irmin Roberts *(second unit photography)*; Francisco Day *(assistant director)*; George Tomasini *(editor)*; Edith Head *(costumes)*; Wally Westmore *(makeup)*

RELEASE DATE: April 21, 1954
RUN TIME: 103 minutes, color

RIGHT: MGM was not the only studio capable of lush glamour photography. Some of her most stunning portraits were taken at Paramount for *Elephant Walk*.

SUMMARY: Ruth meets Ceylon plantation owner John Wiley in London and after a whirlwind courtship they marry. He takes her to his home in Ceylon—a mansion known as Elephant Walk. There Ruth observes an instant change in her husband's personality, which eventually draws her to the handsome Dick Carver. John becomes cold and brooding, haunted by the mysteriously portentous memory of his late father, as well as the tangible menace of the herd of elephants that threatens to cut a path straight through Elephant Walk in search of water. Add to this toxic mix an outbreak of cholera and the result is a tale of ominous action without a moment's letup.

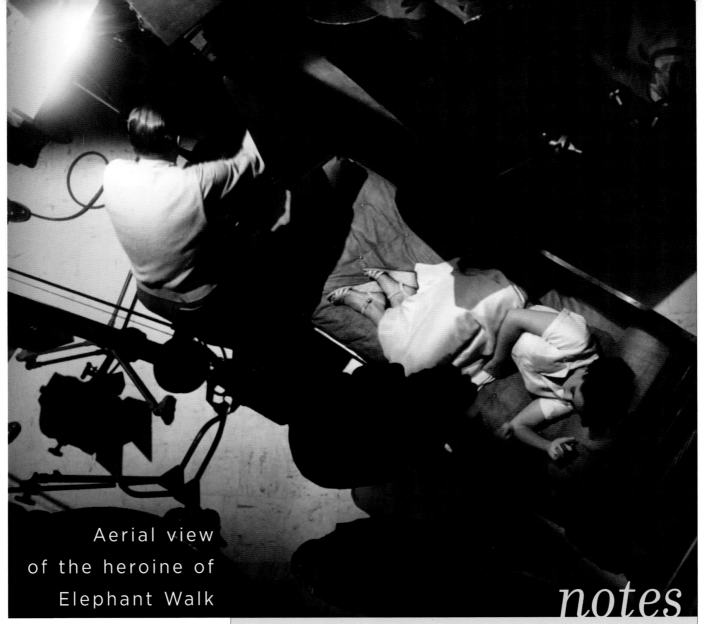

Aerial view of the heroine of Elephant Walk (the mansion's name), exhausted in the midst of a cholera outbreak

notes

PARAMOUNT PICTURES PRODUCER IRVING ASHER HAD ELIZABETH Taylor in mind for the female lead when he first conceived of making *Elephant Walk*. She was pregnant with son Michael when he first requested a loan out from MGM and was to give birth only a month prior to the start of principal photography, making her happily unavailable. Asher then obtained the services of Vivien Leigh for the film, and cast and crew departed for Ceylon (the former name of Sri Lanka) to shoot exteriors. After weeks in the heat of South Asia, Leigh's fragile mental and physical health was depleted, she suffered from exhaustion, and shortly after returning to America to complete filming she suffered a nervous breakdown.

A replacement for Leigh was needed in a hurry. Since Elizabeth had by then given birth and was suitably recovered, Asher turned again to his first choice of leading lady, borrowing her from MGM for the sum of $150,000. Elizabeth's and Leigh's similarities of coloring and build allowed Asher and director William Dieterle to retain much of the footage that had been shot in Ceylon. As a result, in the location long shots, it is Vivien Leigh and not Elizabeth Taylor that one sees. They were also still able to utilize the majority of the costumes that Edith Head had created for Leigh by letting out seams and remodeling just a few. But like her predecessor in the role, Elizabeth did not

walk away from the production unscathed. A wind machine blew a bit of steel into her eye and she had to be hospitalized.

Peter Finch, the man who a few years later was to have played Julius Caesar to Elizabeth's *Cleopatra*, costarred, along with Dana Andrews. The lush, picturesque setting of Ceylon and a herd of elephants were the other major players in the film. *Elephant Walk* was part of a movement of films discovering new locales around the world besides more familiar alternatives to the U.S.—European and Latin American settings that were prevalent in films of the 1930s and '40s. Movies of the '50s such as *King Solomon's Mines*, *The Snows of Kilimanjaro*, *Mogambo*, and *Elephant Walk* intrigued the American public about far-off places in Africa and Southeast Asia. Ultimately in *Elephant Walk*, Elizabeth was aglow in Technicolor, the sets were luxurious, and the elephant-stampede finale all combined to make it a spectacle for the eye. Reviews of the day were tepid at best, but the film is undeniably intriguing and holds the viewers' attention for a fast-paced 103 minutes.

> *Elephant Walk was part of a movement of films discovering new locales around the world.*

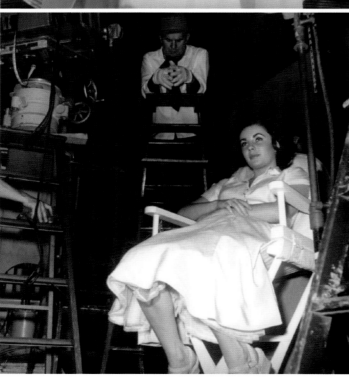

"Unfortunately, the script that John Lee Mahin prepared from the Robert Standish book is lengthy and hackneyed in the build-up, and William Dieterle's direction does not provide anything more than gaudy panoramas of a tropical palace to fascinate the eye. Miss Taylor's performance of the young wife is petulant and smug. Mr. Andrews is pompous as the manager. And Mr. Finch, as the husband, is just plain bad. Abraham Sofaer as the native major-domo wears moustachios like a Turkish highwayman's and has the best chance to be intriguing. But he does little more than roll his eyes."

—*The New York Times* (Bosley Crowther)

"The novelty of the Ceylon backgrounds and pictorial beauty are recommendable points in *Elephant Walk*, an otherwise leisurely romantic drama that strolls leisurely through an hour and 42 minutes. Miss Taylor and Andrews appear more natural in their star spots [than Finch], thus have more impact."

—*Variety* ("Brog")

CLOCKWISE FROM TOP LEFT: She was only a bird in a gilded cage: Ruth Wiley in all her glory. | An outtake—there was very little laughter in the menacing mood of the movie | Dana Andrews and company review some of the glorious portraits made of Elizabeth in connection with the film. | The reaction to seeing a herd of elephants overtake one's home | Observing the action from the sidelines

Beau Brummell

METRO-GOLDWYN-MAYER

CAST

Stewart Granger.............. *Beau Brummell*

Elizabeth Taylor .... *Lady Patricia*

Peter Ustinov ....*Prince of Wales*

Robert Morley ....*King George III*

James Donald ....*Lord Edwin Mercer*

James Hayter .... *Mortimer*

Rosemary Harris ....*Mrs. Fitzherbert*

Paul Rogers ....*William Pitt*

Noel Willman...........................*Lord Byron*

Peter Dyneley .... *Midger*

CREDITS

Sam Zimbalist *(producer)*; Curtis Bernhardt *(director)*; Karl Tunberg *(screenplay)*, based on play by Clyde Fitch; Oswald Morris *(photography)*; Richard Addinsell *(music)*; Alfred Junge *(art director)*; A. W. Watkins *(sound)*; Frank Clarke *(editor)*; Elizabeth Haffenden *(costumes)*; Joan Johnstone *(hairstylist)*; Charles Parker *(makeup)*

RELEASE DATE: October 6, 1954

RUN TIME: 113 minutes, color

SUMMARY: Captain "Beau" Brummell earns the respect of the Prince of Wales by being the only man brave enough to insult him. In time, Brummel becomes an essential member of the crown prince's inner circle and a trusted advisor. Among the aristocrats he meets and falls for the lovely Lady Patricia, who is engaged to another—a far more stodgy man, not half as interesting as Brummell. Their budding love is stunted when Brummell again insults the prince and refuses to make apologies, earning him banishment from court. His pride also means losing Lady Patricia forever, as well as returning to the poverty from whence he came.

RIGHT: A costume test of Elizabeth as Lady Patricia **OPPPOSITE, FROM TOP:** Fetching in her flaxen wig; no one thought to lighten those trademark eyebrows | In costume by Elizabeth Haffenden

"*Beau Brummell* is an elaborate Technicolor period piece, lofty in manner and in principle. Most of the personalities in it are china figures, including Elizabeth Taylor as an eligible maiden of fashion and Rosemary Harris as the prince's favorite. The notable exception is Peter Ustinov's performance, which cuts through the high gloss and rigid poses of fancy-dress history. His lonely, pompous prince is animate and touching, as he captures and vitalizes this movie in a fine character role." —New York *Herald Tribune* (Otis L. Guernsey, Jr.)

"One of the handsomest color pictures ever made—so handsome, indeed, that one feels shabby, just sitting there watching it. . . . The lovely young lady with whom Brummell is supposed to be in love— and who is endowed by Elizabeth Taylor with dazzling beauty and the blossoms of appeal—is a foggy and vacillating creature who is never made sensibly clear . . . it is in the taste and artfulness of design, in the exquisite blendings of colors and in the mellow effects achieved through superlative use of the camera that *Beau Brummell* becomes a lovely film." —*The New York Times* (Bosley Crowther)

THE REAL-LIFE BEAU BRUMMELL CUT A STRIKING FIGURE in Regency-era England with his tailored fashions, and he was credited with bringing into style the modern men's suit and tie. He mingled in aristocratic circles and was quite the character—a dandy, as men who concerned themselves with outward appearance were known in his day. He also had a fall from grace that led him to poverty by the time of his death. The exploits of the rascally Brummell, also known to be a ladies' man, fascinated the general public and his memory was kept alive well into the twentieth century, through numerous stage and screen incarnations.

Lensed in Technicolor and with no expense spared in either luxuriousness or authenticity, Beau Brummell was another finely crafted historical drama from the studio that did them best.

The famous English stage actor Richard Mansfield stepped into Brummell's suits in a celebrated play of 1890 by Clyde Fitch. Fitch's work was later adapted for the silent screen in a 1924 film starring John Barrymore and Mary Astor. Not much had been done on Brummell for quite some time though, when MGM producer Sam Zimbalist decided to bring the fashionable Englishman to the screen once more. Stewart Granger, whom MGM was molding as the hopeful new Clark Gable, was chosen to embody Brummell, and Elizabeth was to portray his decorative light of love, Lady Patricia. Peter Ustinov played a neurotic Prince of Wales and, it should be noted, was deserving of laurels for his performance.

ABOVE, FROM LEFT: *Beau Brummell* was filmed on location in England, with exteriors shot at the historic fifteenth-century Ockwells Manor. | Elizabeth and Michael Wilding with costar Stewart Granger and his actress wife, Jean Simmons | With Stewart Granger. Brummell was not always the easiest person to get along with.

Elizabeth and company again traveled to England for the filming, which took place primarily at the studios at Borehamwood and at England's historic Ockwells Manor. Lensed in Technicolor and with no expense spared in either luxuriousness or authenticity, *Beau Brummell* was another finely crafted, if not momentous, historical drama from the studio that did them best. This was not a film of which Elizabeth was particularly proud. "I was so embarrassing in it," was her critical assessment.

Beau Brummell spots
his love, Lady Patricia.

The Last Time I Saw Paris

METRO-GOLDWYN-MAYER

CAST

Elizabeth Taylor ....*Helen Ellswirth*

Van Johnson..........................*Charles Wills*

Walter Pidgeon ....*James Ellswirth*

Donna Reed....................*Marion Ellswirth*

Eva Gabor............................*Lorraine Quarl*

Kurt Kasznar.....................................*Maurice*

George Dolenz.................*Claude Matine*

Roger Moore..*Paul*

Sandy Descher.......................................*Vicki*

Celia Lovsky ....*Mama*

CREDITS

Jack Cummings *(producer)*; Richard Brooks *(director)*; Julius J. Epstein, Philip G. Epstein, Richard Brooks *(screenplay)*, based on story "Babylon Revisited" by F. Scott Fitzgerald; Joseph Ruttenberg *(photography)*; Conrad Salinger *(music)*; Jerome Kern, Oscar Hammerstein II *(song: "The Last Time I Saw Paris")*; Saul Chaplin *(musical supervisor)*; Cedric Gibbons, Randall Duell *(art directors)*; Edwin B. Willis, Jack D. Moore *(set decorations)*; William Shanks *(assistant director)*; Wesley C. Miller *(sound)*; John Dunning *(editor)*; Helen Rose *(costumes)*; Sydney Guilaroff *(hairstylist)*; William Tuttle *(makeup)*

RELEASE DATE: November 18, 1954

RUN TIME: 116 minutes, color

SUMMARY: While working as a journalist for a newswire service in Paris, Charles Wills falls in love and marries Helen Ellswirth. During their early years together Charles churns out news by day and works feverishly by night on the novel he wants desperately to get published. Helen supports his ambitions while leading a life of frivolity amid the omnipresent revelers of postwar Paris. Life changes after they have a daughter and acquire unexpected funds from an oil well. Helen settles down as Charles's ambition deteriorates into alcoholism. One drunken binge inadvertently leads to Helen's death from pneumonia after Charles locks her out of their home in the middle of a storm. The tragedy changes Charles's life and after proving his stability through success as a novelist, he seeks to reunite with his daughter.

RIGHT: Cast shot, clockwise: Walter Pidgeon, Eva Gabor, Elizabeth, Van Johnson, and Donna Reed

REVIEWS

"Mr. Johnson as the husband is too bumptious when happy and too dreary when drunk; Miss Taylor as the wife is delectable, but she is also occasionally quite dull. Mr. Pidgeon is elaborately devilish, Sandra Descher as the child is over-cute, Donna Reed as the bitter sister is vapid. But the soft soap is smeared so smoothly and that sweet old Jerome Kern tune, from which the title is taken, is played so insistently that it may turn the public's heart to toothpaste. This is something which we wouldn't know."

—*The New York Times*
(Bosley Crowther)

"Richard Brooks's direction has helped bring out the best in Johnson, and it has done the same for Miss Taylor. She is not only a stunning creature but a vibrant one as she flings herself into the role of an impetuous, alluring, pleasure-loving beauty. She wears yellow and red—the colors of gayety—but her performance is such that disillusionment is never out of sight. They are involved in something less than Fitzgerald in *The Last Time I Saw Paris*, but all concerned have done a capable job with the lesser materials at hand."

—New York *Herald Tribune*
(Otis L. Guernsey, Jr.)

FROM TOP: Portrait of the conflicted Helen in *The Last Time I Saw Paris* | A French magazine cover of Elizabeth from the film

notes

THOUGH THE STRAINS OF THE UBIQUITOUS "THE LAST TIME I Saw Paris" are heard throughout the entire movie, it was not its namesake Kern-Hammerstein song but a short story by F. Scott Fitzgerald from which the film took its inspiration. Fitzgerald's story was called "Babylon Revisited," but the studio decided against that title for the film lest audiences think it was another MGM biblical epic.

Far from that, *The Last Time I Saw Paris* was an interesting modern drama set in post–World War II Paris, presented as a mecca for lost souls and American expatriates. Fortunately for Elizabeth the film was only a loose adaptation of Fitzgerald's story, or else she would have found herself with very little to do. The Epsteins and Richard Brooks's script expanded the role of Helen Ellswirth through extensive flashback sequences that comprised the better part of the film. The tale was a soap opera but a good one, and gave Elizabeth one of the most multifaceted roles of her career to date. In the star's own words, "That girl was offbeat with mercurial flashes of instability—more than just glib dialogue." She played her second death scene in the movie (the first was in *Jane Eyre*). Ironically, both deaths were caused by pneumonia, an illness that plagued Elizabeth throughout her life and nearly ended it on more than one occasion.

> *The tale was a soap opera but a good one, and gave Elizabeth one of the most multifaceted roles of her career to date.*

CLOCKWISE, FROM TOP LEFT: A moment with newly installed MGM studio chief Dore Schary | At the Academy Awards with husband Michael Wilding. This ceremony took place in her *Paris* period. | Behind the scenes with Donna Reed

Picking up on strengths from the role or from her costars or director always inspired Elizabeth to go above and beyond. In this case she loved her part but had long since grasped the struggle she had with critics assessing her work. The film's director, Richard Brooks, said years later, "She told me, 'What's the use of my being a good actress? People pay no attention to it, anyway. They just say that, as usual, Elizabeth Taylor looked beautiful.' She began to think of her beauty as a handicap, a liability." No matter how good she was, it was indeed impossible not to comment on the way she looked. Her beauty in this film was enhanced by the costuming of Helen Rose, who used wardrobe to complement not only Elizabeth but her character. Helen Ellswirth enters the film in bohemian-chic black from head to toe, then puts a red plaid jacket over it and wears colorful clothing throughout the balance of the film, reflecting her seemingly happy-go-lucky spirit.

Elizabeth was top-billed in the film, above costars Van Johnson, Donna Reed, Walter Pidgeon, and Eva Gabor. For Johnson, Elizabeth's leading man from *The Big Hangover* and one of MGM's top stars for a decade, it would be his last role under long-term contract to the studio. *The Last Time I Saw Paris* was released in November 1954. It would be an entire year before the public saw her next film. The quick succession of Elizabeth Taylor releases paused as she took a break from moviemaking to give birth to her second child, Christopher Wilding, on February 27, 1955.

CLOCKWISE, FROM TOP LEFT: VE-Day celebration in Paris with Van Johnson and revelers | A party at Maxim's during filming, with friends Judy Garland and Montgomery Clift | Wardrobe test shot, in her dressing-room door | The magazine *Screen Stories* presented novelizations of popular films.

Giant

WARNER BROS.

CAST

Elizabeth Taylor .... *Leslie Benedict*
Rock Hudson .... *Jordan "Bick" Benedict, Jr.*
James Dean .... *Jett Rink*
Carroll Baker .... *Luz Benedict II*
Jane Withers .... *Vashti Snythe*
Chill Wills .... *Uncle Bawley*
Mercedes McCambridge ....*Luz Benedict*
Dennis Hopper .... *Jordan Benedict III*
Sal Mineo .... *Angel Obregón II*
Rodney Taylor .... *Sir David Karfrey*
Fran Bennett .... *Judy Benedict*

CREDITS

George Stevens, Henry Ginsberg *(producers)*; George Stevens *(director)*; Fred Guiol, Ivan Moffat *(screenplay)*, based on novel by Edna Ferber; William C. Mellor *(photography)*; Dimitri Tiomkin *(music)*; Paul Francis Webster, Dimitri Tiomkin *(songs: "Giant," "There's Never Been Anyone Else But You")*; Boris Leven *(production designer)*; Ralph Hurst *(set decorations)*; Fred Guiol *(second unit director)*; Joe Rickards *(assistant director)*; Earl Crain, Sr. *(sound)*; William Hornbeck, Robert Lawrence, Phil Anderson, Fred Bohanan *(editors)*; Marjorie Best, Moss Mabry *(costumes)*; Gordon Bau *(makeup)*

RELEASE DATE: November 24, 1956
RUN TIME: 201 minutes, color

CLOCKWISE, FROM ABOVE RIGHT: George Stevens, Jr., Elizabeth, James Dean, and George Stevens on the 595,000-acre Texas ranch known as Reata | Aging Hudson and Elizabeth was no easy feat for the makeup department. | Filming one of the opening scenes with Rock Hudson | The Benedicts and their babies

SUMMARY: Texas cattle tycoon Bick Benedict visits Maryland to buy a horse and comes back with a high-spirited wife, Leslie. At home on Bick's mammoth ranch, Reata, Leslie finds a less than welcoming sister-in-law, Luz, and ranch hand Jett Rink, who is contemptuous of Bick but privately idolizes Leslie. Leslie and Bick butt heads over her independent spirit and her humanity in defense of local Mexicans. Love sustains them through their differences, and they eventually have three children. Luz dies following a horse-riding accident and in her will she has left a small plot of land to Jett. Jett discovers oil on the land, making him a rich man with power he can easily misuse. Leslie and Bick's daughter (Luz's namesake niece), falls hard for Jett, to her parents' dismay, but she will soon come to her senses. Over the passage of twenty-five years, Leslie and Bick come to a new understanding of each other and now watch over their children and grandchildren.

REVIEWS

"Miss Taylor, required by her role to age 30 years, gives her usual alert, effectual performance in the earlier years of her role, and then displays a new artistry in meeting the sterner demands of parent-hood and grandmotherhood." —*Motion Picture Herald*

"For all its three hours and twenty minutes *Giant* is engrossing story-telling in the best Ferber fashion—with director-producer George (*Shane*) Stevens and a splendid cast helping to make this one of the finest films of this, or any year. In starring roles, Elizabeth Taylor and Rock Hudson reveal new and unsuspected talents, giving by far the most impressive performances of their careers." —*Cue* (Jesse Zunser)

"Under Mr. Stevens' direction, an exceptionally well-chosen cast does some exciting performing. Elizabeth Taylor as the ranchman's lovely wife, from whose point of observation we actually view what goes on, makes a woman of spirit and sensitivity who acquires tolerance and grows old gracefully. And Rock Hudson is handsome, stubborn and perverse but oddly humble as her spouse. However, it is the late James Dean who makes the malignant role of the surly ranch hand who becomes an oil baron the most tangy and corrosive in the film. Mr. Dean plays this curious villain with a stylized spookiness—a sly sort of off-beat languor and slur of language—that concentrates spite. This is a haunting capstone to the brief career of Mr. Dean."

—*The New York Times* (Bosley Crowther)

RIGHT: Elizabeth touches up her own hair; a makeup man freshens her face.
OPPOSITE: Behind the scenes of *Giant* with Hudson and Elizabeth

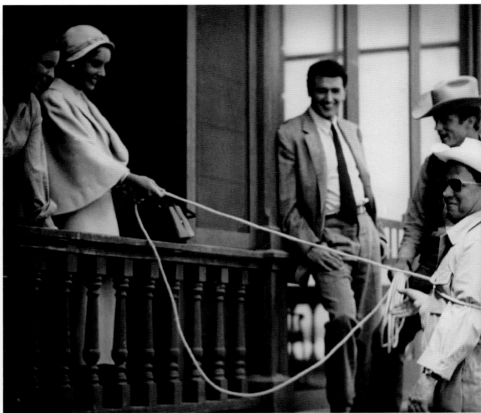

notes

CLOCKWISE FROM TOP LEFT: Feeding water to a puppy. James Dean is in the background. | Mercedes McCambridge, Elizabeth, Hudson, Dean, and George Stevens. Between cast and crew on location there existed a spirit of camaraderie. | A candid shot, as Leslie Benedict | Elizabeth became close with both Dean and Hudson. Others on the set recalled there seemed to exist a bit of rivalry for her friendship between the two men, at least on Dean's part.

ELIZABETH'S BEST ROLE TO DATE CAME NOT FROM THE STUDIO that was managing her career in 1955 but from George Stevens—the man who had given Elizabeth her second best role to date when he directed her in *A Place in the Sun*. *Giant*, the sprawling novel of Texas and three generations of cattle titans, was the distinguished and at times controversial work of Edna Ferber. Ferber's novels and plays had proven to be solid bets for Hollywood over the years, inspiring such cinematic triumphs as *Show Boat*, *Cimarron*, *Dinner at Eight*, *Come and Get It*, *Stage Door*, *Saratoga Trunk*, and *So Big*,.

The dream trio of Elizabeth Taylor, James Dean, and Rock Hudson would star in *Giant*, but none of them was Stevens's first choice when he conceived of the film. For the part of Jett Rink, Stevens considered Alan Ladd, the star of his most recent hit, *Shane*. Grace Kelly, fresh from her Oscar win for *The Country Girl*, was the original selection for the part of Leslie Benedict. Rock Hudson proposed Elizabeth Taylor to Stevens as an alternative when he could not get Grace Kelly. Elizabeth was thrilled to be second choice and back working with Stevens, though it was not entirely a bed of roses. Stevens was known to be tedious at

CLOCKWISE FROM TOP LEFT: A moment with Rock Hudson. Elizabeth called his performance "brilliant." | With James Dean, who they said never stopped toying with that rope throughout filming | Off the set with Dean and a friend

times, as he liked to shoot scenes again and again from different angles. His was a proven formula that produced classic after classic, but he was a director who took his time. In the years since they had worked together on *A Place in the Sun*, Stevens had made two films; while Elizabeth had made nine.

Stevens understood his leading lady as few of her directors ever did. "She was kept in a cocoon by her mother," the director said, "by her studio, by the fact that she was the adored child who had had everything she wanted since she was eight years old. What most people don't know is that there has been a smoldering spirit of revolt in Elizabeth for a long time." The sense of revolt came through onscreen, as Elizabeth was more spirited than ever in *Giant*. She could not have asked for better male costars than Rock Hudson and James Dean to bring this out in her. She became great friends with both, though the two men themselves did not become close. Both were troubled to some degree and confided their secrets to Elizabeth. As with Montgomery Clift, people who were somehow wounded brought out her maternal nature, and she would remain loyal to them and their secrets to the end of their lives. Hudson called her "The most beautiful woman I've ever seen. That's outward beauty and inside, too."

The film was shot primarily on location in the small town of Marfa, Texas, in the summer of 1955. Stevens did nothing to discourage passersby from stopping to have a look at the moviemaking process. On the contrary, he invited locals to work as extras. The cast of the younger generation included a young Dennis Hopper and Carroll Baker, whom Paramount was aggressively promoting. Elizabeth was a year younger than Baker but portrayed her mother. The cross-generational theme of the movie required the three stars to age twenty-five years over the course of the film. Young and beautiful as Elizabeth, Hudson, and Dean were, it posed a great challenge to the makeup department.

Tragedy struck days before production wrapped, on September 30, 1955. While watching dailies on the film, Stevens broke the news that James Dean had died in an auto accident while driving his Porsche 550 Spyder through Salinas,

> "What most people don't know is that there has been a smoldering spirit of revolt in Elizabeth for a long time."
>
> — GEORGE STEVENS

California. The *Giant* company, and the American public, were shocked. Elizabeth was deeply upset. Dean had acted in only three movies in his storied but remarkably short career; yet he had instantly achieved iconic status in the public's memory as the rebel without a cause.

Dean went out on a high note with *Giant*. The film cost Warner Bros. over $5 million to make, but it netted more than $14 million, making it the highest-grossing Warner Bros. film to date. Critics and industry peers loved the film as much as the public did. *Giant* earned ten Oscar nominations including Best Picture and acting honors for Hudson, Dean, and Mercedes McCambridge. The Best Picture award that year went to *Around the World in 80 Days*. If her own film did not win, Elizabeth was happy *Around the World* took home the title, for during the making of *Giant* she was courted like mad by that film's producer, Mike Todd, her future husband.

CLOCKWISE FROM TOP LEFT: A portrait of the period, used for Japanese print | Cementing her fame at Grauman's Chinese Theater, a star honor granted after her performance in *Giant*. Rock Hudson was on hand. | By the time *Giant* premiered, Elizabeth had separated from Michael Wilding. Mike Todd escorted her to the opening.

Raintree County

METRO-GOLDWYN-MAYER

CAST

Montgomery Clift..........*John Shawnessy*

Elizabeth Taylor ....*Susanna Drake*

Eva Marie Saint........................*Nell Gaither*

Nigel Patrick............*Professor Jerusalem Webster Stiles*

Lee Marvin ....*Orville "Flash" Perkins*

Rod Taylor....................*Garwood B. Jones*

Agnes Moorehead.........*Ellen Shawnessy*

Walter Abel......................*T. D. Shawnessy*

Jarma Lewis........................*Barbara Drake*

Tom Drake..............................*Bobby Drake*

CREDITS

David Lewis *(producer)*; Edward Dmytryk *(director)*; Millard Kaufman *(associate producer and screenplay)*, based on novel by Ross Lockridge, Jr.; Robert Surtees *(photography)*; Johnny Green *(music)*; William Horning, Urie McCleary *(art directors)*; Edwin B. Willis, Hugh Hunt *(set decorations)*; Wesley C. Miller *(sound)*; John Dunning *(editor)*; Walter Plunkett *(costumes)*; Sydney Guilaroff *(hairstylist)*; William Tuttle *(makeup)*

RELEASE DATE: December 20, 1957
RUN TIME: 188 minutes, color

RIGHT: As New Orleans belle Susanna Drake **OPPOSITE, FROM TOP:** The stars of *Raintree County*, at center: Eva Marie Saint, Montgomery Clift, and Elizabeth, flanked by, from left: NAME TK, director Edward Dmytryk, MGM studio chief Dore Schary, and NAME TK | Walter Plunkett's costumes for the film earned him an Oscar nomination.

SUMMARY: Belle of New Orleans Susanna Drake visits Indiana's Raintree County and falls for John Shawnessy, who is already engaged to his sweetheart of years, Nell Gaither. Susanna proves irresistible to John, but she makes her hold on him official by telling John, falsely, that she is pregnant with his child. Marrying Susanna is a pleasure for John because he loves her. John's love for Susanna comes without truly knowing her, though; he is unaware of the demons locked within her mind—or the secrets behind the death of her parents and Henrietta, the nanny Susanna so dearly loved. When the Civil War breaks out, abolitionist John joins the Union Army, putting him and Susanna on opposing sides of the political struggle. Susanna is ever more tortured by her dark childhood, eventually landing in an asylum. At war's end John assists in Susanna's recovery and considers a run for Congress. Susanna sees a bright future ahead for her husband in politics, but believes Nell would make a better wife by his side. What Susanna does to achieve her vision for John's happiness is a shock to all of Raintree County.

> *MGM had star power with Elizabeth in the female lead and Montgomery Clift as her costar.*

CLOCKWISE FROM TOP: Arriving with Clift in Kentucky for location filming | Ready to film a scene with Clift | Movie talk between the stars and director Edward Dmytryk

"Millard Kaufman's screenplay is a formless amoeba of a thing, and therein lies the fatal weakness of this costly, ambitious film. The people here are vaporous creatures, without clear personalities or drives, pasted together out of patches of literary clichés and poetic sentiments. What is more, the natures of their problems are too sketchily presented to bring them out. . . . Miss Taylor's daughter of the Deep South is a vain, posey, shallow young thing whose only asset is her beauty."

**—The New York Times
(Bosley Crowther)**

"To say that it moves at a snail's pace is to insult the snail. Director Edward Dmytryk could not have made a more sluggish drama if he projected magic lantern slides on the screen. . . . Elizabeth Taylor, as the frightened and pathetic wife, is the best of the actors."

**—New York Herald Tribune
(William K. Zinsser)**

CLOCKWISE FROM TOP: The stars between takes | With one of her best friends, "Monty" Clift | Candid shot with Clift | The two friends comforted each other through their respective dramas during filming.

notes

Signing autographs for fans on the set | On the set with son Michael | Behind the scenes with Lee Marvin **BELOW:** A southern belle with a delicate grip on reality

MGM HAD ASPIRATIONS OF MOUNTING A PRODUCTION ON THE scale of *Gone with the Wind* with their screen adaptation of *Raintree County*, Ross Lockridge, Jr.'s novel of the Civil War–era South. The book was one of the bestsellers of 1948 and MGM quickly snapped up the film rights. Screenwriters tackled the assignment of producing a suitable script over the course of six years. The task was completed by Millard Kaufman, and *Raintree County* was finally ready to go before the cameras in April 1956. Cast and crew went on location to Kentucky and Tennessee, though the story was set in Indiana and New Orleans.

One innovation selected at the outset was that *Raintree County* would be photographed in a new widescreen process called Camera 65, which presented audiences with a wider-than-ever aspect ratio of 2.76:1. However, theaters were not equipped for the format and technical difficulties involving the audio ultimately caused it to be released in standard CinemaScope, familiar to audiences and theaters since 1953.

Though the Camera 65 gimmick proved disappointing, MGM had star power with Elizabeth in the female lead and Montgomery Clift as her costar. Elizabeth had not worked with her friend since *A Place in the Sun*, when he inspired her to want to become a truly fine actress and not just a decorative one. Elizabeth had never had any formal training. "If I have learned anything about acting," she later said, "I learned it from my peers and the director." Clift was certainly among those who taught her what it meant to push herself further when it came to acting: "Monty was the most emotional actor I have ever worked with, and it is contagious."

The joy of working with Clift again turned to tragedy in the midst of filming when, driving home from a party at Elizabeth's, groggy from mixing alcohol and prescription drugs, Clift was in a car crash just off of Elizabeth's property. She ran to his aid, got in the car, and consoled him until the paramedics arrived. Clift was hospitalized and had to undergo reconstructive surgery on his face. The production of *Raintree County* was halted until Clift was ready to return to

work. He did come back, but it was as a changed man, emotionally and physically marred. Elizabeth comforted her friend as best she could and got him through the rest of filming. He was commendable in *Raintree County*, but the change in him was evident.

Elizabeth needed comforting herself during production. Her marriage to Michael Wilding was ending, not through any great difference between them but mostly through sheer boredom. Elizabeth said, "After a while, we had nothing to talk about but what happened at the studio that day." Enter film producer Mike Todd, bringing excitement into her life. He was a dynamo in the industry and in his private life, known for his larger-than-life personality. Elizabeth was enthralled by him almost from the start. During the making of his colossal all-star production *Around the World in 80 Days* in 1955, he wooed Elizabeth with diamonds and charm. Twenty-five years her senior and with a high-profile image of his own to maintain, he was not threatened by Elizabeth's fame, as past boyfriends and husbands had been. He was also an earthy, worldly man with whom twenty-four-year-old Elizabeth could learn and mature. Friend and producer Joe Mankiewicz observed, "More than anyone realizes, Mike was responsible for the intellectual and emotional awakening of this girl."

> *"If I have learned anything about acting, I learned it from my peers and the director."*
>
> —ELIZABETH TAYLOR

CLOCKWISE FROM LEFT: Elaborate costuming was required for this period drama. | A makeup test shot | Stepping out of her dressing room for a wardrobe test

FROM LEFT: Elizabeth at a press conference | At the film's premiere with Mike Todd. They were married by then.

Between Montgomery Clift's injuries, the failure of her second marriage, and the transformative courtship with Mike Todd, young Elizabeth had many more emotional experiences from which to draw in her work. Conscious of this or not, Elizabeth's acting was improving with each performance, and as Susanna Drake in *Raintree County* she earned her first Academy Award nomination as Best Actress. She lost to Joanne Woodward in *The Three Faces of Eve*, but Elizabeth was honored by the recognition from the industry.

When all was said and done, *Raintree County* took a massive job to edit down to a manageable length. MGM made versions of varying lengths available to theaters of the day, but the official extended cut (the version available today) was 188 minutes. The movie was produced on what was at that time a staggering budget of $5 million. It made a profit of $1 million, which was on the plus side but not approaching the success of some of Elizabeth's prior films.

> *As Susanna Drake in Raintree County she earned her first Academy Award nomination as Best Actress.*

After making *Raintree County* Elizabeth took over a year off from movies and got her first taste of the jet-setting lifestyle for which she would later be known, by traveling to far-off places with Mike Todd. She married him on February 2, 1957. More time off was necessary before and after the birth of their daughter, Liza Todd, born August 6, 1957.

Cat on a Hot Tin Roof

METRO-GOLDWYN-MAYER/ AVON PRODUCTIONS

CAST

Elizabeth Taylor	Maggie
Paul Newman	Brick Pollitt
Burl Ives	Big Daddy
Jack Carson	Gooper
Judith Anderson	Big Momma
Madeleine Sherwood	Mae
Larry Gates	Dr. Baugh
Vaughn Taylor	Deacon Davis
Deborah Miller	Trixie

CREDITS

Lawrence Weingarten (producer); Richard Brooks (director); Richard Brooks, James Poe (screenplay), based on play by Tennessee Williams; William Daniels (photography); William A. Horning, Urie McCleary (art directors); Henry Grace, Robert Priestly (set decorations); Dr. Wesley C. Miller (sound); William Shanks (assistant director); Ferris Webster (editor); Helen Rose (costumes); William Tuttle (makeup); Sydney Guilaroff (hairstylist)

RELEASE DATE: September 20, 1958
RUN TIME: 108 minutes, color

RIGHT: With Paul Newman, as Brick and Maggie

SUMMARY: The Pollitt family gathers in New Orleans to celebrate Big Daddy's sixty-fifth birthday. All except Big Daddy know that his health is precarious. When he will die, either of his sons, Brick or Gooper, stand to see the bulk of a vast inheritance. Big Daddy favors Brick and his wife, Maggie, to Gooper and his tribe of "no-neck monsters," but the behavior of Brick, an ex–football hero with an inexplicable aversion to the sultry Maggie, gives Big Daddy pause. Maggie tries as best she can to make Brick desire her, and to decipher the true nature of Brick's relationship with his best friend Skipper. Gooper and family tumble over themselves to get into Big Daddy's good graces while Maggie can achieve that with just a smile. Greed, sexual tension, love, and deception all collide in a birthday blowout.

ABOVE: An ensemble cast consisting of Burl Ives, Paul Newman, Judith Anderson, Elizabeth, Madeleine Sherwood, and Jack Carson

"*Cat on a Hot Tin Roof* is not only a powerful film, it is a conscientious and honest expression of all that is most important in Tennessee Williams' extraordinary play from which it is derived. There are some muffled areas, not unnaturally, but it remains a work of rare intensity in which one staggering domestic crisis follows another and underlying morality overflows into matters of universal significance. . . . [Miss Taylor] gives a great deal of conviction and contributes much to the movie's basic reality."

—New York *Herald Tribune*
(Paul V. Beckley)

"An all-fired lot of high-powered acting is done in *Cat on a Hot Tin Roof*. Burl Ives, Paul Newman, Elizabeth Taylor, Judith Anderson, Jack Carson, and two or three more almost work and yell themselves to pieces making this drama of strife within a new-rich Southern family a ferocious and fascinating show. . . . As a straight exercise in spewing venom and flinging dirty linen on a line, this fine Metro-Goldwyn-Mayer production in color would be hard to beat. It is done by superior talents, under the driving direction of Richard Brooks, making even the driest scenes drip poison with that strong, juicy Williams dialogue. And before the tubs full of pent-up fury, suspicion, and hatred are drained, every major performer in the company has had a chance to play at least one bang-up scene."

—*The New York Times*
(Bosley Crowther)

"What is the victory of a cat on a hot tin roof?" . . .

"Just stayin' on it, I guess. Long as she can."

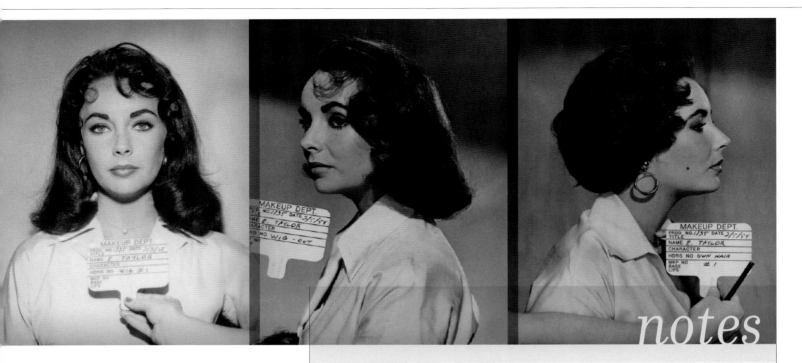

ABOVE: Finding the look of Maggie "the cat," seen in a series of hairstyle test shots

> ### Elizabeth threw herself into work to take her mind off of the pain of losing Todd.

ABOVE: Grief-stricken widow, at Mike Todd's funeral **OPPOSITE CLOCKWISE FROM TOP LEFT:** A token from Big Daddy, Burl Ives | Richard Brooks was floored by how much Elizabeth had grown as an actress. "What brought it about," he said, "was life, pain, the necessity to work under adverse conditions as an artist and a woman, after years of an incredibly sheltered existence." | On the set with director Richard Brooks | Burl Ives and Elizabeth

TENNESSEE WILLIAMS'S PULITZER PRIZE–WINNING PLAY *Cat on a Hot Tin Roof* laid the groundwork for one of the most sizzling, passionate performances ever committed to the screen in Hollywood. The play had debuted on Broadway in March 1955, directed by Elia Kazan and starring Barbara Bel Geddes and Ben Gazzara as Maggie and Brick. When MGM purchased the rights, the studio hired Burl Ives and Madeleine Sherwood to re-create their original roles, but for the film adaptation MGM cast powerhouse stars Paul Newman and Elizabeth as the protagonists. With director Richard Brooks at the helm, the company began principal photography on March 6, 1958.

Elizabeth fell ill with bronchitis soon after, preventing her from accompanying her husband on a jaunt to New York two weeks into filming, when Todd was to receive an honor from the National Association of Theater Owners as "Showman of the Year." She saw him off when he boarded his private plane, the Lucky Liz, on March 22, 1958, and never saw him again. The plane crashed in New Mexico, and Mike Todd was killed on impact. A devastated Elizabeth took to her bed and was inconsolable. Three weeks later, she worked up the determination to go back to work. Cast and crew were extremely supportive. People noticed she was not eating. When it came time to film the scene in which the family sits around an outdoor table eating, Richard Brooks insisted on filming the scene over and over again, so that Elizabeth would get her nourishment.

Elizabeth threw herself into work to take her mind off of the pain of losing Todd. "I was lucky I had someone else to become," she later said. "When I was Maggie was the only time I could function. The rest of the time I was a robot." Brooks observed that the tragedy "helped her grow up. . . . She was enough of a pro and enough of an actress to know this was something that you use—that you use honorably, because to be the best that you can every time you come to bat

was part of her credo." She immersed herself in the role and threw raw emotion into her performance. At times it was difficult. If she would get overly emotional Brooks would direct her to "Use it!"

In particular Brooks later said he depended on Elizabeth to put across points of Tennessee Williams's play that had been softened or edited out entirely for the censors. The subtext of Brick's homosexuality vanished except for hints that came through in some of Elizabeth and Paul Newman's scenes. Brooks told Elizabeth that he was relying on this unspoken message to come from her. Through to the end of filming in May 1958, Elizabeth was at the top of her game in terms of acting. Fortunately, she was also surrounded by a top-notch cast performing at the same level. Elizabeth and Newman both received Academy Award nominations, as did Brooks, William Daniels for his cinematography, Brooks's collaboration with James Poe on the screenplay, and the film itself for Best Picture.

There were no Oscar wins, but a $17.5 million gross showed that audiences came out en masse. A driving force behind the public interest was the scandal in which Elizabeth was embroiled at the time the film was released. While grieving for Mike Todd, she cried on the shoulder of his best friend, Eddie Fisher, and they fell into an affair. Fisher, of course, was married to Elizabeth's close friend, actress Debbie Reynolds. The ensuing Liz-Eddie-Debbie scandal rocked the nation and Elizabeth, once the picture of a grieving widow with whom all were sympathetic, was vilified and called a home wrecker in all manner of media feeding the public. Some have speculated that it cost her the Oscar that year, which went to Susan Hayward for her performance in *I Want to Live!* The public indignation died down over time, and Elizabeth wed Eddie Fisher on May 12, 1959, shortly before going to work on her next film, *Suddenly, Last Summer.*

Elizabeth's portrayal of Maggie in *Cat on a Hot Tin Roof* came about under the most trying of circumstances but she made it a signature performance. In later iterations on stage and screen, Maggie was played by Natalie Wood, Elizabeth Ashley, Jessica Lange, Kathleen Turner, and Ashley Judd, but none generated the excitement of Elizabeth Taylor oozing frustration, love, anger, sorrow, and sex appeal in one of her greatest performances.

> *While grieving for Mike Todd she cried on the shoulder of his best friend, Eddie Fisher, and they fell into an affair.*

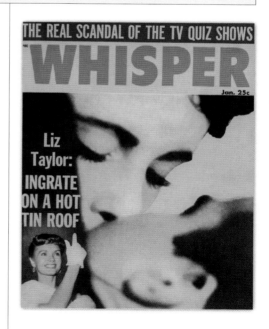

OPPOSITE, CLOCKWISE FROM LEFT: "That woman's got life in her body." Elizabeth was nominated for her performance both by the Hollywood and British motion picture academies. | "She was absolutely great," said Brooks of her performance. | The target of one of the "no-neck monsters" **FROM TOP:** Attending the Academy Awards with Eddie Fisher, 1959 | One of the more colorful magazine covers at the time of the Liz-Eddie-Debbie drama. The public was just getting over the scandal of Lana Turner's daughter Cheryl Crane killing Lana's boyfriend, Johnny Stompanato, in defense of her mother. It was a lot for movie fans to take in a short time.

Suddenly, Last Summer

COLUMBIA PICTURES

CAST

Elizabeth Taylor .... *Catherine Holly*

Katharine Hepburn... *Mrs. Violet Venable*

Montgomery Clift.............. *Dr. Cukrowicz*

Albert Dekker.................... *Dr. Lawrence J. Hockstader*

Mercedes McCambridge............ *Mrs. Grace Holly*

Gary Raymond...................... *George Holly*

Mavis Villiers............................. *Ms. Foxhill*

Patricia Marmont .... *Nurse Benson*

Joan Young.......................... *Sister Felicity*

CREDITS

Sam Spiegel *(producer)*; Joseph L. Mankiewicz *(director)*; Gore Vidal, Tennessee Williams *(screenplay)*, based on play by Tennessee Williams; Jack Hildyard *(photography)*; Malcolm Arnold, Buxton Orr *(Music)*; Oliver Messel *(production design, costumes)*; William Kellner *(art director)*; Scott Slimon *(set decorations)*; A. G. Ambler, John Cox, Peter Thornton *(sound)*; Bluey Hill *(assistant director)*; William Hornbeck, Thomas G. Stanford *(editors)*; Norman Hartnell *(Katharine Hepburn's costumes)*; Jean Louis *(Elizabeth Taylor's costumes)*; David Aylott *(makeup)*; Joan White *(hairstylist)*

RELEASE DATE: December 22, 1959

RUN TIME: 114 minutes, black and white

SUMMARY: Catherine Holly has been in a mental asylum since the demise of her cousin Sebastian, whose brutal murder she witnessed. The traumatic events which caused his death remain unspoken, locked away in her memory. Consumed with the desire to silence Catherine about Sebastian's death and peculiar life, his mother, Violet Venable, attempts to arrange for niece Catherine to be lobotomized. Dr. Cukrowicz entertains the notion when Mrs. Venable offers funding to improve conditions at his mental institution. But over time the doctor and Catherine develop a close connection and his goal becomes to help her. When the truth about Sebastian's death finally comes pouring out of Catherine, it is more shocking than anyone could have imagined.

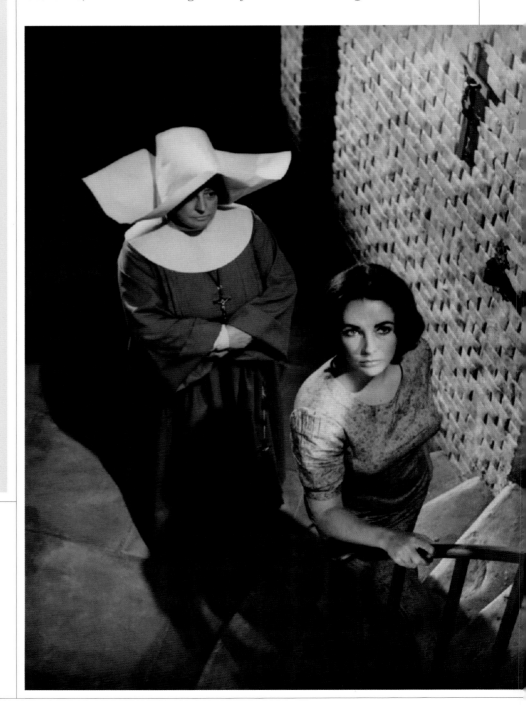

RIGHT: As the institutionalized Catherine Holly

Catherine is ready to tell her story.

"*Suddenly, Last Summer* goes further than any one has previously cared, I won't say dared, to go. It will be almost certainly so alien to most audiences I doubt they will be able to show it much sympathy, not because it is poorly done, but because of its essentially poetic strength. . . . Miss Hepburn's performance [is] splendid, as one would expect. And if there were any doubts about the ability of Miss Taylor to express complex and devious emotions, to deliver a flexible and deep performance, this film ought to remove them."

—New York *Herald Tribune*
(Paul V. Beckley)

"People who leap to conclusions may assume the trouble is that Sam Spiegel and his crew that made the picture were compelled to go easy with the ugly words. They may suspect that because the true nature of the most-talked-of character could not be tagged (he was obviously a homosexual, as well as a sadist of some sort, in the play) and because the precise and horrible details of his death could not be explained (he was literally eaten by urchins), the point of it all is missed. There's no doubt that a great deal of the feeling of dank corruption that ran through the play has been lost or pitifully diluted by a tactful screening of the words. And certainly what should be thoroughly shocking in the flashback scenes of the focal character's death is only confusing and baffling, because you can't really see what's happening, and the lady who is describing the occasion is much less vivid and exact than she could be."

—*The New York Times*
(Bosley Crowther)

FROM TOP: Taking in the sun at a Spanish beach | On the set, ready to film

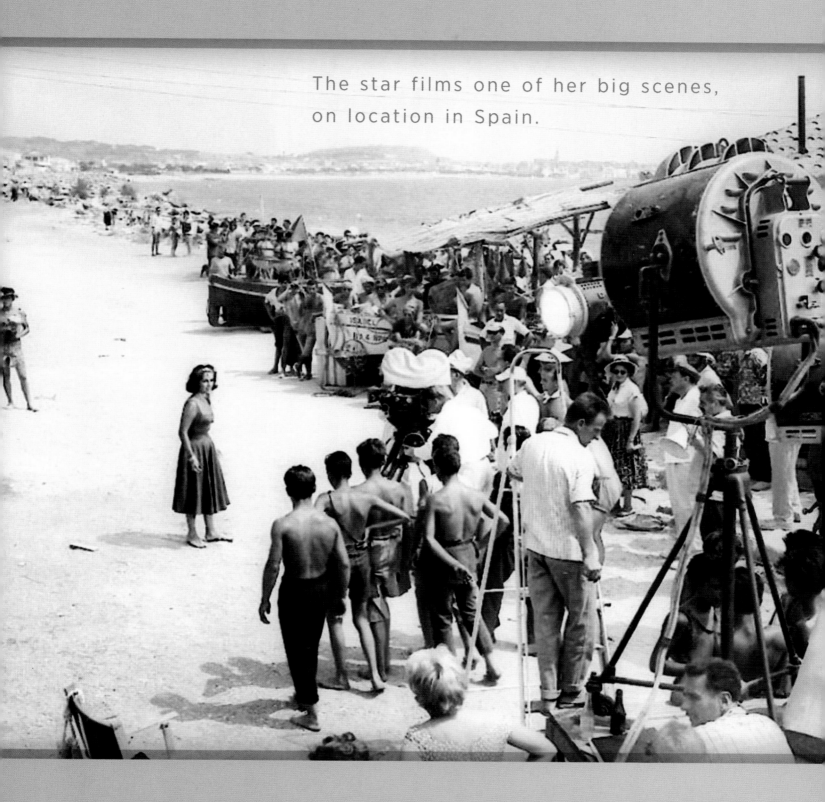

The star films one of her big scenes, on location in Spain.

notes

> "She is close to being the greatest actress in the world, and so far she has done it mostly by instinct."
>
> —JOSEPH MANKIEWICZ

ELIZABETH'S EXPERIENCE WITH TENNESSEE WILLIAMS material in *Cat on a Hot Tin Roof*, a pinnacle in her career thus far, led her to take on *Suddenly, Last Summer*, even though it presented far more challenges than *Cat* in terms of turning it into a film for mass consumption. *Suddenly, Last Summer* was originally a one-act play primarily involving two women in a single garden setting, that was presented off-Broadway as part of a Tennessee Williams double bill under the name *Garden District*.

Patricia Neal, who had starred in a London stage production, expected to re-create her role in the movie, but director Joseph Mankiewicz instead hired Elizabeth Taylor. He had every confidence in the actress Elizabeth had grown to be. He said, "She is close to being the greatest actress in the world, and so far she has done it mostly by instinct. She is still a primitive, sort of the Grandma Moses of acting." Elizabeth concurred with the latter part of Mankiewicz's statement, saying "I'm a completely instinctive actress. I've never had any lessons. I try and become the character."

As *Cat on a Hot Tin Roof* had conditioned her to do, Elizabeth gave herself completely to the role. Though embroiled in the aftermath of the love triangle involving Eddie Fisher and Debbie Reynolds, Elizabeth was still very much grieving the loss of Mike Todd and that made her vulnerable on the set. While enacting her big monologue in the garden, where she describes the scene of cannibalism she witnessed, Elizabeth became so emo-

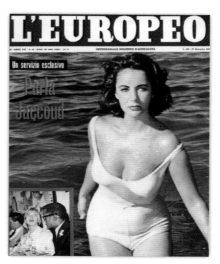

tional she had to excuse herself from the set. "I thought she had gone to freshen up," Mankiewicz recalled, "but then one of the wardrobe women came over and said, 'Do you know that Miss Taylor is sitting all alone behind the set, crying?' I found her, and she had broken up completely. I was amazed because she had such great instinctive and understanding of the pain and suffering of the character she was playing. She kept saying, 'That poor girl!' Then she went back and completed what I think is one of the finest pieces of acting in any motion picture ever made."

Throughout the filming at England's Shepperton Studios, it was a difficult time for Elizabeth. Though she had married Eddie Fisher two weeks before production began, she continued to venerate Mike Todd. One journalist who visited their hotel room during the making of *Suddenly, Last Summer* was struck by the only photo in her and Fisher's room—there was a giant likeness of Mike Todd looking down upon them. And she was still wearing Todd's $92,000 engagement ring.

Equally, if not more, troubled by ill health and private crises than Elizabeth was her costar, Montgomery Clift. She was reunited with her great friend onscreen for the third and final time in *Suddenly, Last Summer*. "A friend who stands by you is worth a thousand rubies," Elizabeth once said. She and Clift had seen each other through many difficult times and though they never worked

together again, they continued to cherish each other's friendship until Clift's death in 1966. She had learned a great deal from him from the moment they began making *A Place in the Sun*, and now it was Elizabeth who was receiving the major accolades. Both she and costar Katharine Hepburn, hauntingly memorable as the eccentric Mrs. Venable, received Academy Award nominations as Best Actress for their respective roles in *Suddenly, Last Summer*. Both being nominated in the same category for the same film seemed to split the vote, and the Oscar that year went to Simone Signoret in *Room at the Top*.

The film performed well, bringing in $6.3 million at the box office. In addition to her acting, there was the famous scene of Elizabeth in a white swimsuit in Spanish waters that garnered a great deal of press. The movie was not uniformly a critical triumph. Bosley Crowther of *The New York Times* panned the film. His review alluded to sensational details of a story involving cannibalism, homosexuality, sadism, and all manner of corruption. Screenwriter Gore Vidal was convinced Crowther's lurid details only helped drive audiences to see *Suddenly, Last Summer*.

ABOVE, FROM LEFT: With Fisher at the Academy Awards in 1960 | Elizabeth and Eddie Fisher arrive in London to make *Suddenly, Last Summer*. Her children came as well. Eddie appeared as an extra on the beach in the film, too. | At the Academy Awards. She was nominated that year as Best Actress.

> "*A friend who stands by you is worth a thousand rubies.*"
> —ELIZABETH TAYLOR

OPPOSITE, CLOCKWISE FROM TOP: On the set with son Christopher. Her children always traveled with her on location. | In costume as Catherine. Her wardrobe in the film was the work of Jean Louis. | At the premiere of *Suddenly, Last Summer*

Scent of Mystery

MIKE TODD COMPANY

CAST

Denholm Elliott .... *Oliver Larker*

Peter Lorre .... *Smiley*

Beverly Bentley .... *Decoy Sally*

Paul Lukas .... *Baron Saradin*

Liam Redmond .... *Johnny Gin*

Leo McKern .... *Tommy Kennedy*

Peter Arne .... *Robert Fleming*

Diana Dors .... *Winifred Jordan*

Mary Laura Wood .... *Margharita*

Elizabeth Taylor .... *cameo*

CREDITS

Mike Todd, Jr. *(producer)*; Jack Cardiff *(director)*; Gerald Kersh, William Rose *(screenplay)*, based on story by Kelley Roos; John von Kotze *(photography)*; Harold Adamson, Mario Nascimbene, Jordan Ramin *(music)*, Franco Ferrara *(musical director)*; Vincent Korda *(production design, art director)*; Dario Simoni *(set decorations)*; Murray Spivak *(sound)*; James E. Newcom *(editor)*; Charles Simminger *(costumes)*; Neville Smallwood *(makeup)*

RELEASE DATE: January 12, 1960

RUN TIME: 125 minutes, color

SUMMARY:

Tourist Beverly Bentley mysteriously disappears from a Spanish tourist destination and an international incident ensues as shady and honorable characters and even imposters traipse in and out to either uncover new information or further muddy the mystery. In the end, the girl is found alive and well.

REVIEWS

"There is a strong smell of the midway about Michael Todd Jr.'s *Scent of Mystery*, a color film accompanied by odors that opened at the Warner Theatre last night. As theatrical exhibitionism, it is gaudy, sprawling and full of sound. But as an attempt at a considerable motion picture it has to be classified as bunk. . . . It is an artless, loose-jointed "chase" picture set against some of the scenic beauties of Spain, which, indeed, are the most attractive and rewarding compensations of the show. And whatever novel stimulation it might afford with the projection of smells appears to be dubious and dependent upon the noses of the individual viewers and the smell-projector's whims."   —*The New York Times* **(Bosley Crowther)**

notes

THE SON OF ELIZABETH'S LATE HUSBAND, MIKE TODD, JR., had his first producing effort with *Scent of Mystery*, a gimmick film that introduced Smell-o-Vision. It was an unsophisticated process that involved pumping out odors related to what was unfolding on the screen. A scene in a rose garden, for example, prompted a spray like fresh blooms. Not all theaters were equipped for Smell-o-Vision. Audiences did not take to the gimmick and critics considered it pure nonsense. Elizabeth, who had an interest in the film with Mike Todd, Jr., made a cameo appearance that was small but critical. She proves to be the crux of the story—she's the missing girl all have been searching for over the course of the 125-minute run time.

BUtterfield 8

METRO-GOLDWYN-MAYER

CAST

Elizabeth Taylor .... *Gloria Wandrous*

Laurence Harvey .... *Weston Liggett*

Eddie Fisher .... *Steve Carpenter*

Dina Merrill .... *Emily Liggett*

Mildred Dunnock .... *Mrs. Wandrous*

Betty Field .... *Mrs. Fanny Thurber*

Jeffrey Lynn .... *Bingham Smith*

Kay Medford .... *Happy*

Susan Oliver .... *Norma*

George Voskovec .... *Dr. Tredman*

CREDITS

Pandro S. Berman (*producer*); Daniel Mann (*director*); Kathryn Hereford (*associate producer*); Charles Schnee, John Michael Hayes (*screenplay*), based on novel by John O'Hara; Joseph Ruttenberg, Charles Harten (*photography*); Bronislau Kaper (*music*); George W. Davis, Urie McCleary (*art directors*); Gene Callahan, J. C. Delaney (*set decorations*); Hank Moonjean, John Clarke Bowman (*assistant directors*); Ralph E. Winters (*editor*); Helen Rose (*costumes*); Sydney Guilaroff (*hairstylist*)

RELEASE DATE: November 4, 1960

RUN TIME: 109 minutes, color

RIGHT: Elizabeth as Gloria Wandrous

SUMMARY: Gloria Wandrous is a high-priced Manhattan model and party girl accustomed to a revolving door of men in and out of her life—wealthy, respected "gentlemen," often of good families and bad marriages. One of these is Weston Liggett. At the outset neither has any respect for the other—and possibly not even for themselves. They mistreat each other until eventually falling head over Gloria's stiletto heels in love. Weston is married to wife Emily, and Gloria comes to feel herself undeserving of his love, at least until she has had time apart in a new town to reform and atone for her past. Weston's pursuit of Gloria in his car puts an end to it all in a dramatic twist of events.

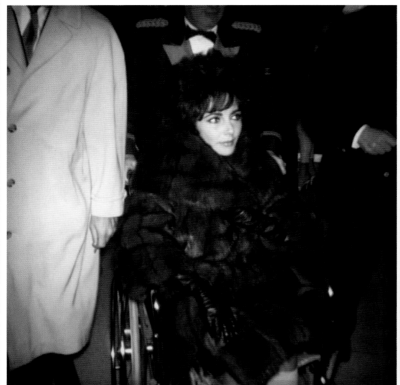

ABOVE AND RIGHT: At the airport in London, Elizabeth returns home following her near-death experience. BELOW: Arriving in Los Angeles at the end of her long journey back from England

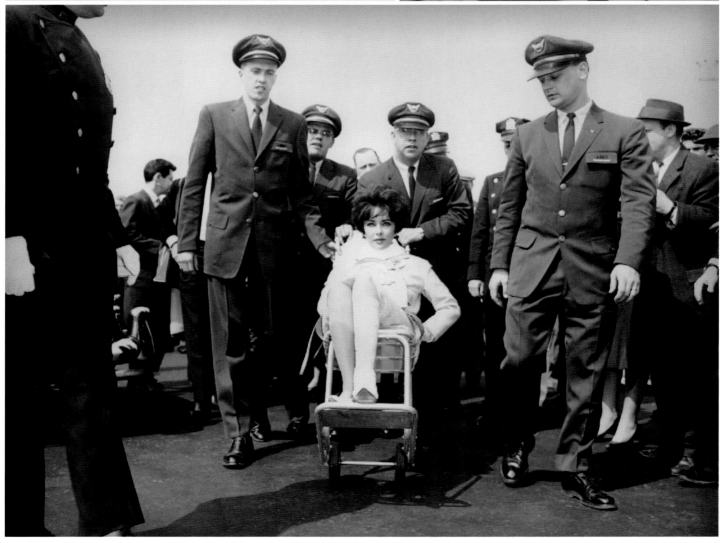

"In *BUtterfield 8* the object seems to have been to make some unpleasant people attractive. Dressmakers and interior decorators must have worked overtime on it, and, of course, Elizabeth Taylor, who has a crackling effect on the screen, would dress up a rag picker's shack, but the effect only makes things ambiguous and cancels out the hard, brittle definitions that the theme promises."

—New York *Herald Tribune* (Paul V. Beckley)

"In the first place, it has Miss Taylor, playing the florid role of the lady of easy virtue, and that's about a million dollars right there. 'I was the slut of all times,' she tells her mother in one of those searing scenes wherein the subdued, repentant playgirl, thinking she has found happiness, bares her soul. But you can take it from us, at no point does she look like one of those things. She looks like a million dollars, in mink or in negligée. . . . Mildred Dunnock is excellent as the mother of Miss Taylor. So is Betty Field as the mother's friend. When these two cut up Baby, the film is livelier than it has a right to be. Dina Merrill is lovely and simple as Mr. Harvey's wife. Only Eddie Fisher, as a boyhood friend of the frantic playgirl, seems like something dragged in from left field."

—*The New York Times* (Bosley Crowther)

TOP: A bandage to cover the scar from her tracheotomy did not stop Elizabeth from going out often. **LEFT:** Candid shot during production

notes

PRODUCER WALTER WANGER OFFERED ELIZABETH THE opportunity to star in his upcoming film, *Cleopatra*, in 1959. After negotiating a landmark $1 million contract, Elizabeth was set to do the film, but she owed one more picture to MGM to conclude what she came to look upon as a period of servitude to the studio after nearly two decades under contract. Elizabeth would have made anything they wanted just to get out from under her obligations, but then and for the rest of her life, she remained vocal about her great distaste for *BUtterfield 8*, always describing it in colorful terms.

The story was based on a 1935 novel by John O'Hara that MGM at times had considered attempting to put on the screen, but through the era of the Production Code, they kept the racy story on the back burner. It was a soap opera—a slick, stylish, expensive one—which was a specialty for MGM, and filled with camp dialogue that littered the script by John Michael Hayes and Charles Schnee. The deal for Elizabeth to appear in the film was sweetened when director Daniel Mann agreed to cast her husband Eddie Fisher in a supporting role. Lawrence Harvey, Dina Merrill, and the unexpectedly great twosome of Mildred Dunnock and Betty Field rounded out the cast.

Shot on location in New York, production took place during the first three months of 1960. When it was over, Elizabeth's tenure as a studio contract player was up, but she did not receive any sort of send-off. She said, "After I had ended my eighteen years of servitude at MGM, wouldn't you expect a phone call, or a

LEFT: Collecting the Best Actress Oscar for *BUtterfield 8* in April 1961. She later reflected, "I was filled with gratitude when I got it. . . . But it was for the wrong picture. Any of my previous nominations were more deserving."

telegram, or one wilted rose? Or some kind of goodbye? I got nothing. Some of the stars say that at least the man at the studio gate says goodbye to you. But even this didn't happen."

As a literal exit to a great career at the studio it was inauspicious but, lo and behold, she received an Academy Award nomination as Best Actress for *BUtterfield 8*. Before she could find out if she won or not, disaster nearly struck. While in London later that year and into 1961 for the filming of *Cleopatra*, Elizabeth contracted double pneumonia. An emergency tracheotomy saved her life and instantly put her back in the public's favor. Thousands of letters were sent to her sick bed. Elizabeth said, "I never knew there was so much love in the world."

Elizabeth and Fisher attended the Academy Awards in Los Angeles in 1961. When her name was announced as winner for Best Actress, a hush fell over the crowd, followed by a roar of applause. After accepting her award Elizabeth said, "I don't really know how to express my gratitude. I guess I will just have to thank you with all my heart." Many in the industry saw the win more as an acknowledgment of her fine work in *Cat on a Hot Tin Roof* and *Suddenly, Last Summer* than for *BUtterfield 8*. Elizabeth, forever after, maintained that she got the award because she had almost died.

TOP SPREAD, FROM LEFT: Elizabeth and Eddie Fisher get lunch on the set. The cast received much praise, but Fisher was roundly panned by the critics. | A scene with Laurence Harvey, with whom she became friends offscreen | An after party following the Academy Awards. Audrey Hepburn is seen at right. | A candid shot during production

> *As a literal exit to a great career at the studio it was inauspicious but, lo and behold, she received an Academy Award nomination as Best Actress for BUtterfield 8.*

Cleopatra

TWENTIETH CENTURY FOX

CAST

Elizabeth Taylor .... *Cleopatra*

Richard Burton .... *Mark Antony*

Rex Harrison......................... *Julius Caesar*

Pamela Brown.................... *high priestess*

George Cole.................................. *Flavius*

Hume Cronyn .... *Sosigenes*

Casare Danova .... *Apollodorus*

Kenneth Haigh................................ *Brutus*

Martin Landau..*Rufio*

Roddy McDowall ....*Octavian*

CREDITS

Walter Wanger *(producer)*; Joseph L. Mankiewicz *(director)*; Joseph L. Mankiewicz, Ranald MacDougall, Sidney Buchman *(screenplay)*, based on histories by Plutarch, Suetonius, Appian and book *The Life and Times of Cleopatra* by C. M. Franzero; Leon Shamroy, Claude Renoir, Piero Portalupi *(photography)*; Ray Kellogg, Andrew Marton *(second unit directors)*; Alex North *(music)*; Forrest E. Johnston, C. O. Erickson, Saul Wurtzel *(production managers)*; John De Cuir *(production design)*; Jack Martin Smith, Hilyard Brown, Herman Blumenthal, Elven Webb, Maurice Pelling, Boris Juraga *(art directors)*; Walter M. Scott, Paul S. Fox, Ray Moyer *(set decorations)*; Bernard Freericks, Murray Spivack *(sound)*; Fred R. Simpson *(assistant director)*; Dorothy Spencer *(editor)*; Irene Sharaff, Vittorio Nino Novarese, Renie *(costumes)*; Alberto de Rossi *(makeup)*; Vivienne Zavitz *(hairstylist)*

RELEASE DATE: June 12, 1963

RUN TIME: 320 minutes, color

SUMMARY: Queen Cleopatra of Egypt seeks to secure her throne through an alliance with Julius Caesar of Rome. In Rome she wins not only the emperor's support but his heart. They have a child, Caesarion, whom Cleopatra aims to see become ruler of the Roman Empire. The love affair, coupled with mounting tensions in Rome, leads to Julius Caesar's eventual assassination. Mark Antony, Caesar's would-be successor to the throne, forms a military alliance with Cleopatra against his rival, her brother Octavian. The legendary love affair that ensues between Cleopatra and Mark Antony is set against a backdrop of war, treachery, regal opulence, and deadly ambition.

TOP LEFT AND BOTTOM RIGHT: Elizabeth as Cleopatra **TOP RIGHT AND BOTTOM LEFT:** Opulence was poured into every set. **OPPOSITE:** Lavish expenditures and scandalous headlines notwithstanding, Elizabeth's interpretation became the predominating image of the legendary Cleopatra.

"Has anybody ever told you that you're a very pretty girl?" Burton's first line for Elizabeth was quite true, if unoriginal.

REVIEWS

"Physically, *Cleopatra* is as magnificent as money and the tremendous Todd-AO screen can make it. Sad to say, however, the deep-revolving, witty Mankiewicz fails most where most he hoped to succeed. As drama and as cinema, *Cleopatra* is riddled with flaws. It lacks style both in image and in action." *—Time*

"This most publicized film of our (if not all) time is at best a major disappointment, at worst an extravagant exercise in tedium. It depends, of course, on what you have been waiting for. Certainly if you want to devote the better part of four hours to looking at Elizabeth Taylor in all her draped and undraped physical splendor, surrounded by elaborate sets, all in the loveliest of colors, this is your movie. And if you adjust your focus from time to time, you will get two fine performances by Rex Harrison and Roddy McDowall, the lilting speech of Richard Burton and a couple of parades and divertissements that Flo Ziegfeld or Busby Berkeley might well have master-minded."
—New York *Herald Tribune* (Judith Crist)

"In vocal competition with the clipped precisions of Rex Harrison as Julius Caesar or the poetic sonorities of Richard Burton as Mark Antony, [Elizabeth Taylor] sounds like something dragged in from a minor league. Perhaps one of her faults is that you can understand what she says and the dialogues leave much to be desired. It pains one to reflect that the Liz Taylor, so brutally over-matched here, who started her career with the perfection of *National Velvet* 19 years ago, is over the edge. *Cleopatra* proves an expensive way to demonstrate it."
—New York *Post* (Archer Winston)

"One of the great epic films of our day. . . . Elizabeth Taylor's Cleopatra is a woman of force and dignity, fired by a fierce ambition to conquer and rule the world—at least, the world of the Mediterranean basin—through the union of Egypt and Rome. In her is impressively compacted the arrogance and pride of an ancient queen. Harrison's faceted performance is the best in the film. But Richard Burton is nonetheless exciting as the arrogant Antony. . . . There may be those who will find the length too tiring, the emphasis on Roman politics a bit too involved and tedious, the luxuriance too much. But unless you are one of those skeptics who are stubbornly predisposed to give *Cleopatra* the needle, I don't see how you can fail to find this a generally brilliant, moving and satisfying film."
—*The New York Times* (Bosley Crowther)

TOP ROW FROM LEFT:

Hollywood history is made. Flanked by producer Walter Wanger and Fox executive Buddy Adler, Elizabeth inks the deal that made her the town's highest-paid actress. | "I was never terrified by the bigness of the production. I was a playing a fascinating, complex woman." | In the hospital recovering from pneumonia and a tracheotomy, Elizabeth and Fisher read some of the thousands of letters and telegrams sent by friends and fans | On set in Rome. Elizabeth sits on Eddie Fisher's lap while exchanging words with Richard Burton.

MIDDLE ROW FROM LEFT:

A candid shot during filming. | With her Julius Caesar, Rex Harrison, who earned an Academy Award nomination as Best Actor for the role. Richard Burton said, "There's one thing I'm absolutely certain of—the absolute brilliance of Rex's and Elizabeth's performances. Both of them are extraordinary craftsmen." | On the set with director Joe Mankiewicz and Burton. Due to delays and overtime payments due the stars, in the end it was Burton who got the $1 million paycheck for Cleopatra. Elizabeth's final take was $7 million. | Elizabeth's eye makeup stirred a revival of Kohl eyeliner.

MIDDLE ROW FROM LEFT:

On location with Burton, Rex Harrison, Roddy McDowall, and Hume Cronyn | A world-weary Cleopatra | Capturing the intensity of Cleopatra. Elizabeth told an interviewer her favorite scene was "the one in which Cleopatra hears of her lover Antony's marriage to Octavia. I was so energetic and fierce that I dislocated my thumb." | Elizabeth's children enjoyed the fantasy world of ancient Rome and Alexandria, created before their eyes. Here Elizabeth has a moment with daughter Liza.

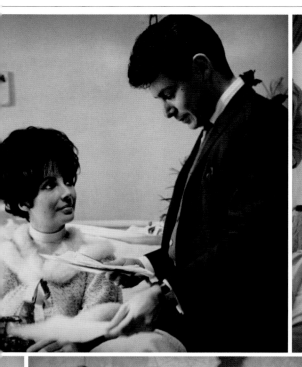

Ready for her close-up as Cleopatra

notes

WHEN TACKLING THE LEGENDARY SUBJECTS OF CLEOPATRA, Julius Caesar, and Mark Antony, it is difficult to imagine how the epic tale behind the making of the film rivaled that which producer Walter Wanger and director Joseph L. Mankiewicz endeavored to bring to the screen. But after an international scandal involving the breakup of two marriages, the near-financial ruin of a major motion-picture studio, the near-death of its star, and expenditures upwards of $40 million, a filmmaking history as storied as Queen Cleopatra herself was the result.

Previous Cleopatras of twentieth-century stage and screen included Helen Hayes, Vivien Leigh, Claudette Colbert, Tallulah Bankhead, Theda Bara, and Katharine Cornell. When Fox conceived of making the film in 1959, studio executive Spyros Skouras considered Joan Collins or Joanne Woodward. Producer Walter Wanger, meanwhile, had only one star in mind: Elizabeth Taylor. Elizabeth had no interest in playing the role, so she asked for $1 million and 10 percent of the gross, never believing she would get it. Wanger was so anxious to see her bring his vision to life that he agreed to pay the highest salary ever paid to an actress at that time. Elizabeth also requested that it be shot in Todd-AO, the widescreen format that had been developed by Mike Todd.

The queenly sum paid to the star notwithstanding, *Cleopatra* got off to a fairly ordinary start with Rouben Mamoulian set to direct. (Mamoulian and Wanger had partnered successfully back in 1933 on Greta Garbo's *Queen Christina*.) Elizabeth's *Elephant Walk* costar Peter Finch had been cast as Julius Caesar and Stephen Boyd would portray Mark Antony. Keeping the $5 million budget for

the film in mind, Wanger thought it would be cost-effective to shoot in the controlled setting of England's Pinewood Studios, setting the stage for all that was to follow, if not for the film itself.

Cast and crew set out in September 1960. The cold, damp weather of England in fall quickly took a toll on Elizabeth's always fragile health. She began calling in sick with what, over the next few months, went from a cold to meningitis to double pneumonia. She went into the hospital in early March 1961 and underwent an emergency tracheotomy to assist her breathing and save her life. "I was desperately ill," she later explained, "coming in an out of comas, for about six days. At one time, the doctor had to announce that I had less than one hour to live. . . . They cut a hole in my throat and inserted a big silver tube to help me breathe." By the end of the month she could sit up in bed and read the thousands of messages from fans and well-wishers who had prayed for her recovery. The fight for her life endeared Elizabeth to the public once more. The Liz-Eddie-Debbie scandal was forgotten.

Elizabeth returned to Los Angeles in time to attend the Academy Awards ceremony in April 1961 to collect her Oscar for *BUtterfield 8*.

> *Cleopatra was not a vamp. She was a highly complicated, intelligent woman who was carried to great heights in her ambition. Elizabeth Taylor has an understanding of this.*

Reminders of her illness could be heard in her gravel-voiced acceptance speech and seen in the bandage covering the healing incision on her neck. Embraced by the public again and recognized with top honors by her colleagues, Elizabeth was appreciative and happy to be alive. She also had $50,000 worth of medical expenses, so she rested up in order to resume work on *Cleopatra* as swiftly as possible. She was the only Queen of the Nile that Wanger wanted. Joseph L. Mankiewicz, who had replaced Mamoulian as director, concurred, so they would wait for her to fully recover.

The film resumed production in the fall of 1961. This time Fox took no chances on exposing Elizabeth to elements that might be detrimental to her health and moved filming to sunny Italy, in and around Cinecittà Studios outside of Rome. Elizabeth traveled with husband Eddie and her children, who delighted in the vacation. Son Michael Wilding said: "The entire city of Alexandria was re-created in Italy. . . . For a kid just seven or eight, it was a fantasy. It was this fantastical playground."

Due to the delays, male leads Peter Finch and Stephen Boyd had opted out of the playground. Rex Harrison was signed to play Julius Caesar and Welsh-born star of stage and screen Richard Burton was brought in as Mark Antony. Burton had first encountered Elizabeth at a party in Los Angeles a decade earlier but they "carefully avoided each other," according to Burton. Still, his initial reaction to her at that first encounter was recorded in his diary: "She was so extraordinarily beautiful that I almost laughed out loud. . . . She was lavish. She was a dark unyielding largesse. She was, in short, too bloody much."

When Burton first arrived in Rome he was friendly with both Elizabeth and Fisher. Then they played their first scene together on January 22, 1962. It was the start of one of the great romances of the twentieth century. Elizabeth was married to Fisher and Burton to his wife of thirteen years, Sybil Williams, but from that first moment the bond between them was so intense that they could not hide what was happening. Mankiewicz cabled back to Walter Wanger: "I have been sitting on a volcano all alone for too long and I want to fill you in on some facts you ought to know. Liz and Richard are not just playing lovers—they are Antony and Cleopatra." Wanger, who himself had once been involved in a scandal for shooting his wife Joan Bennett's lover in the groin, urged Fisher to go home—advice the spurned husband took. Soon the press let the entire world in on La Scandale in Italy. Elizabeth's son, Michael, recalled, "[the paparazzi] were going wild. . . . I remember once we were given permission to use the garden hose on the telephoto lenses that were peering over the wall."

Meanwhile, pyramiding overruns from delays and the most lavish film production ever attempted took Fox to the brink of bankruptcy. The studio continued to pour money into it. When all was said and done, Fox was banking on cashing in on the priceless publicity generated by the Taylor-Burton romance. The inter-

> *When all was said and done, Fox was banking on cashing in on the priceless publicity generated by the Taylor-Burton romance.*

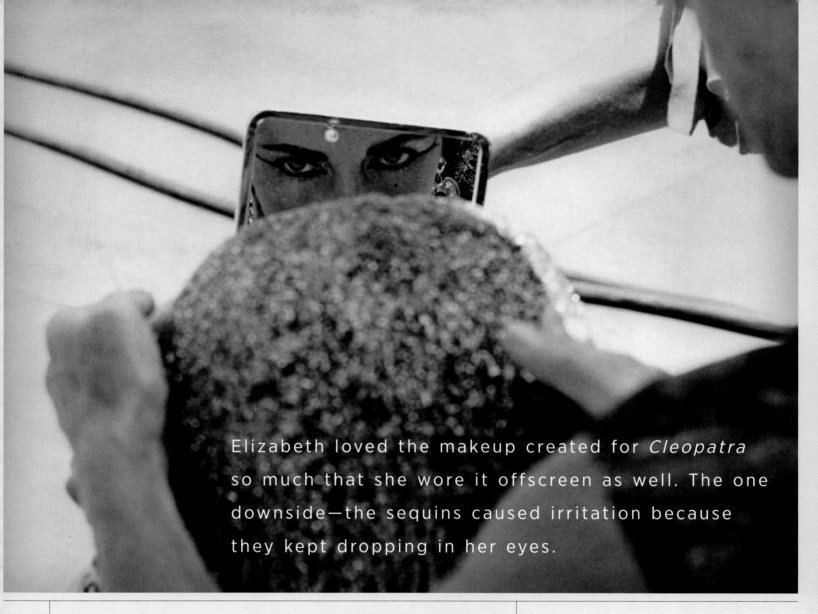

Elizabeth loved the makeup created for *Cleopatra* so much that she wore it offscreen as well. The one downside—the sequins caused irritation because they kept dropping in her eyes.

national headlines generated by the film were matched by the production that Mankiewicz mounted. It was a sumptuous extravaganza filled with regal sets, expansive battle scenes, and no fewer than sixty elaborate costumes crafted for Elizabeth by Irene Sharaff.

Ultimately, Elizabeth was disappointed with the final assemblage of footage, feeling that in editing it down to a manageable length they had cut the heart out of the film and it lacked substance. She had been so invested in the production from both a personal and professional standpoint that she truly wanted it to be a great film. If not for her own sake, she offered to the press, "Rex Harrison is superb, different, remarkable, and brilliant. . . . And I must say that Richard Burton is one of the greatest actors, without question, who has ever worked on the screen or in the theater." Her final assessment was summed up years later when she said, "I really could have done without *Cleopatra*, except for meeting Richard."

Reviews of the film were mixed, at best, but Taylor and Burton drew the public to theaters in droves and in the end *Cleopatra* earned nine Academy Award nominations (including Best Picture) and took home four Oscars. As to Elizabeth, for all her reservations about her performance and the indifference of the critics, she created a truly indelible image that is forever linked with Cleopatra. More often than not, when conjuring visions of the Queen of the Nile, it is kohl-eyed Elizabeth Taylor one sees.

The V.I.P.s

METRO-GOLDWYN-MAYER

CAST

Elizabeth Taylor ....*Frances Andros*

Richard Burton .... *Paul Andros*

Louis Jourdan .... *Marc Champselle*

Elsa Martinelli .... *Gloria Gritti*

Margaret Rutherford........... *the Duchess*

Maggie Smith............................*Miss Mead*

Rod Taylor............................ *Les Mangrum*

Linda Christian ....*Miriam Marshall*

Orson Welles.............................. *Max Buda*

Robert Coote .... *John Coburn*

CREDITS

Anatole de Grunwald *(producer)*; Anthony Asquith *(director)*; Terence Rattigan *(screenplay)*; Jack Hildyard *(photography)*; Miklós Rózsa *(music)*; William Kellner *(art director)*; Pamela Cornell *(set decorations)*; Kip Gowans *(assistant director)*; Frank Clarke *(editor)*; Felix Evans *(costumes)*; Hubert de Givenchy *(Elizabeth Taylor's wardrobe)*; Pierre Cardin *(Elsa Martinelli's wardrobe)*; Vivienne Walker-Zavitz *(hairstylist)*

RELEASE DATE: May, 1963 (U.K.)

September 19, 1963 (U.S.)

RUN TIME: 119 minutes, color

RIGHT: Elizabeth as Frances Andros **OPPOSITE, FROM TOP:** With Richard Burton and Louis Jourdan | With Louis Jourdan | With Burton, playing her estranged husband | With Louis Jourdan, playing her would-be lover

SUMMARY:
Fog rolls in around London airport, putting a halt to all air traffic and affecting the lives of an assorted group of first-class passengers. A dotty duchess attempts to save her estate. Movie mogul Max Buda counts on timeliness to save him a fortune in taxes. Les Mangrum and his secretary Miss Mead need to get to America posthaste to save his business interest. But at the center is the story of Frances and Paul Andros. Frances has come to feel unloved by her shipping magnate husband and plans to leave him for playboy Marc Champselle. While waiting for the fog to lift, Paul tries to win Frances back, but their marriage may be beyond repair. As with their fellow travelers, uncertainty reigns as the clock ticks.

"*The V.I.P.s* is so super deluxe in its lushness and lavishness, with so highly polished a surface that, if you haven't your wits about you, you might, from time to time, mistake it for the solid gold Cadillac it resembles, courtesy of a couple of 24-carat performances by Margaret Rutherford and Maggie Smith. Mr. Burton's performance is graceful and unremittingly gloomy and Miss Taylor's is unremitting; both, of course, are beautiful to look at." **—New York *Herald Tribune*
(Judith Crist)**

"The picture is a satisfying work because it delivers suspense and plot, nicely varied, handsomely acted, and funneled through the medium of some of the world's best publicized performers." **—New York *Post***

"*The V.I.P.s* is, gratifyingly, a lively, engrossing romantic film. . . . The crisis that Miss Taylor and Mr. Burton portray is a fairly solemn business, prickly and soaked in sentiment, in which neither character looks too sensible or good. Particularly the wife, although Miss Taylor plays her appropriately, with a strange sort of icy detachment—almost cruelty—toward both men, and is very lovely to look at, she does not generate much sympathy. Mr. Burton is better as the husband, particularly in the early scenes when he is weathering the shock of discovering the perfidy of his wife. . . . But all right. Their dramatic difficulty, while it may have a sad and shallow look, is sufficiently touching and engrossing to form a solid hub for the film. And around it swirls all this other suspenseful, amusing stuff."

**—*The New York Times*
(Bosley Crowther)**

O SECULO
ilustrado   Nº 1679 • 7-3-70 • preço 5$00

LIZ A DEVORADORA DE DIAMANTES

FROM TOP: The cast, assembled at the grand dinner party on the Andros yacht | Italian magazine cover depicting Elizabeth in the film

notes

ON THE STRENGTH OF THE PUBLICITY GENERATED BY THEIR romance, and by *Cleopatra* in general, Elizabeth and Richard Burton were a box-office dream team for any producer. Burton signed up to do *The V.I.P.s* (then called *International Hotel*) first. When Elizabeth casually offered to do the film with him, producer Anatole de Grunwald leaped at the suggestion. Elizabeth was back working for MGM, though this time there was no commitment to the studio beyond one film. Production took place at Elstree Studios in England between January and March 1963.

From *Cleopatra* to *The V.I.P.s* through the next nine films they would make together, Burton became Elizabeth's favorite costar. She said in 1963, "He's wonderful to work with because he gives you so much. Unlike so many actors, he's not a stone wall. He has electricity." *The V.I.P.s* was among their most successful films. It grossed $14 million worldwide. The story was in what was then often termed the *Grand Hotel* style, wherein the audience is given a glimpse into the world of a group of disparate characters, each with an evolving story of their own. In this case it would be more fittingly compared to *Separate Tables*, another hit multistory film from screenwriter Terence Rattigan. The format allowed an

ensemble cast to shine, in this case including Louis Jourdan, Orson Welles, Margaret Rutherford, Maggie Smith, and Rod Taylor. Rutherford won a Best Supporting Actress Oscar for her role as a slightly batty duchess.

Little known at the time, Terence Rattigan based his screenplay on an incident in the lives of his friends Vivien Leigh and Laurence Olivier. At one time Leigh planned to leave her husband for actor Peter Finch but, as in the film, their flight was delayed, allowing Olivier time to go to the airport and change Leigh's mind. The Oliviers reunited. A similar situation was played out in the film by Elizabeth, Burton, and Louis Jourdan.

After making *The V.I.P.s*, Elizabeth took time off from acting in movies herself and traveled with Burton to the locations of his work. *Becket* kept them based in England through the summer of 1963. *The Night of the Iguana* took them to Puerto Vallarta, Mexico, in the fall. Then it was on to Canada, and later New York, for a stage production of *Hamlet*. They would not be married until March

> *Elizabeth and Richard Burton were a box-office dream team for any producer.*

CLOCKWISE FROM LEFT: As neglected wife Frances Andros | Hairstyling by Vivienne Walker-Zavitz. The diamond tiara had been a gift from Mike Todd. | Elizabeth always enjoyed wearing all or bits of costuming from her films offscreen, in this case to the premiere of *Lawrence of Arabia*.

ABOVE, FROM LEFT: In London during the making of *The V.I.P.s* | Coming out of her dressing room **OPPOSITE, FROM TOP:** A candid shot of Elizabeth and Burton during the production | Elizabeth and Burton in *The V.I.P.s,* the second of eleven films they made together

15, 1964. In the interim Elizabeth was seeking a divorce from Eddie Fisher while Burton's own "Sybil War" raged on. He had been married to Sybil Williams for fourteen years and they had two daughters, Kate and Jessica. Burton struggled with conscience for months before coming to the decision to divorce his wife. Elizabeth embraced her role of impending stepmother. Kate Burton said, "Elizabeth and I got on from the word go. She is an irresistible woman. I loved her and she cared for me, too. I think in a lot of ways, because I wasn't her own child, she could really enjoy me."

> *Elizabeth was never one to sneak around for the sake of public appearances. She had fallen in love with Richard Burton and could not conceal it.*

While Elizabeth and Burton worked out their respective divorces, it was obvious to the world that they were living together wherever they traveled. Elizabeth was never one to sneak around for the sake of public appearances. She had fallen in love with Richard Burton and could not conceal it. They were a combustible pair who fought, laughed, and loved passionately. Elizabeth said, "We find we share the same sense of comedy and the ridiculous. That's why we love each other. We feel exactly the same way about things." Unlike her relationship with Eddie Fisher, which the public never fully accepted, Elizabeth and Burton were an irresistible pair. They were vilified as illicit lovers for a time but then embraced by the public on an international level. The power of Elizabeth and Burton's dynamic coupling could not be denied.

The Sandpiper

FILMWAYS/
METRO-GOLDWYN-MAYER

CAST

Elizabeth Taylor .... *Laura Reynolds*
Richard Burton .... *Dr. Edward Hewitt*
Eva Marie Saint .... *Claire Hewitt*
Charles Bronson .... *Cos Erickson*
Robert Webber .... *Ward Hendricks*
James Edwards .... *Larry Brant*
Torin Thatcher .... *Judge Thompson*
Tom Drake .... *Walter Robinson*
Doug Henderson .... *Paul Sutcliff*
Morgan Mason .... *Danny Reynolds*

CREDITS

Martin Ransohoff *(producer)*; Vincente Minnelli *(director)*; John Calley *(associate producer)*; Ben Kadish *(production supervisor)*; Dalton Trumbo, Michael Wilson *(screenplay)*; Irene Kamp, Louis Kamp *(adaptation)*, based on story by Martin Ransohoff; Milton Krasner *(photography)*; Johnny Mandel *(music)*; Johnny Mandel and Paul Francis Webster *(song: "The Shadow of Your Smile")*; George W. Davis, Urie McCleary *(art directors)*; Henry Grace, Keogh Gleason *(set decorations)*; Franklin Milton *(sound)*; William McGarry *(assistant director)*; David Bretherton *(editor)*; Irene Sharaff *(costumes)*; Sydney Guilaroff *(hairstylist)*; William Tuttle *(makeup)*; Elizabeth Duquette *(Laura's paintings)*; Edmund Kara *(redwood statue)*

RELEASE DATE: June 23, 1965
RUN TIME: 117 minutes, color

RIGHT: Though her twenties were well in the past, Elizabeth was arguably at her most beautiful in this period. **OPPOSITE:** Laura Reynolds lives life as free as a sandpiper.

SUMMARY: Artist Laura Reynolds's free-spirited thinking defies social mores of the day. She lives with her illegitimate son, Danny, in a secluded home on the beach in Big Sur. By putting herself in charge of Danny's education, she isolates the boy from the outside world, until authorities order her to send him to a private school run by Episcopalian minister Dr. Edward Hewitt and his wife, Claire. Dr. Hewitt's staunch conservative views are the opposite of Laura's, yet by challenging each other's strongest convictions they become emotionally involved. They have an affair that results in Laura's open-mindedness expanding to the point of finally enrolling Danny in the private school, where he flourishes surrounded by other young boys. Meanwhile, Dr. Hewitt decides to leave the clergy in hopes of discovering what he truly wants for his future.

REVIEWS

"*The Sandpiper* was made for the voyeurs among us who are willing to pay admission to see Elizabeth Taylor and Richard Burton engage in illicit lovemaking in and out of bed and beach. They do it in Metrocolor and Panavision to boot, with some Big Sur scenery, some pre-freshman sociological chatter and some ludicrous artsy-smarty atmosphere thrown in for the higher thinkers in the crowd."

—New York *Herald Tribune*
(Judith Crist)

"Burton's performance is of his usual high quality, his expressive face and cultured voice adding up to perfection. . . . There is some good drama in *The Sandpiper* and it's a pity that the further it goes the more sudsy it gets. Director Vincente Minnelli should have known better than to let it take on a soap opera aspect."

—New York *Daily News*
(Wanda Hale)

"Built up to give the impression that it is taking a disapproving view of an adulterous affair between a free-thinking woman and an Episcopal clergyman, it is really a slick and sympathetic sanction of the practice of free love—or, at least, of an illicit union that is supposedly justified by naturalness. . . . All the best of it is given to the woman, whom Miss Taylor plays with the lofty and elegant assurance of a chicly dressed, camera-pampered star. Her arty and shallow pretensions of a bold, humanistic philosophy are never intelligently challenged. And Mr. Burton is compelled to play the clergyman in an annoyingly solemn, apologetic way. However, there are a lot of handsome and diverting incidentals in this film—a lot of scenic and environmental details to give it a sophisticated air and look. Much of it was shot on location in the coastal area of California's Big Sur, with the rugged and beautiful seacoast to give the color cameras much grandeur on which to dwell. And Vincente Minnelli, as director, has captured the style and charm of an artist's beach house and the clatter and splash of an artist's friends."

—*The New York Times*
(Bosley Crowther)

> *Reviews were sharply critical of the free love, free-as-a-sandpiper thinking represented by the Laura Reynolds character, but it all holds up considerably better today.*

FROM LEFT: On the Big Sur location with daughter Liza | Elizabeth as Laura Reynolds **OPPOSITE, CLOCKWISE FROM TOP LEFT:** With Morgan Mason, her son in the film | Elizabeth's paintings in the film were the work of Elizabeth Duquette. This is the opening sequence. | With James Edwards and Charles Bronson. Sammy Davis, Jr. was once intended for the role played by Bronson. | Elizabeth and Burton played forbidden lovers in the film.

IN 1964 ELIZABETH AND RICHARD BURTON WERE THE WORLD'S most exciting couple, though by this time they presented a family picture, marrying in March and then adopting a daughter, Maria, later the same year. It was through no shortage of activity that when Elizabeth began work on *The Sandpiper* she had not made a film for more than a year and a half. Burton, meanwhile, had made two movies and starred in a stage production of *Hamlet*.

The Sandpiper began filming amid the spectacular scenery of Big Sur in northern California. It was a hot Indian summer on the location and Elizabeth made use of a small portable fan constantly on the set. From there the production moved to Paris, at the Burtons' request. It was on the voyage to Europe to complete *The Sandpiper* that Elizabeth was reunited with Debbie Reynolds, then traveling with her second husband, wealthy shoe manufacturer Harry Karl. Over dinner together, the hatchet between them was buried once and for all, and they saw a great deal of each other on the ocean voyage to Europe.

TOP, LOWER MIDDLE: With Richard Burton at a reception just after their arrival in Europe **LOWER LEFT:** With Debbie Reynolds aboard the ship to Europe to shoot *The Sandpiper* **LOWER RIGHT:** Signing an autograph for a young fan at the *Sandpiper* premiere in Los Angeles

ABOVE: Amid the star-studded assemblage at the Lido were Maria Callas, Ingrid Bergman, Aristotle Onassis, Guy de Rothschild, Richard Burton, and Elizabeth. **BELOW:** While in Paris filming *The Sandpiper*, Elizabeth and Burton attended the opening of a new review at the Lido nightclub, where spectacular candids were taken, but almost none seen in color.

Vincente Minnelli, who had last worked with Elizabeth fourteen years ago on *Father of the Bride* and its sequel, *Father's Little Dividend*, directed *The Sandpiper* from a script by Michael Wilson and writer Dalton Trumbo, who was once blacklisted as a communist. Critics of the day opined that the views of Trumbo, as presented through his script of *Sandpiper*, were still not in line with the thinking of the general American public. Reviews were sharply critical of the free love, free-as-a-sandpiper thinking represented by the Laura Reynolds character, but it all holds up considerably better today.

Elizabeth negotiated another $1 million salary for the film. She said, "A lot of people may think that *Sandpiper* was written specifically for Richard and me in order to cash in on our notoriety. Actually the script has been knocking around for years and at first they didn't ask Richard to be in it." Now in their third film together, the Burtons were establishing a fine reputation as an acting partnership. Filmways vice president Mike Mindlin spoke of his experience on *The Sandpiper*, saying, "I have found them professional, extremely bright, sensitive, very well meaning, and serious about their work. They are also a hell of a lot of fun to be around." Publicist Cynthia Grenier spent time on the *Sandpiper* set and observed, "They make such a marvelous couple. You see it rarely. There is a very nice feeling of how they play around with each other—mock hostility and jockeying for position."

While not a critical triumph, *The Sandpiper* was a hit with Elizabeth and Burton's enthusiastic fans, ensuring more Taylor-Burton films to come. When the press speculated if Elizabeth would change her professional name to Mrs. Richard Burton, he quipped, "If she were Mrs. Richard Burton on the marquees, I could get top billing at last." *The Sandpiper* had another noteworthy success: the song which played over the titles, "The Shadow of Your Smile," written by Johnny Mandel and Paul Francis Webster, won the Oscar for Best Song.

> *They make such a marvelous couple. You see it rarely. There is a very nice feeling of how they play around with each other—mock hostility and jockeying for position.*
>
> —CYNTHIA GRENIER

OPPOSITE: As the free-spirited Laura Reynolds
ABOVE: The couple drew all attention at the star-studded opening at the Lido during the making of *The Sandpiper*.

Who's Afraid of Virginia Woolf?

WARNER BROS./CHENAULT

CAST

Elizabeth Taylor .... *Martha*

Richard Burton .... *George*

George Segal .... *Nick*

Sandy Dennis .... *Honey*

CREDITS

Ernest Lehman *(producer)*; Mike Nichols *(director)*; Ernest Lehman *(screenplay)*, based on play by Edward Albee; Haskell Wexler *(photography)*; Alex North *(music)*; Richard Sylbert *(production design)*; George James Hopkins *(set decorations)*; M. A. Merrick *(sound)*; Bud Grace *(assistant director)*; Sam O'Steen *(editor)*; Irene Sharaff *(costumes)*; Sydney Guilaroff *(hairstylist)*; Gordon Bau, Ron Berkeley *(makeup)*

RELEASE DATE: June 22, 1966

RUN TIME: 131 minutes, black and white

SUMMARY: George is a professor of history at a university run by the father of his shrewish wife, Martha, who needles him for his failure to rise in the ranks at the school. What Martha and George do best is incite each other to anger with below-the-belt remarks. They are joined for an evening by a young couple, Nick and Honey, and a night of alcohol-fueled revelations, betrayal, and revenge ensues. When Martha crosses the line by talking about their son, George takes his anger out on the guests. Martha takes young Nick to bed with her, and George strikes back where it hurts the most, bringing to light the reality about their son—and George and Martha's deep, ultimate need for each other.

"She's so goddamn good in this—no other way to put it."

—Richard Burton's assessment of Elizabeth's work
in *Who's Afraid of Virginia Woolf?*

LEFT: Costume test shots of Elizabeth as Martha **ABOVE:** Elizabeth was only thirty-three at the time she was offered the role of Martha. It was frightening but she knew it was the role of a lifetime.

"[The film] has given Elizabeth the outstanding acting role of her career. She is nothing less than brilliant as the shrewish, slovenly, blasphemous, frustrated, slightly wacky, alcoholic wife of a meek, unambitious assistant professor of history at a university, over which her father reigns as president. The Albee vehicle has also given Burton a chance to display his disciplined art in the role of the victim of a wife's vituperative tongue."

   —New York *Daily News* (Kate Cameron)

"Here, with a director who knows how to get an actor's confidence and knows what to do with it after he gets it, [Taylor] does the best work of her career, sustained and urgent. Of course, she has an initial advantage. Her acceptance of gray hair and her use of profanity make her seem to be acting even (figuratively) before she begins. ('Gee, she let them show her looking old!' 'Wow, she just said 'Son of a bitch'! A star!') It is not the first time an American star has gotten mileage out of that sort of daring. Miss Taylor does not have qualities that, for instance, Uta Hagen had in the Broadway version, no suggestion of endlessly coiled involutions. Her venom is nearer the surface. But, under Mr. Nichols's hand, she gets vocal variety, never relapses out of the role, and she charges it with the utmost of her powers—which is an achievement for any actress, great or little. . . . In its forthright dealing with the play, this becomes one of the most scathingly honest American films ever made."   **—*The New York Times* (Stanley Kauffmann)**

In conference with director Mike Nichols

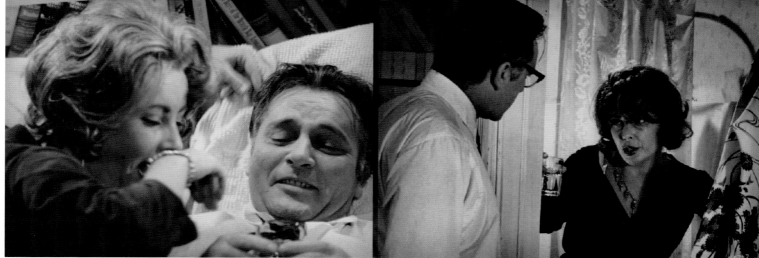

CLOCKWISE, FROM TOP: With George Segal, Sandy Dennis, and Burton. The movie posters read, "You are cordially invited to George and Martha's for an evening of fun and games." | With Richard Burton | "It's a silly thing, letting a bloody play work on you. . . . This one has exorcised several ghosts." The extreme dramatics of the film proved cathartic for the Burtons.

notes

ABOVE: At long last, in the finale, Martha's vulnerability comes shining through.

EDWARD ALBEE'S STARTLINGLY FEROCIOUS DRAMA, *WHO'S Afraid of Virginia Woolf?*, provided Elizabeth with what was arguably the single greatest role of her career, and the star's personal favorite. The smash hit play opened on Broadway October 13, 1962, and had a run of 664 performances. Warner Bros. purchased the film rights for $500,000 and dictated that Tony winners Uta Hagen and Arthur Hill be replaced by box-office attractions to ensure return on a sizable investment.

Writer-producer Ernest Lehman, fresh from his success as screenwriter of *The Sound of Music*, and director Mike Nichols, a Broadway export making his cinematic debut, had the controversial idea of casting Elizabeth in the role of the frumpy, foul-mouthed Martha. Lehman said, "From the very beginning, she kept coming back into my mind." Elizabeth herself was unsure she wanted the

Elizabeth and Burton, one of the world's greatest acting couples

part: "I was absolutely terrified. . . . I thought I was too young, and I hope and trust I'm unlike Martha as a person. It meant I'd have to create a totally different being. I didn't know whether I could." She knew though, that it was the role of a life-time, and Richard Burton ultimately convinced her to take the opportunity. Burton was then signed to star opposite his wife. For the only two other characters in the story, Nick and Honey, George Segal and Sandy Dennis were cast. Dennis was an acclaimed stage actress, and this was touted as her screen debut, though it was not.

Elizabeth began preparing for her role by gaining twenty pounds. She wore a salt-and-pepper wig, prosthetics, and padding to aid in the physical transformation, and extra tight clothing gave the illusion of adding more vol-ume to her frame. Shooting in black and white allowed her to cake on makeup for an aged appearance. Nichols and the cast of four went into three weeks of intense rehearsals beginning July 6, 1965. The actual filming took place in Northampton, Massachusetts, where rain and fog caused numerous delays but provided a fitting backdrop for the story.

ABOVE, FROM LEFT: During rehearsals, with director Mike Nichols | A visit to the set by Marlene Dietrich

Who's Afraid of Virginia Woolf? was by no means an obvious vehicle for the transition from stage to screen. One struggle was opening up the story from the play's single setting to make it cinematic. The biggest departure in the film was adding a roadhouse set. This also brought two fleeting additional characters into the story, a roadhouse manager and waitress, who were portrayed by Frank and Agnes Flanagan. The husband and wife were part of the company who worked on the film every day; Frank as a gaffer, Agnes as Elizabeth's hairdresser.

A greater struggle for the film versus the play was that Albee's dialogue was riddled with phrases which the censors had diligently kept off the screen for decades. Lehman told the press, "We've retained as much as possible of the corrosive controversy of Albee's play—its scathing dialogue, explosive dramatics, and electrifying emotions." The screen adaptation remained remarkably true to Albee, making the film the first to carry the warning tag "No one under 18 will be admitted unless accompanied by his parent."

Many wondered how playing such a ferociously antagonistic couple would affect Burton and Elizabeth. Burton noted, "I think ours is the strongest marriage I know, and *Virginia Woolf* didn't alter that." They came to look at playing George and Martha as a cathartic experience. Elizabeth said "I've never had a better time in my life," but when asked if it was easy to turn off Martha at the end of the day's shooting she admitted, "My God, no. When we first started shooting, I couldn't turn her off at all. She's so complex—vulgar, gross, cruel, and soft as an unborn bird. . . . It seems I've been Martha forever. She's not anyone I'd want to be forever."

Each of the stars put forth their best efforts in the film and earned Oscar nominations for their work. Sandy Dennis took home the award for Best Supporting Actress, and Elizabeth won the honor of Best Actress for her performance as Martha. She was angry that Burton did not also win, but took enormous satisfaction in the completed *Who's Afraid of Virginia Woolf?*, later saying, "I was overcome with such a sense of joy and pride. God, we were good together."

> *Each of the stars put forth their best efforts in the film and earned Oscar nominations for their work.*

The Taming of the Shrew

**ROYAL FILMS INTERNATIONAL/
F.A.I. PRODUCTIONS/
COLUMBIA PICTURES**

CAST

Elizabeth Taylor	*Katharina*
Richard Burton	*Petruchio*
Cyril Cusack	*Grumio*
Michael Hordern	*Baptista*
Alfred Lynch	*Tranio*
Alan Webb	*Gremio*
Giancarlo Cobelli	*the Priest*
Vernon Dobtcheff	*Pedant*
Ken Parry	*Tailor*
Anthony Gardner	*Haberdasher*
Natasha Pyne	*Bianca*
Michael York	*Lucentio*

CREDITS

Richard McWhorter *(executive producer)*; Richard Burton, Elizabeth Taylor, Franco Zeffirelli *(producers)*; Franco Zeffirelli *(director)*; Franco Zeffirelli, Paul Dehn, Suso Cecchi d'Amico *(screenplay)*, based on play by William Shakespeare; Oswald Morris *(photography)*; Nino Rota *(music)*; John De Cuir, Renzo Mongiardino *(production designs)*; Giuseppe Mariani, Elven Webb *(art directors)*; Dario Simoni, Luigi Gervasi *(set decorations)*; Carlo Lastricati, Albino Cocco, Rinaldo Ricci *(assistant directors)*; Peter Taylor *(editor)*; Danilo Donati, Gloria Musetta, Irene Sharaff *(costumes)*; Alexandre de Paris *(Elizabeth Taylor's hairstylist)*; Alberto De Rossi, Giannetto De Rossi, Frank Larue, Ron Berkeley *(makeup)*

RELEASE DATE: March 8, 1967

RUN TIME: 122 minutes, color

SUMMARY: In sixteenth-century Padua, the beauteous and delicate Bianca would be set to marry suitor Lucentio, but for her father, Baptista, who mandates that Bianca may not marry until her older sister Katharina is wed. The problem is, though Katharina be rich and beautiful, she has a fierce personality and is perpetually in a fit of rage. No man is willing to subject himself to a lifetime of her abuse. Then, traveler Petruchio arrives in town to "wive it wealthily." Petruchio cares not that Katharina is a hellion and becomes determined to subdue her. With the help of all Bianca's suitors, who wish to see Katharina married for their own benefit, Petruchio succeeds in making a series of furious and comic events turn Katharina into a gentle, loving wife. Bianca may now marry the steadfast Lucentio.

ABOVE: A shrew ready for taming. Elizabeth came to love a role which at first frightened her with its Shakespearean text. **OPPOSITE:** Petruchio comes to Padua to wive it wealthily, even if it means taming a hellion named Katharina.

REVIEWS

"Franco Zeffirelli's *The Taming of the Shrew* is a film of great visual beauty, a voluptuous feast for those with a hungry eye for the sun-sodden misted glow the Italian director uniquely provides on screen as on stage for Shakespeare's 16th-century Italy, and/or a ravenous one for the exquisite face and décolletage of Elizabeth Taylor. Both scene and set and leading lady are set forth in lavish splendor and in such glowing tones that play and performance can well assume secondary status.'"

—**New York *World Journal Tribune*
(Judith Crist)**

"Director Franco Zeffirelli has made a lusty comedy and a beautiful canvas of *The Taming of the Shrew*. . . . It would be hard to find a better Petruchio than Richard Burton—rip-roaring male in his cups, humorously gutsy in his swagger, stout-hearted in his dual with Katharina, yet with a gleam of tenderness when he finds her softening. Elizabeth Taylor's Kate is more like a furious kitten than a snarling termagant in the earlier scenes, she is irresistible to watch, she speaks her Shakespeare nicely and becomes moving in her final obeisance to her 'lord and master.'"   —**New York *Post*
(Frances Herridge)**

"Having had at one another very roundly and in a serious dramatic vein in their most recent husband-wife tangle, *Who's Afraid of Virginia Woolf?* the Burtons are now turned loose with slapsticks for a free-swinging hit-as-hit-can in this forthrightly campy entertainment. They are refereed by Franco Zeffirelli out of the corner of one winking eye. And if any crusty customer doesn't like it—well, a pox on him!"   —***The New York Times*
(Bosley Crowther)**

notes

WILLIAM SHAKESPEARE'S ZESTFUL ROMANTIC COMEDY *The Taming of the Shrew* was a natural for married actors to play. Forceful fortune-seeker Petruchio and Katharina the shrew were portrayed by famed couple Alfred Lunt and Lynn Fontanne onstage in the mid-1930s and on the screen by the husband-and-wife team of Douglas Fairbanks and Mary Pickford in an early talkie of 1929. Italian producer-director Franco Zeffirelli originally conceived his production as a vehicle for Sophia Loren and Marcello Mastroianni, but ultimately continued the tradition of couples casting with the most famous acting pair in the world, Elizabeth Taylor and Richard Burton.

> The Shakespeare film adaptation was a beautiful Technicolor production with lavish (Oscar-nominated) art direction and costumes.

In addition to starring in the film, Elizabeth and Burton coproduced with Zeffirelli, waiving their usual generous salaries in exchange for a profit share in the movie. *The Taming of the Shrew* was an intriguing follow-up to *Who's Afraid of Virginia Woolf?* It had the shrew in common, though the Shakespeare film adaptation was a beautiful Technicolor production with lavish (Oscar-nominated) art direction and costumes. Elizabeth shed the pounds of *Virginia Woolf* and looked as stunning as ever.

Granted, it was not appearances that concerned Elizabeth with this film, but the acting itself. Burton had much experience with Shakespearean acting, but Elizabeth was apprehensive about it. He was less concerned about how she would fare: "Anything, including Shakespeare, is possible with Elizabeth. Elizabeth is

OPPOSITE, CLOCKWISE FROM TOP LEFT: Katharina the Shrew | Elizabeth always loved riding. Her cloak was by Irene Sharaff, part of the Oscar-nominated costuming team on the movie. | Elizabeth and Richard Burton take on Shakespeare. They had toyed with the idea of doing *Macbeth*, but Elizabeth always maintained that *The Taming of the Shrew* would be more fitting for her.

ABOVE, FROM LEFT: Outside of an Italian restaurant during filming | In Italy, during the making of *The Taming of the Shrew* BELOW: Burton collects a David di Donatello Award for his performance in the film.

shy about her lack of experience in the classical theatre, but she speaks verse with a kind of deadly authority. I think it would be fascinating to have a youngish Lady Macbeth, a sort of femme fatale."To his last comment, Elizabeth replied, "Wouldn't it be better typecasting for me to do *Taming of the Shrew*?" As Burton suspected, Elizabeth eased into the role of Katharina quickly. She improved as the production went on, so much so that nearing the end Elizabeth talked Zeffirelli into reshooting the first day's footage. The movie presented a new challenge for Burton, too, when director Zeffirelli had to leave the production for the last few days of filming. Leaving precise instructions, Zeffirelli entrusted directorial duties to his male star.

> *Zeffirelli later said in his memoirs that making the movie with his friends, the Burtons, was one of the best times he ever had.*

The Taming of the Shrew was filmed at the studios of Dino De Laurentiis in Italy from March through August 1966. The Roman setting, in the color cinematography of Oswald Morris, helped make it a gorgeously spectacular film. Zeffirelli later said in his memoirs that making the movie with his friends, the Burtons, was one of the best times he ever had. For their part, Elizabeth described the production as "one long honeymoon." It was a profitable one at that. *The Taming of the Shrew* drew more than $12 million in gross worldwide, and Elizabeth, Burton, and the film itself won David di Donatello Awards at the Sicilian Film Festival.

Elizabeth's hairstylist, Alexandre de Paris, outdid himself on the movie.

Doctor Faustus

OXFORD UNIVERSITY SCREEN PRODUCTIONS/ NASSAU FILMS/VENFILMS/ COLUMBIA PICTURES

CAST

Richard Burton .... *Doctor Faustus*

Elizabeth Taylor .... *Helen of Troy*

Andreas Teuber .... *Mephistopheles*

Ian Marter .... *Emperor*

Elizabeth O'Donovan .... *Empress*

David McIntosh .... *Lucifer*

Jeremy Eccles .... *Belsebub*

Ram Chopra .... *Valdes*

Richard Carwardine .... *Cornelius*

Richard Heffer .... *Disciple No. 1*

CREDITS

Richard McWhorter, Richard Burton *(executive producers)*; Richard Burton, Nevill Coghill *(directors)*; Nevill Coghill *(screenplay)*, based on play by Christopher Marlowe; Gábor Pogány *(photography)*; Mario Nascimbene *(music)*; John DeCuir *(production design)*; Boris Juraga *(art director)*; Dario Simoni *(set decorations)*; Jacqueline Harvey *(choreographer)*; Gus Agosti *(assistant director)*; David Hildyard, John Aldred *(sound)*; John Shirley *(editor)*; Peter J. Hall *(costumes)*

RELEASE DATE: October 10, 1967 (U.K.); February 6, 1968 (U.S.)

RUN TIME: 93 minutes, color

RIGHT: As the wife of Faustus. Elizabeth appeared in all her glamorous glory in Richard Burton's pet project.

SUMMARY: Doctor Faustus is a dedicated scholar with an insatiable desire to master all the knowledge in the world. He invokes the devil's demon agent, Mephistopheles, out of hell and through him Faustus enters into a pact, granting his soul to the devil in exchange for the knowledge and power which are of paramount importance to him. Over the next twenty-four years, Faustus is to live the life he thinks he wants, filled with gluttony, pride, avarice, lechery, and all the sins that ultimately lead Faustus to a wretched existence. God becomes the doctor's only hope to spare him from an eternity of misery, but the devil will not allow Faustus to break his pact without a fight.

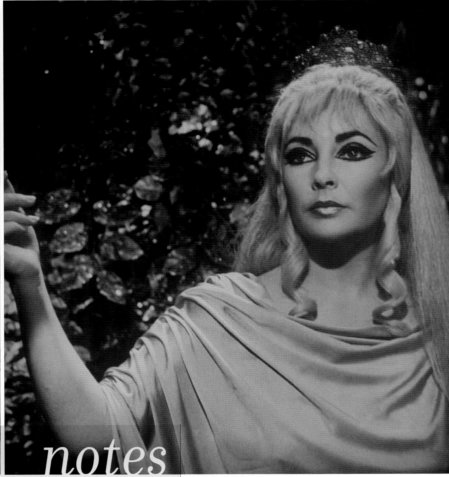

notes

CHRISTOPHER MARLOWE'S PLAY *DOCTOR FAUSTUS*, BASED on a tale of German legend about a man who sells his soul to the devil, first appeared on the stage sometime in the late sixteenth century, with the first known performances taking place in 1594. Many modernized Faustian tragedies appeared on the American screen over the years, among them *The Devil and Daniel Webster* (1941), *Alias Nick Beal* (1949), the classic 1953 musical *The Band Wagon*, and *Damn Yankees* (1958). A straightforward classical treatment was not a popular idea for mass consumption and indeed, such a treatment was never made into a major motion picture in Hollywood,

> *Mute throughout, Elizabeth was presented like a jewel, adorned with glitter, metallic paint, wigs, headdresses, and stunning costuming.*

though it had been done several times in Europe. The success of *The Taming of the Shrew*, however, assisted Richard Burton and coproducer Richard McWhorter in generating financial backing for their classic interpretation of *Faustus*.

The film was based on a stage edition in which Burton had appeared in 1966. (Elizabeth participated too, in a walk-on role.) He was drawn to the production by his alma mater, Oxford University, and specifically by his former tutor, Nevill Coghill. The Burtons provided their services free of charge, with all proceeds going to the Oxford University Dramatic Society. The play was a success, and Burton and Coghill were then inspired to bring it to the big screen.

The movie was filmed both at England's Shepperton studios and Italy's Dino Di Laurentiis studios in September and October 1966. Save for Elizabeth and

CLOCKWISE FROM TOP LEFT: Offscreen with Burton | Elizabeth and Burton give a press conference upon arrival in England for the film's premiere. | Elizabeth and Burton arrive in England to appear in the Oxford University Dramatic Society's production. | At rehearsals for *Doctor Faustus* in Oxford **OPPOSITE:** Elizabeth was stunning in the movie but, many thought, out of place.

Burton, the cast was composed of members of the Oxford University Dramatic Society. Elizabeth appeared in several different roles in the film. Mute throughout, each time she was presented like a jewel, adorned with glitter, metallic paint, wigs, headdresses, and stunning costuming, and each time she appeared more breathtaking than in the previous sighting.

The movie was released in the U.K. in 1967, but Columbia Pictures, the film's U.S. distributor, dragged their feet about releasing the movie and it did not make it to theaters stateside until February 1968. For all the high-minded intentions of the entire company, *Doctor Faustus* was a total failure in reviews and at the box office. Elizabeth's supreme glamour was appreciated, though not seen by many as appropriate to the production. But the greater criticisms were directed at the manner in which the play had been truncated and liberties taken with the dialogue. Reviews noted that in the scenes representing the Pageant of the Seven Deadly Sins, two sins were missing and in the remaining five Marlowe's original words were inexplicably interspersed with passages from the author's other works, including *Edward II* and *Tamburlaine*.

Doctor Faustus, Elizabeth and Burton's sixth film together, was their first that was not a hit. After one film apart they would be back together, removed from classical settings.

REVIEWS

"In spite of Christopher Marlowe's deplorable failure to provide her with a speaking part, Elizabeth Taylor manages to steal the devil's own thunder in *Doctor Faustus*."
—*Newsweek* (J. M.)

"Probably one of the most desperately non-commercial enterprises in motion picture history, this *Doctor Faustus* derives from the Taylor-Burton foray into Oxford last year. The result is a curio unlikely to recover its negative cost."
—*Variety* ("Otta")

"The whole enterprise has the immense vulgarity of a collaboration (almost Faustian, really) in which Academe would sell its soul for a taste of the glamour of Hollywood; and the stars are only too happy to appear awhile in the pretentious friar's robes from Academe. The Burtons, both of whom act themselves as carried over from *The Comedians*, are clearly having a lovely time; at moments one has the feeling that *Faustus* was shot mainly as a home movie for them to enjoy at home. One or the other of them is almost constantly on camera—in various colors, flavors, and shades and lengths of hair. Miss Taylor, who never speaks a word, plays almost all the female parts, from Faustus's devil wife through Helen of Troy and Alexander's Paramour. In this last role, she is, for some reason, frosted all over with silver—like a pastry, or a devaluated refugee from *Goldfinger*."
—*The New York Times* (Renata Adler)

Reflections in a Golden Eye

**JOHN HUSTON-RAY STARK/
WARNER BROS.-SEVEN ARTS**

CAST

Elizabeth Taylor .... *Leonora Penderton*

Marlon Brando .... *Major Weldon Penderton*

Brian Keith ..... *Lt. Colonel Morris Langdon*

Julie Harris .... *Alison Langdon*

Zorro David .... *Anacleto*

Gordon Mitchell .... *stables sergeant*

Irvin Dugan .... *Captain Murray Weincheck*

Fay Sparks .... *Susie*

Robert Forster ...... *Private L. G. Williams*

CREDITS

John Huston, Ray Stark *(producers)*; John Huston *(director)*; C. O. Erickson *(associate producer)*; Chapman Mortimer, Gladys Hill *(screenplay)*, based on novel by Carson McCullers; Aldo Tonti *(photography)*; Toshiro Mayuzumi *(music)*; Stephen Grimes *(production design)*; Bruno Avesani *(art director)*; William Kiernan *(set decorations)*; Vana Caruso, Edward Folger *(assistant directors)*; John Cox, Basil Fenton-Smith, Leslie Hodgson *(sound)*; Russell Lloyd *(editor)*; Dorothy Jeakins, Anna Maria Fea *(costumes)*; Alexandre de Paris *(Elizabeth Taylor's hairstylist)*; Frank LaRue *(makeup)*

RELEASE DATE: October 13, 1967

RUN TIME: 108 minutes, color

SUMMARY: Major Weldon Penderton is a strictly disciplined (though occasionally violent) army officer whose latent homosexual desires make him indifferent to his sexy wife, Leonora. Leonora, who is also given to violent displays, is having an affair with the higher-ranking Lt. Colonel Morris Langdon. Langdon, too, is married. His wife Alison's failure to have a child led to a mental breakdown during which she sliced off her own nipples. While Langdon carries on his affair with Leonora, his wife is comforted only by her effeminate male best friend, Anacleto. Penderton, meanwhile, has taken an interest in young Private Williams, whose unusual habits include riding horseback naked and spying on Leonora. Williams's continued obsession with the major's wife ultimately leads to a tragic finale.

REVIEWS

"*Reflections in a Golden Eye*, John Huston's version of the late Carson McCullers' novel, starring Elizabeth Taylor, Marlon Brando, Julie Harris, and Brian Keith, is a picture of superlative performance, occasional marvels and psychopathia sexualis. Brando has never been greater. Brian Keith and Elizabeth Taylor are superb . . . . It is the kind of picture that brings bated breath almost to the end."

New York *Post* (Archer Winsten)

"[Miss Taylor] is erratic, showing genuine arrogance and cruelty in some scenes, but too often letting her bitchy housewife be merely postured and shrill. . . . The fact that the script of Chapman Mortimer and Gladys Hill follows Mrs. McCuller's book down to this melodramatic murder may be commendable as fidelity, but it does not do well for the significance and plausibility of the drama itself. Neither does Mr. Huston's odd and pretentious use of color to convey the notion of reflections in a golden eye." **—*The New York Times* (Bosley Crowther)**

"Elizabeth Taylor, her beautiful violet eyes glazed by weird photography, plays a hussy, a bold, vulgar woman, belittling and loathing her impotent husband, Marlon Brando, whose face is expressionless in an unearthly glow."

—New York *Daily News* (Wanda Hale)

OPPOSITE BOTTOM: Elizabeth and Brando. The force of their star power alone would have made the film a classic, but the highly unusual drama that unfolds earned it a cult following.

As Leonora Penderton, in one of the most offbeat films of her career

notes

PLAYING THE PART OF AN ARMY OFFICER HARBORING suppressed homosexual tendencies while married to a sadistic, sexually voracious wife, was far from the most coveted role of the year for an actor in 1966. Neither Richard Burton nor Lee Marvin wanted the part, though Elizabeth remained fascinated by the idea of translating Carson McCullers's *Reflections in a Golden Eye* to the big screen. McCullers's story first appeared as a serial in the October–November 1940 issues of *Harper's Bazaar*, and was subsequently published as a novel in 1941. The book's themes of homosexuality and voyeurism, among a host of other explosive topics, made it impossible material on which to base a film at the time. When Ray Stark and John Huston conceived of making it into a film in the more permissive mid-'60s, Elizabeth agreed to do it, with or without Burton. His declining the film made it the first on which she worked without him since *BUtterfield 8*.

> *Both Elizabeth and Burton thought Brando a fine choice as costar, though working with him was an interesting experience, to say the least.*

Elizabeth lobbied to get former costar and dear friend Montgomery Clift hired for the movie. Clift's physical frailties were well known, and doors were closed to him in terms of insurance required for him to make the film. Elizabeth wanted him for the role so badly that she was willing to forego a portion of her salary to insure her friend. Clift's death from a heart condition at age forty-five, in July 1966, shocked Elizabeth and put *Reflections in a Golden Eye* on hold for the next few months. When production commenced in October 1966, Marlon Brando was in the lead role. Director Huston filmed scenes with some of his cast in Long Island, New York, before the company left for Rome for the balance of the production. Elizabeth's clout was such that she could ask that the film be made at De Laurentiis studios in Italy, even if the story's setting was an army post in Georgia.

Both Elizabeth and Burton thought Brando a fine choice as costar, though working with him was an interesting experience, to say the least. Elizabeth recalled years later, "He was full of rubbish and tried to intimidate you, but I wasn't scared of him. . . . He'd forget his lines and right at the end of the take, ask [the director] 'Can we do another one?' So you start all over again and then he'd get to the end of it and then have to keep doing it again until he was happy."

Peopled by a cast of characters that were intriguing, though far from likable, while playing out an altogether sordid story, *Reflections in a Golden Eye* did not find a huge audience. Further alienating viewers upon its initial release was a colorization technique that gave the film a sepia, or "golden," hue, emphasizing certain objects within the frame in another color. This stylized approach was not well-received and was abandoned in favor of straightforward Technicolor for general release. Time has worn well on the offbeat film though, and it has become a cult classic and favorite among fans of Taylor and Brando.

Richard Burton, who was on the set often during production said, "Marlon and Elizabeth's personalities, to say nothing of their physical beauty, are so vast that they have got away with murder." But he was a fan of Brando's work. Long before the making of *Reflections in a Golden Eye*, Burton said in an interview, "Elizabeth is terribly like Marlon Brando, who I think is the best actor America has ever had. She has the same qualities I would use to describe Marlon—slow-moving, quiet, with a suggestion of infinite power. Both of them never move directly toward an object. An actor like myself lunges right at it. Instead, they circumlocute the object, sort of meander around it. They are evasive, and you can't quite catch them. That's why they are such remarkable stars." Undeniably, the movie is worth viewing, if only for the pairing of Elizabeth Taylor and Marlon Brando.

OPPOSITE FROM LEFT: Still in costume for *Reflections*, Elizabeth and Brando made a small Italian film to promote blood donation. Each started the drive off by giving a pint. | A film crew at work. Director John Huston stands behind the camera. The scene shows Elizabeth, Brian Keith, and Julie Harris. Brando is hidden by Huston in the background. **ABOVE:** With Marlon Brando, playing her homosexual husband

The Comedians

MAXIMILLIAN/
TRIANON FILMS/
METRO-GOLDWYN-MAYER

CAST

Richard Burton .... *Brown*

Elizabeth Taylor .... *Martha Pineda*

Alec Guinness .... *Major H. O. Jones*

Peter Ustinov .... *Ambassador Manuel Pineda*

Paul Ford .... *Smith*

Lillian Gish .... *Mrs. Smith*

Georg Stanford Brown ..... *Henri Philipot*

Roscoe Leigh Browne .... *Petit Pierre*

Gloria Foster .... *Mrs. Philipot*

James Earl Jones .... *Dr. Magiot*

CREDITS

Peter Glenville *(producer/director)*; Graham Greene *(screenplay)*; Henri Decaë *(photography)*; Laurence Rosenthal *(music)*; François de Lamothe *(art director)*; Robert Christidès *(set decorations)*; Jean-Michel Lacor *(assistant director)*; Jonathan Bates, Jacques Carrère *(sound)*; Françoise Javet *(editor)*; Alexandre de Paris *(Elizabeth Taylor's hairstylist)*; Frank La Rue *(makeup)*

RELEASE DATE: October 31, 1967

RUN TIME: 150 minutes, color

RIGHT: Peter Ustinov played her boorish husband in the movie. **OPPOSITE:** With Richard Burton, as lovers Brown and German-accented Martha

SUMMARY: The oppressive political climate of Haiti under the rule of despotic "Papa Doc" Duvalier comes to light in the stories of a group of travelers inhabiting a once first-class hotel run by Brown. While trying to maintain appearances at his establishment, Brown enters into an affair with Martha, the rigid but amorous German-born wife of oafish Ambassador Manuel Pineda. The jovial Major Jones conceals a double life as an arms dealer helping the dictatorship. The Smiths act as missionaries hoping to bring solace to the people until the certain danger they are in dawns on them with its deadly grip. As unrest encroaches, the cynical Brown begins to suspect there is more to life than his own selfish existence and he joins the Haitian rebels.

REVIEWS

"*The Comedians*, skillfully adapted by Grahame Greene from his own recent novel, is a thoughtful, thought-provoking work."

—*Saturday Review* (Arthur Knight)

"Burton does a workmanlike job of playing Brown, however uninspiring, since he has little to do to inspire an audience and therefore elicits no sympathy for his pains to right some political matters. Miss Taylor is, of course, beautiful and as always is good as a bad woman, a very unsympathetic woman in this case."

—New York *Daily News* (Wanda Hale)

"The tired and disgusted hotel owner is played with fine acerbity and bristling boredom by Richard Burton, [but] he's a fellow we've all endured many times. Likewise, the lady is another familiar and predictable type. Elizabeth Taylor simply plays her so cruelly and confidently that she appears more ferocious than usual, especially in the kissing scenes. The husband is the customary cuckold as played politely by Peter Ustinov. And Alec Guinness comes on bright and breezy as the British boaster who turns out to be a fraud. All together, these characters contribute

only a moderately interesting account of apathy and personal self-indulgence in the midst of a nation undergoing terrible trial. . . . But what is arresting and disturbing is the atmosphere that surrounds this curious island of mechanical people. Mr. Glenville has crowded his picture with a vivid and convincing *mise-en-scène* of a hot country boiling with anger and frustration under an unseen dictator (he is glimpsed just once from the side) and with characters and cultural indications that reek of menace and mystery."

—*The New York Times* (Bosley Crowther)

notes

GRAHAME GREENE, THE ACCLAIMED AUTHOR BEST KNOWN
for brilliantly bringing to life the atmosphere of displaced souls and political
uncertainty of post–World War II Europe in his novel *The Third Man*, published
The Comedians in 1966. It was an insider's view of the political unrest and
oppression that the citizens of Haiti endured under the rule of François "Papa
Doc" Duvalier and his feared paramili-
tary force, the Tontons Macoutes. Greene
teamed with producer-director Peter Glenville to commit his tale to film, and wrote
the screenplay himself.

An illustrious cast was rounded up for
the production, including Alec Guinness,
Peter Ustinov, silent-screen legend Lillian Gish, and a young James Earl Jones.
Richard Burton, who had previously acted
under Glenville in *Becket*, was at the center of the story, with Elizabeth at his side
providing a romantic subplot and an air of beauty amidst a sinister setting. These
"comedians," all acting out their own agendas in the proceedings, were played up
as the perfect ensemble in the film's publicity tagline: "They lie, they cheat, they
destroy . . . they even try to love."

Given the subject matter, the story's true location of Haiti was out of the
question as the place to film. Some footage was shot in France, but primarily, a
believable background was provided by Dahomey, Benin. The company arrived
to begin production in January 1967, and the West African country proved more

ABOVE: On location with director Peter Glenville OPPOSITE: On location in the West African
nation of Benin

> *Though the title and story on the surface of*
> The Comedians *was somewhat glossy and
> contrived, the backdrop of turmoil was
> straightforward and genuinely chilling.*

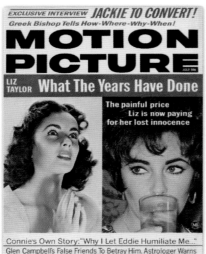

than inviting to its visiting celebrities and film crew. The stars got to visit the palace of Beninese leader Christophe Soglo, who was said to be quite taken with Elizabeth. It was a brief moment in history as Soglo's rule was overthrown by a new regime later the same year. During production, a short film was made called "The Comedians in Africa," featuring all of the stars in behind-the-scenes footage and discussing the troubles they faced during filming. The documentary short is included as a special feature on the DVD release of the film.

The Comedians premiered in October 1967 and the of-the-moment drama immediately caused a firestorm of publicity caused by the indignant reaction of the Haitian government, which called the movie "an inflammatory libel against . . . one of the most beautiful, peaceful, and safest countries in the Caribbean." History can speak for the accuracy of Greene's work. Though the title and story on the surface of *The Comedians* was somewhat glossy and contrived, the backdrop of turmoil was straightforward and genuinely chilling. Lillian Gish fared best among the cast, earning a Golden Globe nomination as Best Supporting Actress. Elizabeth was pleased to be back working with Burton after making one film apart from him. In this, their seventh screen partnership, she again proved she was content to be working with her husband and did not need to shine solo in the spotlight.

TOP: Outside of a restaurant in the south of France, where portions of the film were shot LEFT: A magazine depicting the jet-setting superstar during the making of *The Comedians*. Fans loved her adventures, even if *Motion Picture* saw fit to dig up a photo of an impossibly angelic Elizabeth in the 1940s for comparison. OPPOSITE: The crew sets up to film Elizabeth and Burton in the bed scene.

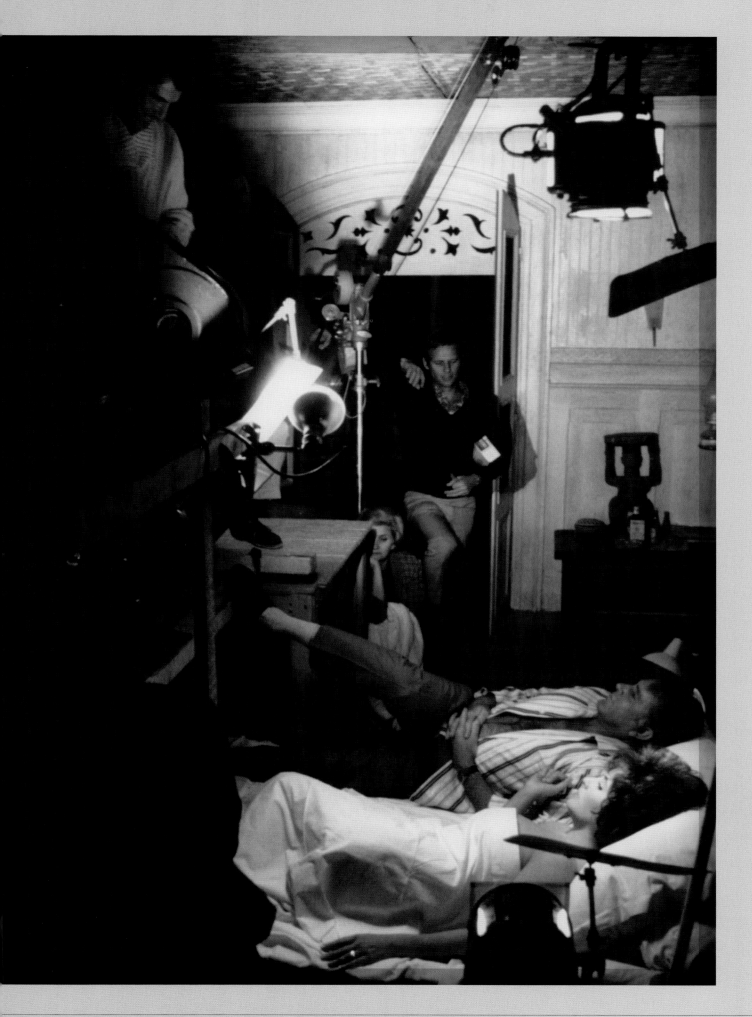

Boom!

UNIVERSAL PICTURES

CAST

Elizabeth Taylor ... *Flora "Sissy" Goforth*
Richard Burton .... *Chris Flanders*
Noël Coward .... *the Witch of Capri*
Joanna Shimkus .... *Miss Black*
Michael Dunn .... *Rudi*
Romolo Valli .... *Doctor Luilo*
Fernando Piazza .... *Etti*
Veronica Wells .... *Simonetta*
Howard Taylor .... *journalist*

CREDITS

John Heyman, Norman Priggen *(producers)*; Joseph Losey *(director)*; Lester
Persky *(associate producer)*; Tennessee
Williams *(screenplay)*, based on play *The
Milk Train Doesn't Stop Here Anymore* by
Tennessee Williams; Douglas Slocombe
(photography); John Barry *(music)*; Don
Black, John Dankworth *(song: "Hidea-
way")*; Richard MacDonald *(production
design)*; Les Hammond, Gerry Hum-
phreys *(sound)*; Carlo Lastricati *(assistant director)*; Reginald Beck *(editor)*;
Annalisa Nasalli Rocca, Tiziani of Rome
(costumes); Frank La Rue, Ron Berkeley
(makeup); Alexandre de Paris *(as Claude
Ettori)* *(Elizabeth Taylor's hairstylist)*

RELEASE DATE: May 26, 1968
RUN TIME: 113 minutes, color

RIGHT: Listening attentively to *Boom!* director Joseph Losey. Costar Joanna Shimkus,
who later married Sidney Poitier, is seen
behind Elizabeth.

SUMMARY: Sissy Goforth, a wealthy widow who has buried five husbands, reigns with an iron fist over a private island in the Mediterranean. Ever-declining health portends her time may be up next, though she will never admit weakness. Sissy's sole activity at her villa is to belt out dictation of her memoirs to her secretary, Miss Black, between occasional visits from her dear friend, the Witch of Capri. Sissy's world is shaken up by the unexpected arrival of poet Chris Flanders. The man is also known as the Angel of Death for his habit of being on hand at the demise of many a wealthy matron. His presence brings new life to the island for a time and awakens feelings in Sissy not felt for years. But how long will the budding amour—and Sissy herself—last?

CLOCKWISE FROM TOP: With the Witch of Capri, Noël Coward | The Angel of Death seems to be working true to form as Sissy succumbs to a coughing fit. | Setting up a shot against the backdrop of the Sardinian coastline

REVIEWS

"Boom! Boom! Boom! That's the effect that the screen's most exciting team, Elizabeth Taylor and Richard Burton, will have on most people in their new picture. . . . Universal's weirdly fascinating drama is a tour de force for Elizabeth Taylor who doesn't hesitate to play to the hilt the role of Flora Goforth, a dynamic woman with a touch of insanity. Burton's magnetic personality and the superb quality of his voice captures and holds the viewer's attention."
— **New York** *Daily News* **(Wanda Hale)**

"Mr. Williams can always write beautiful set pieces—moving, enigmatic parables about life and death, flashes of sardonic humor and passages of lengthy exposition that contain more drama than the surface action of the film. However, in *Boom!* they're like bright little clearings in an otherwise dim forest. Miss Taylor, who is not a subtle actress, has no trouble with the robust, shrewish aspects of the multimillionaire from One Street, Ga., but it's impossible to see the vulnerability in the woman Williams described as 'a universal human condition.' . . . As the Angel of Death, Mr. Burton is earnest and mellifluous. The one unequivocal success is a brief appearance by Noël Coward as the Witch of Capri, Mrs. Goforth's wickedly gossipy friend."
— *The New York Times* **(Vincent Canby)**

FROM TOP: Noël Coward, Richard Burton, and Joseph Losey observe as Elizabeth takes kabuki instruction for a brief scene. | With Burton and Michael Dunn

CLOCKWISE FROM TOP: With director Joseph Losey | Losey instructs stars Coward and Elizabeth. | Elizabeth was on crutches after slipping on the deck of their yacht in Portofino, where they greeted Rex Harrison. | When traveling Elizabeth and Burton lived on their yacht, known as the traveling kennel for dogs. This is shortly after completion of *Boom!*

FROM LEFT: A family road trip during a day off from filming. All of her children are seen: Michael, Maria, Liza, and Christopher | A candid, in transit between Venice and Sardinia, where the film was shot

TENNESSEE WILLIAMS'S *THE MILK TRAIN DOESN'T STOP HERE Anymore* was a play written with the flamboyant stage actress Tallulah Bankhead in mind and reportedly inspired by the Marchesa Luisa Casati, an even more flamboyant European socialite of the early twentieth century, known at her eccentric best for walking around town with a pair of cheetahs on leashes. The Williams story existed in several iterations over the years. It began as the short story "Man Bring This Up the Road!," from which the play was drawn. *Milk Train* then saw two versions on Broadway, both of which failed to meet the success expected of the celebrated Williams. The play opened in January 1963 starring Hermione Baddeley. That show closed after a fairly brief sixty-nine performances, but in that time Baddeley earned a Tony nomination as Best Actress in the lead role of Sissy Goforth, a juicy character for any strong female actress. Williams then saw his muse, Tallulah Bankhead, revive the show in 1964, to only more disappointing results as the play closed just three days after its debut.

If anyone could remove the curse from *Milk Train* for the film adaptation, it was thought that Elizabeth Taylor was the one to do it. After all, big-screen versions of the Williams plays *Cat on a Hot Tin Roof* and *Suddenly, Last Summer* had been supremely successful in her capable hands. *Milk Train*, however, did not seem an ideal Williams vehicle for her, as she was admittedly too young, vital, and healthy-looking in the role of the aging, dying Sissy. Still, she played the role with her usual gusto, and succeeded in presenting an engrossing characterization under the direction of Joseph Losey.

The costarring role of the Angel of Death/Chris Flanders, had been portrayed on the stage by Tab Hunter, indicating that a younger man would be most appro-

priate for the part. Sean Connery was Williams' first choice, but he passed on the project, leaving the door open for Elizabeth and Richard Burton to again join forces on the screen. Another departure from the original play was the casting of Noël Coward as the Witch of Capri. The character was originally female, but it hardly mattered: Coward was superb in the role. Also in the cast was Elizabeth's brother, Howard Taylor, who made a cameo early in the film.

Another highlight of the movie, ultimately released under the title of *Boom!* instead of *Money Train*, was the work of production designer Richard MacDonald. His art direction made the film a sight to behold, though credit for the film's beauty must obviously also go to location shooting on the picturesque Mediterranean coast of Sardinia, Italy. Tennessee Williams ultimately said he was proud of *Boom!* but, like past versions of *Money Train*, it was not profitable after a lavish $10 million had been expended on the production.

> *For all its scattered strong points, Boom! was Elizabeth and Burton's third successive film that failed to deliver at the box office.*

For all its scattered strong points, *Boom!* was Elizabeth and Burton's third successive film that failed to deliver at the box office. They now took some time to make films individually though, as ever, they traveled together wherever work took them. Elizabeth said, they were "incapable of being sweet stay-at-homes, sweet lie-a-beds." The Burtons' home, more often than not in this period, was their yacht, *Kalizma* (a conglomeration of the names of their daughters Kate, Liza, and Maria).

Secret Ceremony

CAST

Elizabeth Taylor .... *Leonora*

Mia Farrow .... *Cenci*

Robert Mitchum .... *Albert*

Peggy Aschcroft .... *Hannah*

Pamela Brown .... *Hilda*

Michael Strong .... *Dr. Walter Stevens*

Angus MacKay .... *Vicar*

Robert Douglas .... *Sir Alex Gordon*

George Howell .... *first cleaner*

CREDITS

John Heyman, Norman Priggen *(producers)*; Joseph Losey *(director)*; George Tabori *(screenplay)*, based on story "Ceremonia Secreta" by Marco Denevi; Gerald Fisher *(photography)*; Richard Rodney Bennett *(music)*; Richard MacDonald *(production design)*; John Clark *(art director)*; Leslie Hammond, Hugh Strain *(sound)*; Richard Dalton *(assistant director)*; Reginald Beck *(editor)*; Klara Kerpen, Susan Yelland *(costumes)*; Marc Bohan *(Elizabeth's costumes)*; Alex Garfath *(makeup)*; Alexandre de Paris *(Elizabeth's hairstylist)*

RELEASE DATE: October 23, 1968

RUN TIME: 109 minutes, color

SUMMARY: Cenci, a strange young girl, becomes attached to a prostitute who bears a striking resemblance to her mother, whose death Cenci never accepted. In turn the woman, Leonora, feels a connection to Cenci because she reminds her of her own dearly departed daughter. She plays the role of Cenci's real mother, stepping into the late woman's enviable wardrobe and assuming her place as head of a rich home. To Cenci's paternal aunts, Leonora pretends to be the sister of the girl's late mother. But one person not buying her story is Cenci's estranged stepfather, Albert, who harbors an incestuous passion for the girl. Cenci is too unstable to realize the wrong he does her, but shortly after Albert's arrival, his presence combined with increasingly mixed emotions about Leonora leads the girl to commit suicide. Leonora enacts revenge on Albert.

RIGHT: Elizabeth and Mia Farrow, a disturbing (and disturbed) twosome in *Secret Ceremony*

ABOVE: Elizabeth mourns her daughter. Farrow's character transfers her affection for her late mother to a mysterious woman she runs into on a public bus.

REVIEWS

"Mia Farrow has given an extraordinarily touching portrait of a wistful girl seeking something in her mentally disturbed loneliness. Elizabeth Taylor, by turns forceful and vulgar, is a definite person, though far from recognizable as any kind of prostitute of public record." —New York *Post* (Archer Winsten)

"*Secret Ceremony* is Joseph Losey's best film in years—incomparably better than *Accident*. The opulent, lacquered decadence works well this time, with Mia Farrow as a rich, mad orphan, whose mother Elizabeth Taylor pretends to be and, in effect, becomes. Robert Mitchum is good as Miss Farrow's stepfather, in a relationship as violent and complicated as relationships in movies like *Accident* and *Reflections in a Golden Eye* tend to be. In all the elaborate fetishism and dragging prose, there is a touching story of people not helping enough. There is also a ceremonial quality—coffins like cribs, parallelisms, people reunited in death—that turns crude and embarrassing at times; although I don't usually like this colored genre of sick ritual film, I rather liked this one." —*The New York Times* (Renata Adler)

notes

Rosemary's Baby and already famous as the child-bride (and soon to be divorcée) of Frank Sinatra, Mia Farrow was Hollywood's newest sensation. The team from *Boom!*, producers John Heyman and Norman Priggen and director Joseph Losey, had the brainstorm to star Farrow opposite Hollywood's longest-running (though at thirty-six by no means old) sensation, Elizabeth Taylor. The screenplay by George Tabori that they were preparing to film was a strange one filled with ambiguous, disturbing, and oftentimes violent characters, and box-office insurance by way of the stars would be vital to give the feature an inherently saleable quality lacking in its story.

> *The relationships between all of the women in the film are interesting, if not precisely drawn out or explained.*

Secret Ceremony was indeed bizarre, but like so many films of the period, takes on a quality of fascination in latter-day viewings as a work of art that seems far removed from the present-day world. The relationships between all of the women in the film are interesting, if not precisely drawn out or explained. Alongside Farrow and Elizabeth, the top supporting roles were played by Peggy Ashcroft and Pamela Brown. Robert Mitchum was third-billed though he comes into the proceedings quite late and winds up in a tragic end for his troubles. It was a women's film all the way.

Unusual roles were no longer unusual for Elizabeth, as she played them fairly frequently. Farrow, too, showed daring in her choice of roles, particularly for an actress just getting her footing in the Hollywood firmament. Renata Adler in *The New York Times* lamented, "from Rosemary, the lapsed Roman Catholic

ABOVE FROM LEFT: Elizabeth was no stranger to unusual roles by the late 1960s. | Convinced the woman is her late mother come back to her, young Cenci dotes on the mysterious, beautiful lady. **OPPOSITE FROM TOP LEFT:** Black was a predominant color in the dark story. Farrow's famous blonde bob was covered by a long, black fright wig. | With Robert Mitchum, who played the sinister Albert | Preparing for an important scene | This scene of Elizabeth and Farrow taking a bath together was cut from television screenings—that and many other scenes.

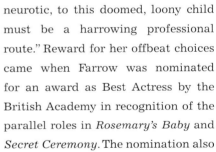

> *The tale of* Secret Ceremony *proved too hot to handle when it was offered up for the mass exposure afforded by television.*

neurotic, to this doomed, loony child must be a harrowing professional route." Reward for her offbeat choices came when Farrow was nominated for an award as Best Actress by the British Academy in recognition of the parallel roles in *Rosemary's Baby* and *Secret Ceremony.* The nomination also acknowledged her performance in the romantic drama *John and Mary.*

The tale of *Secret Ceremony* proved too hot to handle when it was offered up for the mass exposure afforded by television. NBC joined forces with the film's production company, Universal Pictures, in producing an alternate, sanitized version for TV screens. Suggestions of prostitution, child molestation committed by Mitchum's character, a lesbian relationship (or at least thoughts on the part of Farrow's Cenci), and a scene showing Elizabeth and Farrow in the bath together, were stripped from the print for television. New scenes, involving none of the stars or makers of the film, were shot to offer exposition and explanation of some of the greater lapses in continuity in the story—which were mostly caused by the TV editor's scissors in the first place—and to show that no crime went unpunished in the film. The interest factor in the doctored version of *Secret Ceremony* now makes such prints a treasure among collectors.

ABOVE FROM LEFT: A test shot for *Secret Ceremony*. This wig was never used in the film; Farrow got to wear one though. | Elizabeth, as ever, got along well with her costar, Mia Farrow. **LEFT:** The film was shot on location in London. During their time there Elizabeth and Richard Burton attended a wedding with *Boom!* costar Noël Coward.

The Only Game in Town

TWENTIETH CENTURY FOX

CAST

Elizabeth Taylor ....*Fran Walker*
Warren Beatty ....*Joe Grady*
Charles Braswell.........................*Lockwood*
Hank Henry.......................................*Tony*
Olga Valéry.......................................*Hooker*

CREDITS

Fred Kohlmar *(producer)*; George Stevens *(director)*; Frank D. Gilroy *(screenplay)*, based on play by Frank D. Gilroy; Henri Decaë *(photography)*; Maurice Jarre *(music)*; Herman Blumenthal, Auguste Capelier *(art directors)*; Walter M. Scott, Jerry Wunderlich *(set decorations)*; Jo De Bretagne, David Dockendorf *(sound)*; Robert Doudell *(assistant director)*; William Sands, John W. Holmes, Pat Shade *(editors)*; Mia Fonssagrives, Vicki Tiel *(Elizabeth's costumes)*; Alexandre de Paris *(Elizabeth's hairstylist)*; Frank La Rue *(Elizabeth's makeup)*

RELEASE DATE: January 21, 1970
RUN TIME: 113 minutes, color

SUMMARY: Fran Walker is a showgirl attempting to save enough money to escape Las Vegas, a place which she has come to revile. She meets Joe Grady, a cocktail-lounge piano player who forms an immediate crush on her. Fran gives in to temptation and sleeps with him if only to take her mind off the disappointing reality of her affair with a married man named Lockwood. Fran and Joe agree to a no-strings-attached living situation in which they keep each other company while keeping Fran's mind off Lockwood and keeping Joe's penchant for gambling in check so he can save enough money to leave Las Vegas. Lockwood comes back into Fran's life with a vengeance but she eventually has the courage to leave him once and for all. The only problem left? Getting Fran and Joe to admit they are madly in love with each other.

RIGHT: In the movie with Beatty. He is ready to move more quickly than she is.

notes

THE ONLY GAME IN TOWN WAS THE SCREEN ADAPTATION OF a play by Frank D. Gilroy that debuted on Broadway at the Broadhurst Theatre on May 20, 1968, and then closed after just sixteen performances. Tammy Grimes and Barry Nelson fulfilled the two lead roles of a play consisting of just three characters. In spite of its failure to enthuse Broadway audiences, Twentieth Century Fox purchased the screen rights to the play for $750,000 and hired Frank Gilroy to write the screenplay himself. George Stevens, who had directed Elizabeth in two of her greatest films, *A Place in the Sun* and *Giant*, was to be reunited with his violet-eyed leading lady after a thirteen-year hiatus from working together.

The studio wanted Elizabeth to star in *The Only Game in Town* so badly that producer Fred Kohlmar agreed to shoot a movie set in Hollywood's neighboring desert town of Las Vegas in far-off Paris, where Elizabeth wanted to be so that she would not be separated from Richard Burton, who at the time was making *Staircase* in the City of Light. Exteriors and establishing shots were filmed by a second unit in Las Vegas. Location filming in Paris cost the company a considerable sum, in addition to the $1,250,000 salary paid for Elizabeth's acting services. What Elizabeth wanted in those days she could get, but it was not out of diva posturing on her part. She simply had certain requirements to make a film and producers could take it or leave it. Going back to *Cleopatra*, when she asked for $1 million because she never dreamed she would get it and did not care if they turned her down, not caring if she did a film she was not passionate about empowered Elizabeth to make whatever demands she wanted.

Elizabeth was to star opposite Frank Sinatra in *The Only Game in Town* at the time the film was originally set to go into production, but the starting date had to be postponed due to a recurrence of overwhelming back pain suffered by Elizabeth. By the time she was again prepared to work, Sinatra had to bow out of the production and was replaced by the brother of Elizabeth's great friend Shirley MacLaine: the hot young star of *Bonnie and Clyde*, Warren Beatty.

Elizabeth was wildly miscast in the role of a blushing ingénue that she had outgrown in every respect more than a decade ago. As production got underway, Burton, on the set much of the time, particularly to mock-scowl at Elizabeth and Beatty during their love scenes, began to feel Elizabeth had made a terrible mistake by agreeing to do the film. He thought it was pure rubbish and, typically, exaggerated to the press for the sake of amusement, "The awful thing is that it's turned me off drink! . . . If it was anyone else of course I'd pack my bags, head for the hills, and go and live in a Trappist monastery, but this woman is my life."

The film ultimately took six months and $11 million to make. The dynamite trio of George Stevens, Elizabeth Taylor, and Warren Beatty failed to produce a successful film, and it would be the director's last after a predominantly stellar filmography that encompassed *The Diary of Anne Frank*, *Shane*, *The More the Merrier*, *Alice Adams*, and a host of other classics. *The Only Game in Town* generated a mere $1.5 million gross in the U.S. After a succession of box-office disappointments, Elizabeth's drawing power was seriously called into question.

OPPOSITE, CLOCKWISE FROM TOP LEFT: At a party at Maxim's in Paris during filming | On the set with a young fan | Grocery shopping with Beatty | A lot of star power went into *The Only Game in Town*, to no avail.

Anne of the Thousand Days

HAL WALLIS PRODUCTIONS/ UNIVERSAL PICTURES

CAST

Richard Burton .... *King Henry VIII*

Geneviève Bujold .... *Anne Boleyn*

Irene Papas .... *Queen Catherine of Aragon*

Anthony Quayle .... *Cardinal Wolsey*

John Colicos .... *Thomas Cromwell*

Michael Hordern ... *Count Thomas Boleyn*

Katharine Blake .... *Elizabeth Boleyn*

Valerie Gearon .... *Mary Boleyn*

Michael Johnson .... *George Boleyn*

Elizabeth Taylor .... *masked maiden*

CREDITS

Hal Wallis *(producer)*; Charles Jarrott *(director)*; Richard McWhorter *(associate producer)*; Bridget Boland, John Hale *(screenplay)*; Richard Sokolove *(adaptation)*, based on play by Maxwell Anderson; Arthur Ibbetson *(photography)*; Georges Delerue *(music)*; Mary Skeaping *(choreographer)*; Maurice Carter *(production design)*; Lionel Couch *(art director)*; Peter Howitt, Patrick McLoughlin *(set decorations)*; Simon Relph *(assistant director)*; Richard Marden *(editor)*; Ivy Baker Jones, Margaret Furse *(costumes)*

RELEASE DATE: December 18, 1969

RUN TIME: 145 minutes, color

SUMMARY: In sixteenth-century England, King Henry VIII is obsessed with producing a male heir to the throne. After many stillbirths and now past her child-bearing years, his wife, Queen Catherine of Aragon, is deemed useless even though she has given him one daughter. The king sets his sights on the lovely young Anne Boleyn, who he means to take as a mistress only. Anne's refusal to bed with the king out of wedlock leads him to contrive to have his marriage to Queen Catherine annulled. In doing so he breaks from the Church but gets his wish of freedom to marry Anne. The new queen gives him a second legitimate daughter but no son. Anne's inability to give him what he wants, coupled with her fiery personality, lead him to new political machinations that end in her beheading. King Henry is then free to take his third of six wives, Jane Seymour.

notes

THE HISTORY OF HENRY VIII AND HIS SECOND OF SIX WIVES,
Anne Boleyn, was told many times on both stage and screen in years prior to
1969. Producer Hal Wallis, whose hits of a generation earlier included *Little
Caesar* and *Casablanca*, based his film on the play *Anne of the Thousand Days*
by Maxwell Anderson, which had been a success on Broadway in 1948 starring
Rex Harrison. Richard Burton, in the lead role, as well as several other major
players in production of the movie, fared equally well. The film was nominated
for ten Academy Awards, including Best Picture, Best Actor, and Best Actress.
Costume designer Margaret Furse was the only one to take home an award, but
Anne of the Thousand Days was nevertheless considered an unqualified success.

The same, unfortunately, could not be said of the movies Elizabeth made
apart from Burton in this period, but husband and wife continued to support
each other in every professional move. They were also frequently physically on
hand during production. Thus came about Elizabeth's cameo in *Anne of the Thousand Days*. The historical drama was not the kind that lent itself to revealing
inside jokes, so Elizabeth appeared masked only, as a member of the court who
intrudes on Queen Catharine at prayer time. The joke was reported in the press,
with some calling it callous of her to replace an otherwise gainfully employed bit
player. Elizabeth and Richard's daughters, Liza and Kate, also got in on the act
as unbilled maidens.

REVIEW

"This *Anne of the Thousand Days*
is one of those almost unbearably
classy movies, like *A Man for All
Seasons* and *Becket,* that have a
way of elevating the reputations of
moviemakers without doing much
for the art. It's been photographed
in color and with care in all sorts of
lovely English settings; the Tudor
costumes are chic and seemingly wrinkle-free; it has a score
by Georges Delerue that is mostly
alarums and excursions, punctuated
by an occasional madrigal, and it
makes an extremely complex period
in English history (the Reformation)
comprehensible by defining it in
terms of private personalities who
were also public figures."
—*The New York Times* (Vincent Canby)

Anne of the Thousand Days was only one of many Richard Burton films on which Elizabeth was a constant presence. As their individual film schedules permitted, Elizabeth and Burton were frequent visitors to the sets of each other's movies. They were even known to persuade producers to change the locations of films they were making so that they could be near each other when both were working. Presented here are shots of Elizabeth in connection with Richard Burton movies.

ABOVE: Arriving in England to make *The Spy Who Came in from the Cold* **OPPOSITE, CLOCKWISE FROM TOP LEFT:** Richard Burton, Elizabeth, and Peter O'Toole during the making of *Becket* | At the premiere of *Where Eagles Dare* | In Puerto Vallarta during the filming of *The Night of the Iguana* | On the set of *The Klansman* | Taking snapshots on the set of *Becket*

X, Y & Zee *(Zee & Co.)*

ZEE FILM/
KASTNER-LADD-KANTER
PRODUCTIONS/
COLUMBIA PICTURES

CAST

Elizabeth Taylor .... *Zee Blakeley*

Michael Caine .... *Robert Blakeley*

Susannah York .... *Stella*

Margaret Leighton .... *Gladys*

John Standing .... *Gordon*

Mary Larkin .... *Rita*

Michael Cashman .... *Gavin*

Gino Melvazzi .... *head waiter*

CREDITS

Elliott Kastner *(executive producer)*; Alan Ladd, Jr., Jay Kanter *(producers)*; Brian G. Hutton *(director)*; Edna O'Brien *(screenplay)*; Billy Williams *(photography)*; Stanley Myers *(music)*; Peter Mullins *(art director)*; Arthur Taksen *(set decorations)*; Colin Brewer *(assistant director)*; Bob Jones, Cyril Swern *(sound)*; Jim Clark *(editor)*; Beatrice Dawson *(costumes)*; Allan McKeown *(hairstylist)*; Alex Garfath *(makeup)*

RELEASE DATE: January 21, 1972

RUN TIME: 110 minutes, color

SUMMARY: Zee and Robert Blakeley move among a free-wheeling social set in London. At a party Robert finds the direct opposite of his explosive wife in the form of a placid blonde dress designer named Stella. Robert begins an affair with her and eventually falls in love. Zee refuses to let another woman steal her husband without a fight. She tries everything from befriending Stella to reigniting the passion in bed with Robert to finally attempting suicide, but Robert and Zee's miserable marriage is beyond saving and he remains infatuated with Stella. Stella has revealed to Zee that she was expelled from school for developing romantic feelings for a nun, and this prompts Zee's next move. She goes to Stella and sweet-talks her into bed. Robert arrives on the scene and realizes what has transpired. What will happen for the threesome next—parting ways, two pairing off, or three together—is anybody's guess.

ABOVE: Portrait of Elizabeth in the role of Zee **OPPOSITE FROM TOP:** Michael Caine and Elizabeth have a stormy marriage in *X, Y & Zee.* | With Michael Caine

"As directed by Mr. Hutton, who made one of my favorite idiotic action movies (*Where Eagles Dare*), *X, Y & Zee* never misses an opportunity to overstate a line, a point or a mood, or simply to confuse the few things that, from the delicacy of the original (not televised) version of *Three Into Two Won't Go*, I take to be Miss O'Brien's sensibilities. . . . Mr. Hutton allows [Taylor] to play Zee as if she were the ghost of whores past, present, and future, clanking her jewelry, her headbands, her earrings, and her feelings behind her like someone out to haunt a funhouse."   **—The New York Times (Vincent Canby)**

"At the beginning of *X, Y & Zee* Elizabeth Taylor, peering out of blue lamé eye shadow like a raccoon, seemed ridiculous and—well, monstrous. But as the picture went on, I found myself missing her whenever she wasn't onscreen (when Michael Caine and Susannah York were acting immaculately), and I'm forced to conclude that, monstrous though she is, her jangling performance is what gives this movie its energy. . . . I don't think she's ever before been as strong a star personality."   **—New Yorker (Pauline Kael)**

"Elizabeth Taylor goes on an all-out campy rampage, pulling out every stop in her first performance in over a year. And it's her best since *Who's Afraid of Virginia Woolf?* . . . Remember how Bette Davis used to upstage everything and everyone, especially in films like *Now, Voyager*? Well, Miss Taylor does the same thing in this movie. She spews out four-letter words all over the place, screws up her face into strange and wildly funny expressions, and obviously has a good time with this role."   **—Newton North**

notes

ELIZABETH GOT TO USE EVERY ACTING TRICK IN THE BOOK in her performance as Zee Blakeley, a willful woman caught in a turbulent love triangle that ends in her going to bed with her husband's mistress. Undoubtedly, once she was out from under the control of MGM, Elizabeth showed no fear in her choice of roles and sank her teeth into every performance, good or bad for her career though it may have been judged. In *X, Y & Zee* she ran the gamut of emotional histrionics: loving, hating, and playing passionately, from seducing her husband to seducing his lover. Based on an original screenplay by Edna O'Brien called *Three Into Two Won't Go*, the film ends in ambiguity, but O'Brien's original work took the triangular love story a step further, ending with husband, wife, and mistress in a threesome.

> ## Elizabeth showed no fear in her choice of roles and sank her teeth into every performance.

ABOVE: As Zee Blakeley **OPPOSITE, CLOCKWISE FROM TOP LEFT:** With Margaret Leighton, the wife of Michael Wilding, Elizabeth's second husband | Behind the scenes of *X, Y & Zee* | Richard Burton visits the set.

Zee and Co. was the film's original title in England, where it was made in 1971 under the direction of Brian G. Hutton, who had recently produced the hit action film *Where Eagles Dare* with Richard Burton. *X, Y & Zee*'s leading man was Michael Caine, with whom Elizabeth spent most of the proceedings onscreen in bitter fighting. The "other woman" was Susannah York, a delicate blonde British actress who had tread similar territory playing a lesbian in the drama *The Killing of Sister George*. There was also a small but showy role in the film for actress Margaret Leighton, the wife of Elizabeth's second husband, Michael Wilding.

Elizabeth's hair, makeup, and costumes were about as over the top as the character she played. Zee's wardrobe consisted of exotic print ponchos, dresses, and caftans, all accessorized with bangles, rings, hippy beads, and headbands. Designer Beatrice Dawson said, "Elizabeth has definite ideas as to what suits her. She likes her clothes to be amusing—then she can enjoy wearing them; she likes to see a strong challenge in them—so that she needs to set them off; she needs

dramatic color schemes. I chose brilliant color combinations—dramatic black and white, yellow/orange, purple/pink, orange/cerise. Above all, [Elizabeth] likes her clothes to be unrestrictive. She feels happiest in loose clothes because she's a very active, alive woman—both on the set and in real life."

American film critics wildly disagreed in their opinions of Elizabeth's performance in *X, Y & Zee*, but there was no doubt as to her success in the film from the Italian motion picture academy. Elizabeth was awarded a David di Donatello for Best Foreign Actress for her work as the egocentric, volatile Zee.

Under Milk Wood

TIMON PRODUCTIONS/
THE RANK ORGANIZATION (U.K)/
ALTURA FILMS (U.S.)

CAST

Richard Burton .... *First Man*

Elizabeth Taylor .... *Rosie Probert*

Peter O'Toole .... *Captain Tom Cat*

Glynis Johns .... *Myfanwy Price*

Vivien Merchant .... *Mrs. Pugh*

Siân Phillips .... *Mrs. Ogmore-Pritchard*

Victor Spinetti .... *Mog Edwards*

Ryan Davies .... *Second Man*

Angharad Rees .... *Gossamer Beynon*

Ray Smith .... *Mr. Waldo*

Talfryn Thomas .... *Mr. Pugh*

CREDITS

Jules Buck, Peter James, Hugh French *(executive producers)*; John Comfort *(producer)*; Andrew Sinclair *(director, screenplay)*, based on play by Dylan Thomas; Robert Huke *(photography)*; Brian Gascoigne *(music)*; Geoffrey Tozer *(art director)*; Dominic Fulford *(assistant director)*; Cyril Collick *(sound)*; Willy Kemplen, Greg Miller *(editors)*

RELEASE DATE: January 27, 1972 (U.K.);
January 21, 1973 (U.S.)
RUN TIME: 87 minutes, color

RIGHT: As Rosie Probert, the whore so loved by Captain Cat **OPPOSITE:** With Peter O'Toole

SUMMARY: The world of the small Welsh fishing village of Llareggub and its inhabitants is brought to life through a series of episodic stories. At the outset, a narrator informs the viewer that they are hearing and witnessing the dreams of the colorful cast of villagers. Captain Cat recalls his seafaring adventures and the whore he loved in his youth, Rosie Probert. Sweet shop owner Myfawny Price has sweet dreams of Mog Edwards. Mrs. Ogmore-Pritchard thinks on her late lamented husbands. Schoolmaster Mr. Pugh dreams of doing away with the shrewish Mrs. Pugh. When all awake, life goes on in Llareggub and the viewer has a unique understanding of the characters' innermost thoughts.

notes

WELSH POET DYLAN THOMAS'S FINAL MAJOR WORK, AND perhaps his most famous, was *Under Milk Wood*, a lengthy episodic play written for radio which had been performed occasionally onstage as well. The verbose play was never intended for the visual medium of cinema, but director Andrew Sinclair undertook the challenge with gusto, soon lining up a cast headed by Peter O'Toole as Captain Cat and Richard Burton as narrator, Voice One. The movie was filmed in Wales, in the area in which Burton had grown up, which made the project one especially close to his heart. Sinclair supplemented his cast with town locals.

Through Burton, Sinclair secured Elizabeth to make a cameo appearance as Rosie Probert, the memorable love of Captain Cat's youth. Because it was such a small role, Elizabeth asked that she not be billed as one of the film's stars, but producer Jules Buck knew a good thing when he had it. He refused, stating Elizabeth's contract dictated that she receive star billing. Thus Elizabeth's face and name loomed large on all advertising material produced for *Under Milk Wood*, though she actually appears for less than a few minutes.

> *Because it was such a small role, Elizabeth asked that she not be billed as one of the film's stars, but producer Jules Buck knew a good thing when he had it.*

Hammersmith Is Out

J. CORNELIUS CREAN FILMS INC./CINERAMA

CAST

Elizabeth Taylor ... *Jimmie Jean Jackson*
Richard Burton ... *Hammersmith*
Peter Ustinov ... *Doctor*
Beau Bridges ... *Billy Breedlove*
Leon Ames ... *General Sam Pembroke*
Leon Askin ... *Dr. Krodt*
George Raft ... *Guido Scartucci*
John Schuck ... *Henry Joe*
Marjorie Eaton ... *Princess*
Lisa Jak ... *Kiddo*

CREDITS

Alex Lucas *(producer)*; Peter Ustinov *(director)*; Stanford Whitmore *(screenplay)*; Richard H. Kline *(photography)*; Dominic Frontiere *(music)*; Robert Benton *(set decorations)*; Newton Arnold *(assistant director)*; David Blewitt *(editor)*; Edith Head *(Elizabeth's costumes)*; Claudye Bozzacchi *(hairstylist)*; Ron Berkeley *(makeup)*

RELEASE DATE: May 12, 1972
RUN TIME: 108 minutes, color

RIGHT: With Beau Bridges, as the alliteratively named Billy Breedlove and Jimmie Jean Jackson **OPPOSITE:** Off set during the making of *Hammersmith Is Out*. Elizabeth was not afraid to take chances with fashion.

SUMMARY: The criminally insane Hammersmith is locked away in a mental institution from which he wishes to attain freedom. He convinces asylum orderly Billy Breedlove to assist in his escape. In return for Billy's invaluable aid, Hammersmith says that he will help Billy obtain all the money and power in the world that he desires. With Billy's girlfriend, a hash-slinger named Jimmie Jean Jackson, at their side, the escapees embark on a series of wild adventures. From owning a go-go club to running international businesses to taking over Washington, D.C., each enterprise increases their wealth and power exponentially. Equally swelled is the size of Billy's head, a problem which is left for Jimmie Jean and Hammersmith to remedy—once and for all.

R E V I E W S

"The film, a comment on the materialism of the times and the dissatisfaction it breeds, holds attention under the direction of actor Peter Ustinov, but it is superficial. The script by Stanford Whitmore is peppered with bawdy language. Only the scenery, filmed on location in and around Cuernavaca in Mexico, is beautiful. Acting is above average with Burton in a subdued, deadly role. Miss Taylor does well as the waitress, her beauty, though matured, still with her. Bridges manages not to be overshadowed by the two."

—New York *Daily News* (Ann Guarino)

"*Hammersmith Is Out* is another of those heavy-handed 'the criminally insane are running the world' parables that almost comes off—but not quite, in spite of Elizabeth Taylor and Richard Burton giving their best performances of recent years."

—*New York* (Judith Crist)

"An outrageously funny, free-wheeling farce that qualifies as a true sleeper, if any film starring Elizabeth Taylor and Richard Burton can be so defined."

—*Newsweek* (Paul D. Zimmerman)

"*Hammersmith Is Out* is both too elaborate and not quite witty enough to be especially convincing as contemporary morality comedy. . . . Both Bridges and Miss Taylor display a certain vulgar, ratty charm that is often funny. Not so funny are Burton and Ustinov (who, in addition to directing, plays Hammersmith's keeper), but this may simply be a matter of ordinary material that has not been improved by direction or editing."

—*The New York Times* (Vincent Canby)

notes

RIGHT: With Richard Burton, playing Hammersmith, the mental patient with a murderous streak **OPPOSITE:** As Jimmie Jean

HAMMERSMITH IS OUT, A COMEDIC MODERN SPIN ON FAUST, would be Elizabeth and Richard Burton's final time together on the big screen, though they would next be paired in the twin TV movies *Divorce His/Divorce Hers*. *Hammersmith* was financed by mobile-home magnate J. Cornelius Crean, in his first dip into the arena of motion pictures. He hired an equally inexperienced producer under him, Alex Lucas, and Peter Ustinov to direct. Ustinov was an actor and a fine one, with Oscars to show for it, but he had few credits to his name as a director. He also portrayed one of the main characters in the film, the owner of the mental institution from which Hammersmith escapes.

Elizabeth and Burton thought the entire production would be a lark and had fun with it. To do the film they were even willing to forego their usual high salaries in return for a large profit share in the film. They were thrilled to be able to shoot the movie in Cuernavaca, Mexico, near a home the Burtons had in Puerto Vallarta. Burton had considerable experience playing Faust. In this case his titular role of Hammersmith was heir apparent to Mephistopheles, or perhaps the devil himself in his criminal ways. Elizabeth wore a shaggy blonde wig for most of the film in her role as a roadhouse waitress. At first the look and her accent are overwhelmingly distracting, but her characterization of Jimmie Jean grows comically endearing as the story unfolds. Beau Bridges, in a role once planned for Robert Redford, provided additional laughs as Billy Breedlove.

Hammersmith Is Out was released to theaters in May 1972, but only distributed to a limited number of major cities. Later that year, Crean partnered with Cinerama to get the film out in wider release. Even then, the film did not generate a great deal of excitement either with the ticket-buying public or among critics. It was, however, appreciatively welcomed at the Berlin International Film Festival, where Elizabeth was given the award for Best Actress.

> *Elizabeth and Burton thought the entire production would be a lark and had fun with it.*

Divorce His/Divorce Hers

TV Movie

HARLECH TELEVISION/ABC

CAST

Richard Burton .... *Martin Reynolds*

Elizabeth Taylor .... *Jane Reynolds*

Carrie Nye .... *Diana Proctor*

Barry Foster .... *Donald Trenton*

Gabriele Ferzetti .... *Turi Livicci*

Daniela Surina .... *Franca*

Thomas Baptiste .... *minister*

Ronald Radd .... *Angus McIntyre*

Rudolph Walker .... *Kaduna*

Mark Colleano .... *Tommy Reynolds*

Rosalyn Landor .... *Peggy Reynolds*

Eva Griffiths .... *Judith Reynolds*

CREDITS

John Heyman *(executive producer)*; Terence Baker, Gareth Wigan *(producers)*; Waris Hussein *(director)*; John Hopkins *(screenplay)*; Ernst Wild, Gábor Pogány *(photography)*; Stanley Myers *(music)*; Ray Stannard *(production design)*; Ian Whittaker *(set decorations)*; Wolfgang Glattes, Francesco Cinieri *(assistant directors)*; John Bloom *(editor)*; Edith Head *(Elizabeth Taylor's costumes)*; Dorothy Edwards *(costumes)*; Alexandre de Paris *(hairstylist)*; Ron Berkeley *(Richard Burton's makeup)*; Alberto De Rossi *(Elizabeth Taylor's makeup)*

RELEASE DATE: February 6, 1973

RUN TIME: 144 minutes, color

SUMMARY: After eighteen years of marriage, Martin and Jane Reynolds' relationship has come to an end. How they reached this impasse is told in flashback and flash-forward his-and-hers memories. Martin's work causes separations and eventually apathy; they quarrel over matters concerning their three children; and both husband and wife fall into affairs. Through all the pain they cause each other, Martin and Jane remain deeply connected to one another, but only time will tell if they can ever make their marriage work again.

notes

DIVORCE HIS/DIVORCE HERS WAS A STORY ABOUT THE FAILURE of a marriage told from both the husband and wife's perspectives. The tale unfolded in two separate made-for-television movies, *Divorce His* and *Divorce Hers*, which aired in the ABC "Movie of the Week" series. They were rather epic TV productions, understandably so starring Elizabeth Taylor and Richard Burton. Filming took place in Bavaria and Rome at no little expense to the producers. Elizabeth and Burton, ultimate big-screen stars that they were, were not well versed in the common practices of television filming. Measures of expediency and cost-saving were not their strong suits, but ABC knew anything they worked on would generate a raft of publicity.

Elizabeth and Burton's actual marriage was on the rocks. His brother, Ifor, passed away in 1972, after a fall he took following a night of drinking with Burton. Burton felt enormous guilt over his brother's death and his drinking intensified. Elizabeth kept up with him and that often led to bitter quarrels. "Our natures do not inspire domestic tranquility," Burton later said. *Divorce His/Divorce Hers* would be their last of eleven screen partnerships. Over the years he may have consistently won more praise than Elizabeth in terms of acting, but in the end Burton gave his wife credit for his success in films: "Elizabeth has taught me most of what I know about acting for the screen. Above all she's taught me to take it seriously instead of just doing it for the money."

OPPOSITE: With Richard Burton **ABOVE, FROM LEFT:** As Jane and Martin Reynolds | The legendary duo in their final film together

REVIEWS

"The production can claim one unusual distinction: both parts are equally and excruciatingly boring. . . . Miss Taylor looks good and Mr. Burton sounds good. Leave it at that."

—*The New York Times*
(John J. O'Connor)

"When you're a Liz Taylor-Richard Burton watcher just about anything goes. As long as the beauteous Liz's hair is styled by Alexandre of Paris, she's dripping in jewels by Kenneth Lane, and she's wearing Edith Head designs, who could ask for anything more unless it's the resonant voice of Richard Burton on the glamorous scene?" —**New York** *Daily News*
(Kay Gardella)

Night Watch

JOSEPH E. LEVINE AND BURT PRODUCTIONS/ AVCO EMBASSY

CAST

Elizabeth Taylor	*Ellen Wheeler*
Laurence Harvey	*John Wheeler*
Billie Whitelaw	*Sarah Cooke*
Robert Lang	*Appleby*
Tony Britton	*Tony*
Bill Dean	*Inspector Walker*
Michael Danvers-Walker	*Sergeant Norris*
Rosario Serrano	*Dolores*
Pauline Jameson	*secretary*
Linda Hayden	*girl in car*

CREDITS

George W. George, Martin Poll *(producers)*; Brian G. Hutton *(director)*; Tony Williamson *(screenplay)*; Evan Jones *(additional dialogue)*, based on play by Lucille Fletcher; Billy Williams *(photography)*; John Cameron *(music)*; Peter James *(set decorations)*; Scott Wodehouse *(assistant director)*; John Jympson *(editor)*; Yvonne Blake *(costumes)*; Claudye Bozzacchi *(hairstylist)*; Ron Berkeley *(makeup)*

RELEASE DATE: August 10, 1973 (U.S.)

RUN TIME: 99 minutes, color

RIGHT: As Ellen Wheeler

SUMMARY: Ellen Wheeler, a widow haunted by the death of her first husband in a horrifying auto accident, does not get the attention she needs from her second husband, John, and spends much time alone, allowing her mind to wander. From a window of her posh London home she says she witnesses a murder in the house next door. Police turn up no evidence of a crime having been committed. This begins a series of (seemingly) false alarms set off by Ellen. All the while the police attempt to calm her while diligently following through on her leads; John humors her; Ellen's friend Sarah attempts to be consoling; and the neighbor continues to carry out suspiciously timed planting projects of odd sizes. All eventually come to the end of their rope and whodunit leaves everyone in at the finish appalled.

REVIEWS

"*Night Watch* isn't a breathless, frightening thriller of the Hitchcock kind, although there are scenes reminiscent of some Hitchcock films. Its one burst of graphic violence may remind you of the shower scene in *Psycho*. But it is a riveting mystery laced with fine acting, and some of the other things audiences love: atmosphere, right down to the Chagalls and Matisses on the townhouse walls, and of course Miss Taylor's eye-catching wardrobe designed by Valentino. Miss Taylor gives a fascinating performance."

—*Christian Science Monitor*
(Louise Sweeney)

"Elizabeth Taylor, and about time, has got herself a good picture and a whodunit at that. More than one Music Hall patron seemed to be stumbling from the first showing of *Night Watch* yesterday in stunned delight at the windup, a gorgeously brazen, logical swindle. . . . [With] beautiful color photography and Miss Taylor agonizing in some dazzling Valentino finery, it's easy to play a smug Sherlock. But the glossy intimacy only deepens the surprise of the climax, a hair-raising stalk in the house next door, yeastily directed by Brian G. Hutton. Miss Taylor churns up a fine, understandable lather of nerves. Mr. Harvey is properly sleek, Miss Whitelaw makes a peppery parrot, and Mr. Lang is neat. The deliciously cunning postscript may make you feel like a perfect fool. Once in a while it's fun." —*The New York Times*
(Howard Thompson)

notes

Like Hammersmith Is Out, Night Watch *was something of a pet project for Elizabeth, as her first attempt at mystery-suspense.*

NIGHT WATCH WAS BASED ON A PLAY THAT HAD A SUCCESSFUL run on Broadway in 1972, playing at the Morosco Theatre for a total of 121 performances starring Joan Hackett and Len Cariou. The suspense-filled mystery was the work of Lucille Fletcher, the author of the equally tense radio play *Sorry, Wong Number*, which was later turned into a hit film. George W. George, the producer of the stage production of *Night Watch*, oversaw the transition of the work from stage to screen himself, hiring Elizabeth's *X, Y & Zee* director, Brian Hutton, to guide the way.

Tweaks from play to film included a location change from Manhattan's Murray Hill to London, where the film was made in 1973. The film also trimmed the array of suspects featured in the original play. In spite of this tightening of the story, the film sees no loss of activity and appears to be littered with red herrings, which Hutton seemed to drop in a jarringly obvious manner but which served to make the ending all the more shocking to audiences not familiar with Fletcher's play. In *Night Watch*, which is not well known and is underrated today, Hutton and his cast created an atmosphere of suspense surrounding a perpetually panicked Elizabeth Taylor reminiscent of certifiable classics *Gaslight* and *Rear Window*. Elizabeth herself was a wow at the center of it all, never letting up the hysterics for a moment, culminating in a bombshell of a finale.

Like *Hammersmith Is Out*, *Night Watch* was something of a pet project for Elizabeth, as her first attempt at mystery-suspense. She truly wanted to make the movie even though its budget was less than customary for her, so she was willing to gamble by accepting a percentage of the profits rather than a high up-front salary. Her husband in the film was played by *BUtterfield 8* leading man Laurence Harvey. *Night Watch* would be one of his final screen appearances. During filming he suffered severe stomach pains and had to be rushed to the hospital for emergency surgery. He was diagnosed with stomach cancer and died three months after *Night Watch* released in the U.S., in November 1973. In an interview before his death, Harvey spoke of his desire to work with his friend Elizabeth again and offered the tribute, "She is the most talented screen actress in the world today. Professionalism without equal."

OPPOSITE: With Harvey, in one of his final films **RIGHT:** A wardrobe test for *Night Watch*

Ash Wednesday

SAGITTARIUS PRODUCTIONS/
PARAMOUNT PICTURES

CAST

Elizabeth Taylor .... *Barbara Sawyer*

Henry Fonda .... *Mark Sawyer*

Helmut Berger .... *Erich*

Keith Baxter .... *David*

Maurice Teynac .... *Dr. Lambert*

Margaret Blye .... *Kate Sawyer*

Monique van Vooren ..... *German woman*

Henning Schlüter .... *bridge player*

Dino Mele .... *Mario*

Kathy Van Lypps .... *Mandy*

CREDITS

Dominick Dunne *(producer)*; Larry Peerce *(director)*; Jean-Claude Tramont *(screenplay)*; Ennio Guarnieri *(photography)*; Maurice Jarre *(music)*; Philip Abramsom *(art director)*; Steven Barnett *(assistant director)*; Marion Rothman *(editor)*; Annalisa Nasalli Rocca *(costumes)*; Edith Head *(Elizabeth Taylor's costumes)*; Alexandre de Paris *(Elizabeth Taylor's hairstylist)*; Alberto De Rossi *(makeup)*; Dr. Rodolphe Troques *(technical advisor)*

RELEASE DATE: November 1, 1973

RUN TIME: 99 minutes, color

RIGHT: As Barbara Sawyer, rejuvenated

SUMMARY: At age fifty-five and on the verge of losing her husband Mark, Barbara Sawyer makes a desperate attempt to endear him again by undergoing extensive face and body plastic surgery procedures. She has it done secretly at a hospital in Switzerland peopled by a cross-section of wealthy (and often famous) patients looking to shave decades off their appearance, including David, a well-known photographer who befriends Barbara. All goes perfectly and a slimmed-down and stunning Barbara travels to a ski lodge where she is to be reunited with Mark. As Mark's arrival is continually delayed, Barbara makes friends and has a one-night affair with a young playboy. At last, Mark arrives and is impressed by his wife's physical transformation back into the woman he first married, but it does not change the fact that he has fallen in love with another woman.

"Despite the off-putting title, *Ash Wednesday* proves Elizabeth Taylor's best vehicle in years. . . . The change from ugly duckling to swan is, of course, every actress' dream role, and Liz makes the most of it, looking even younger than her actual off-screen years. . . . Jean-Claude Tramont's screenplay, directed by Larry Peerce, makes one remember why millions of people used to enjoy movies."

—*Village Voice* (Roger Dooley)

"Fonda is excellent in his climactic appearance, an unusually superb casting idea. Taylor's performance also is very good, after discounting the before-and-after visuals which sometimes evoke unduly excessive huzzahs for 'acting' that really belong to the makeup crew. But relative to many of her recent roles, this is one of the strongest and most effective in some time. Her beauty remains sensational."

—*Variety* ("Murf")

"*Ash Wednesday* has some shock effect in its early surgical scenes, showing us how the subcutaneous tissue is removed (what we really see is chicken fat) to firm up the skin under Barbara's eyes and other organs. Mostly the film is interested in what Barbara is going to wear next. This is not a male chauvinist's conception of a woman, but her hairdresser's, full of envy, awe and superficial compassion."

—*The New York Times* (Vincent Canby)

FROM TOP: Behind the scenes with her longtime hairstylist, Alexandre de Paris | With *Ash Wednesday* director Larry Peerce

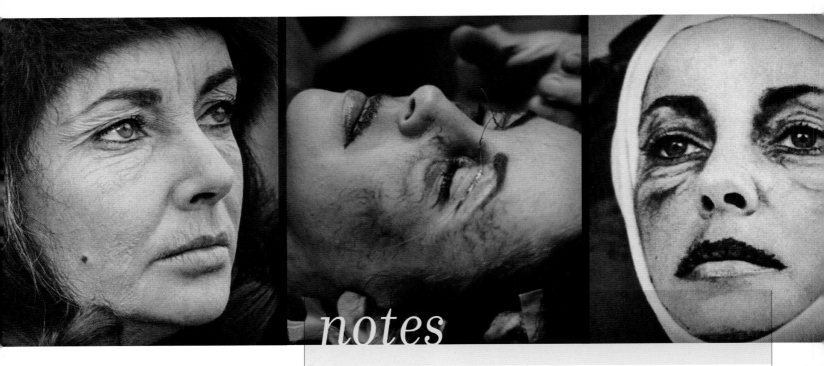

notes

ASH WEDNESDAY HAS BECOME A LATTER-DAY FAVORITE AMONG Elizabeth Taylor fans. She was uniquely believable in the story of a woman who turns back the hands of time through an extensive series of head-to-toe plastic surgeries because in the post-operative scenes, Elizabeth looked slimmer and more beautiful than she had in years. It almost gave one the eerie feeling that the procedures seen happening on the screen had actually taken place. Indeed, there was some complaint from the more faint-of-heart moviegoers as to the film's realism because during the plastic surgery sequences, studio scenes were intercut with actual footage of procedures performed by experts from a hospital of the day like the one in the film, run by Dr. Rodolphe Troques, the film's technical advisor. Viewed today it is interesting to hear talk of such then-novel procedures as chemical peels. If it still makes viewers squeamish, in its own time the discussions and descriptions were all the more shocking as futuristic concepts.

> ## It tells an engrossing yet simple story and in its visual intensity could even work as a silent movie.

FROM LEFT: The transformation of Barbara from where she started; to surgery; and post-operative bandaging; and the stunning end results

Filmed in Italy, largely at the Cortina d'Ampezzo ski resort, *Ash Wednesday* is both thought-provoking and lovely to behold, from the first opening montage of photos to the finish. It tells an engrossing yet simple story and in its visual intensity could even work as a silent movie. Or as an early talkie, hearkening back as it does to the three-hankie soap operas of an earlier period in films, like a drama Ruth Chatterton or Irene Dunne would have done in the early 1930s.

Elizabeth's performance in the film was restrained and most effective and she was nominated for a Golden Globe as Best Actress. Elizabeth was not known for this more reserved kind of acting but she understood its value on film, saying at the time of *Ash Wednesday*, " . . . the emotion has got be there behind your eyes, behind your heart. You can never act superficially and get away with it. It all had to show in the eye. The slightest movement will speak volumes."

Ash Wednesday was a true women's film. Henry Fonda's role is essentially a cameo appearance. Through the character of Barbara Sawyer's remembrances and discussions with friends and her daughter, his story has pretty much all unfolded before we ever see Fonda. All the while though, the audience anticipates his arrival because of the montage in the opening credits in which Fonda's image is superimposed into photos of Elizabeth primarily from the '50s. As a result, as Barbara talks about her husband throughout the movie, we are set up to picture Fonda. Keith Baxter as her friend from the plastic surgery clinic had more screen time than Fonda and used it well. He demonstrated a good rapport with Elizabeth onscreen that is interesting to note considering that Baxter had been up for the role of Mark Antony in *Cleopatra* at the time Rouben Mamoulian was director, before Joe Mankiewicz took the reins and cast Richard Burton.

Elizabeth played the mother of Margaret Blye in *Ash Wednesday*. Blye was only ten years younger than Elizabeth but because Elizabeth was playing a woman fifteen years older than she actually was, the casting worked. What was more troubling about playing a woman of advanced age was the process of making her look believable. Elizabeth said, "Playing an old bag doesn't bother me in the least, but the damn latex makeup drove me crazy." Beyond the heavy makeup, prosthetics, and padding, Elizabeth also suffered through a bout of German measles during the production and dealt off screen with the highly publicized breakup of her marriage to Richard Burton (for the first time). As ever, hardships could not keep Elizabeth down for long and on the contrary, seemed to bring out the best in her. *Ash Wednesday* was well-received in its day and decades later is fondly remembered by her admirers.

OPPOSITE FROM TOP: With Helmut Berger, as her young lover in the film | With Henry Fonda **ABOVE:** Wearing a costume from the movie during production, Elizabeth and Richard Burton attended a performance at the La Scala Opera House in Milan.

> *"The emotion has got be there behind your eyes, behind your heart. You can never act superficially and get away with it."*
> —ELIZABETH TAYLOR

That's Entertainment!

METRO-GOLDWYN-MAYER/ UNITED ARTISTS

COHOSTS APPEARING AS THEMSELVES:

Fred Astaire

Bing Crosby

Gene Kelly

Peter Lawford

Liza Minnelli

Donald O'Connor

Debbie Reynolds

Mickey Rooney

Frank Sinatra

James Stewart

Elizabeth Taylor

CREDITS

Jack Haley, Jr. (producer/director/writer); Daniel Melnick (executive producer); Gene Polito, Ernest Laszlo, Allan Green, Ennio Guarnieri, Russell Metty (photography); Jim Liles, Robert Hoag (optical supervisors); Henry Mancini (music); Jesse Kaye (music supervision); Richard Bremerkamp, Claude Binyon, Jr., David Silver (assistant directors); Lyle Burbridge, William L. McCaughey, Aaron Rochin, Harry W. Tetrick, Hal Watkins (sound); Bud Friedgen, David E. Blewitt (editors); Mort Feinstein (MGM film librarian)

RELEASE DATE: June 21, 1974

RUN TIME: 135 minutes, color and black and white

RIGHT: At the premiere of *That's Entertainment!* with Sammy Davis, Jr.

REVIEW

"[*That's Entertainment*] is a documentary at heart, the sort of compilation feature that depends largely on the genius of others, a movie made by ravaging earlier movies, and, as such, a movie that one shouldn't feel too kindly towards. Theoretically, anyway. Actually, however, *That's Entertainment* is a consciousness-raising delight, an immediate high, a revue that doesn't only evoke the past but, in addition, lays the past out there to compete with the present on its own terms. And, as any ponderous, sober-minded documentary should, it asks a question: what the hell ever happened to the movie musical?" —*The New York Times* (Vincent Canby)

notes

IN AN ERA OF 1970S REALISM, WRITER-PRODUCER-DIRECTOR Jack Haley, Jr. saw a need to produce an antidote of escapism for audiences nostalgic for the glamour of the studio days. No studio of the Golden Era loomed larger or more extravagant than MGM, thus upon the fiftieth anniversary of its formation, *That's Entertainment!* was assembled as a salute to the studio's greatest musicals and the performers who made them great. The film utilized clips from such beloved movies as *The Wizard of Oz*, *The Band Wagon*, *Singin' in the Rain*, and *Gigi*. Looking glamorous in her own wardrobe and jewelry, Elizabeth was one of eleven MGM-star cohosts who introduced various segments of *That's Entertainment!* Besides her cohosting duties, Elizabeth also contributed to the entertainment by way of clips from *Cynthia* and *A Date with Judy*.

Elizabeth's sequence was filmed in Rome, but those of other cohosts were filmed at MGM, and offered some of the last footage ever filmed of the studio's famed back lot before it became part of a housing development. The sad fate the back lot would bring added poignancy to the intrinsic nostalgia of the production. *That's Entertainment!* proved to be a hit with audiences. It inspired a sequel, *That's Entertainment! II*, released in 1976, followed much later by a third edition in 1994.

Identikit *(The Driver's Seat)*

RIZZOLI/AVCO EMBASSY

CAST

Elizabeth Taylor .... *Lise*

Ian Bannen .... *Bill*

Guido Mannari .... *Carlo*

Mona Washbourne ...... *Mrs. Helen Fiedke*

Luigi Squarzina .... *lead detective*

Maxence Mailfort .... *Pierre*

Andy Warhol .... *English lord*

Anita Bartolucci .... *saleswoman*

Gino Giuseppe .... *police commissioner*

Marino Masé .... *traffic policeman*

CREDITS

Nello Meniconi *(executive producer)*; Franco Rossellini *(producer)*; Giuseppe Patroni Griffi *(director)*; Giuseppe Patroni Griffi, Raffaele La Capria *(screenplay)*, based on novel by Muriel Spark; Vittorio Storaro *(photography)*; Franco Mannino *(music)*; Mario Ceroli *(art director)*; Andrea Fantacci *(set decorations)*; Albino Cocco, Aldo Terlizzi *(assistant directors)*; Franco Arcalli *(editor)*; Gabriella Pescucci *(costumes)*; Mirella Ginnoto, Giancarlo Novelli *(hairstylists)*; Giuseppe Capogrosso, Stefano Trani *(makeup)*

RELEASE DATE: May 20, 1974 (Monaco); October 10, 1975 (U.S.)

RUN TIME: 102 minutes, color

SUMMARY: Lise is a mysterious solo traveler across Europe who attracts attention wherever she goes because of her loud clothing, layers of makeup, and quick-to-flare personality. On a trip to parts unknown to meet persons not clearly defined, Lise has a series of adventures that land her in the arms of many men whose lives she changes with a deadly touch. Each encounter adds pieces to the puzzle the police are putting together on Lise. The journey seems to be a constant search for her "boyfriend," but no one is a better companion to her than an eccentric older Canadian woman named Mrs. Fiedke. Could the young man of whom Mrs. Fiedke speaks so much be the one to satisfy Lise's search . . . for the perfect man to kill her?

"*The Driver's Seat* is a strange, morbid, but intensely fascinating, psychological study of a woman going mad that provides Elizabeth Taylor with her most colorful and demanding role in years. She meets the challenge with imperial efficiency. With dark blue circles around her eyes and raspberry-tinted sunglasses, she had a ball and so does the audience. . . . The film is cleverly structured, alternating glimpses of her daily activities with police interrogations of the people she meets in her bizarre encounters, so you really don't know if you are watching flashbacks or flash-forwards until the final dénouement."

—New York *Daily News*

"Giuseppe Patroni Griffi's *The Driver's Seat* is quite possibly one of the best films Elizabeth Taylor has made in her long career. Taylor, under Griffi's firm direction, gives a beautifully controlled and hypnotic performance in which she relays much about this character with subtle vocal inflections. Never once does she rely on her natural beauty, which has been toned down considerably for the film."

—*Hollywood Reporter* (Ron Pennington)

notes

"IDENTIKIT" REFERS TO A COMPOSITE PICTURE OF A CRIMINAL constructed from the descriptions provided to police by witnesses. It describes perfectly the structure of this Italian production from filmmaker Giuseppe Patroni Griffi that Elizabeth made in Germany and Italy in August and September 1973. In the U.S. the picture was known as *The Driver's Seat* and in some markets, fittingly, as *Psychotic*. It was based on a fascinatingly unusual novella that first appeared in the *New Yorker* in 1970 by Muriel Spark (perhaps best known as the author of *The Prime of Miss Jean Brodie*), about a manic female traveler who adversely affects the lives of every male she encounters while at the same time searching for the right moment for her own downfall. The film is of added interest for containing a rare feature film performance by pop artist Andy Warhol as an English lord.

> *The film is of added interest for containing a rare feature film performance by pop artist Andy Warhol as an English lord.*

The movie had a lavish premiere in Monte Carlo in May 1974 hosted by Elizabeth's friends Princess Grace and Prince Rainier. With tickets sold at $500 a piece, it served as a benefit for Grace's favorite charity, the Monaco Red Cross. The

triumvirate of prince, princess, and Elizabeth Taylor brought a flood of media attention to the world premiere of *Identikit*, so much so that it stole the spotlight from the Cannes Film Festival, which was hosting a ball of their own at the same time. (The festival had officially passed on screening *Identikit* during the season's events.) Attendees to the premiere included Franco Zeffirelli, Ursula Andress, Andy Warhol, Paulette Goddard, Elsa Martinelli, Salvador Dalí, Vittorio de Sica, Aristotle Onassis, and Stavros Niarchos. Avco Embassy bought the rights to distribute the film in North America and released it only in select markets in the U.S. beginning in October 1975.

> *Elizabeth was reportedly uncharacteristically tense during filming due to her deteriorating relationship with Richard Burton.*

Elizabeth was reportedly uncharacteristically tense during filming due to her deteriorating relationship with Richard Burton. She did not discuss her troubles, though was unsettled by the impending divorce. At the time Burton was also in Italy, to film *The Voyage* with Sophia Loren. Burton and Loren would soon be joined by Elizabeth's *Identikit* costar, Ian Bannen, who recalled, "There was no mention of Richard [by Elizabeth] until, as I was leaving to join him in Palermo, she told me to give him her love when I saw him." While making *Identikit*, Elizabeth was photographed in Salerno, Italy, consoling herself with a new man to whom she had been introduced by her friend Peter Lawford, erstwhile California used-car dealer Henry Wynberg. Elizabeth's first divorce to Burton would be official in June 1974, before she made her next film, but it was, of course, far from the final word on the Taylor-Burton love saga.

The Blue Bird

LENFILM/WENKS FILMS/
TOWER INTERNATIONAL/
TWENTIETH CENTURY FOX

CAST

Elizabeth Taylor .... *Queen of Light/*
Mother/Witch/Maternal Love

Jane Fonda .... *Night*

Ava Gardner .... *Luxury*

Cicely Tyson .... *Tylette*

Robert Morley .... *Father Time*

Harry Andrews .... *The Oak*

Todd Lookinland .... *Tyltyl*

Patsy Kensit .... *Mytyl*

Will Geer .... *Grandfather*

Mona Washbourne .... *Grandmother*

George Cole .... *Dog*

CREDITS

Edward Lewis, Edward Joseph (*executive producers*); Paul Maslansky, Paul B. Radin, Lee Savin (*producers*); George Cukor (*director*); Aleksei Kapler, Hugh Whitemore, Alfred Hayes (*screenplay*), based on play *L'Oiseau Bleu* by Maurice Maeterlinck; Jonas Gritsius, Freddie Young (*photography*); Irwin Kostal, Andrei Petrov (*music*); Lionel Newman (*music coordinator*); Leonid Jakobson, Igor Belsky (*choreographers*); Brian Wildsmith (*production design*); Valeri Yurkevich (*art director*); Stanford C. Allen, Tatyana Shapiro (*editor*); Marina Azizyan, Edith Head (*costumes*); Sydney Guilaroff (*hairstylist*)

RELEASE DATE: April 5, 1976
RUN TIME: 99 minutes, color

SUMMARY: Young Tyltyl and Mytyl go on a quest for the Blue Bird of Happiness. Along their journeys, the children are able to conjure the human essences of animate and inanimate entities such as Night, Luxury, Cat, Dog, Sugar, and Bread. From each of these beings Tyltyl and Mytyl learn essential truths about life, but the greatest wisdom of all comes from the Queen of Light, who reveals to the children that the Blue Bird of Happiness is not in far-off lands but can be found nestled in one's own backyard.

FROM LEFT: A candid shot behind the scenes of *The Blue Bird* | Transforming herself into the Queen of Light

REVIEWS

"Though the film has about it a kind of lumbering tackiness that I associate with Soviet stage spectacle, I suspect that the Russian version of this co-production might be a lot more interesting than ours. For one thing, Russian audiences apparently love 'The Blue Bird,' the chef d'oeuvre of the Belgian-born playwright who allowed Stanislavsky to stage the world premiere at the Moscow Art Theater in 1908. This love and familiarity with the work might possibly have inspired Soviet film makers to bring to it a consistency of character and style, as well as a decisive point of view, completely absent from the hyphenated production we have here. . . . The English-language screenplay, by Hugh Whitemore and Alfred Hayes, would tax the inspirations of anyone. What could Mr. Cukor possibly have suggested to Miss Taylor to help her read a line like, 'I am the light that makes men see/The radiance in reality'? Keep a straight face, perhaps? The actress has some creditably funny moments as a witch and some not-so-good as a peasant mother who darns socks." —*The New York Times*

"Maurice Maeterlinck's early century fantasy will, in this filming, bore kids when adults are mildly interested, and vice versa."   —*Variety* ("Murf")

"*The Blue Bird* works so hard on making history that it forgets to make sense. . . . Cukor's direction has nothing to do with the celebrated Hepburn-Tracy era, or with the funny-sad comedy-drama that he helped to perfect in Hollywood's better days. Some of his fantasy scenes look like rip-offs from a junior-high pageant. But the veteran filmmaker deserves credit for making even a matinee crazy quilt from the uneven conception and silly songs he had to work with." —*Christian Science Monitor* (David Sterritt)

notes

BELGIAN AUTHOR MAURICE MAETERLINCK'S PLAY, *L'OISEAU BLUE*, debuted at the Moscow Art Theatre in 1908. Thereafter, producers have embraced the children's fantasy story in numerous adaptations, including three Broadway stage productions, two U.S. silent movies, an opera, an animated film from Russia in 1970, and most famously, a 1940 Shirley Temple movie produced by Twentieth Century Fox as their purported answer to Judy Garland in *The Wizard of Oz*. In spite of the minimal success of previous film adaptations, the 1970s edition directed by George Cukor had lofty ambitions, with producer Edward Lewis announcing to the press that *The Blue Bird* would be made on a grand scale with an all-star cast, and a budget upward of $12 million.

ABOVE: In *The Blue Bird*. Playwright Maeterlinck also wrote a little-known sequel called *The Blue Bird and the Betrothal*.

Twentieth Century Fox linked up with the Lenfilm Studio to make this the first Soviet-American joint film production utilizing a cast and crew comprised of both Russian and American talents. Filming would take place in Moscow and Leningrad. *The Blue Bird* was placed in the capable hands of George Cukor, award-winning director of *The Philadelphia Story*, *A Star Is Born*, and *My Fair Lady*, among other classics. An impressive cast headed by Elizabeth Taylor, Ava Gardner, Jane Fonda, and Cicely Tyson was assembled for the film. Katharine Hepburn and Shirley MacLaine were original cast selections but backed out of the production, which is the route others came to wish they had chosen.

It would take a director of Cukor's stature to withstand the flurry of behind-the-scenes difficulties that plagued *The Blue Bird*. First was the language barrier that existed between the Russian cast and crew and their American counterparts, making Cukor resort to a form of sign language on desperate occasions. Cinematographer Jonas Gritsius had to be replaced when Cukor discovered that he had never shot a film in color, resulting in a murky quality to all of the early footage he had shot. The frigid weather was a trial for some, though not as big an issue as the food turned out to be, necessitating edible imports to be shipped from England.

> *It would take a director of Cukor's stature to withstand the flurry of behind-the-scenes difficulties that plagued* The Blue Bird.

ABOVE, FROM LEFT: In her Maternal Love role | At the wrap party with director George Cukor | For Cukor and his cast and crew, a champagne toast was in order when *The Blue Bird* mercifully reached its conclusion. | A portrait from *The Blue Bird* period

Actor James Coco subsisted on bread and butter only for a time and eventually suffered a gallbladder attack that necessitated that he be replaced by George Cole in the role of Dog. Coco later said, "They tell us the movie will finish by August, but not by August of what year. I understand Elizabeth Taylor is having Christmas cards printed."

When all was said and done, the total cost of *The Blue Bird* was $15 million. Production totaled a trying seven months during which time Jane Fonda talked politics to the Russians and George Cukor accused Cicely Tyson of putting a voodoo jinx on the film. Elizabeth suffered from her recurring back pains and was ill with amoebic dysentery and dehydration throughout the production, causing more delays as she was vital to the movie, playing four roles. This came after she had also just endured a lung cancer scare. It was during production of this film that Elizabeth offered one of her most famous quotes to reporter Rex Reed: "I've been through it all, baby. I'm Mother Courage."

Just as production mercifully wrapped on *The Blue Bird*, Elizabeth made headlines again by announcing that she and Richard Burton were reunited. Their second marriage took place on October 10, 1975, at Chobe National Game Park in Botswana. They had never resolved the issues that had separated them two years earlier. Elizabeth said, "I married him the second time because I no longer cared if he stopped drinking. I just wanted to be married to him." Their reunion would last only four months. Love alone could not sustain them. Burton's daughter, Kate, said, "I don't think anybody, least of all them, could have told you why it worked or why it didn't."

> *"I've been through it all, baby. I'm Mother Courage."*
>
> —ELIZABETH TAYLOR

Victory at Entebbe

TV Movie

DAVID L. WOLPER PRODUCTIONS/ABC

CAST

Richard Dreyfuss............*Colonel Yonatan Netanyahu*

Burt Lancaster...................*Shimon Peres*

Julius Harris................*President Idi Amin*

Anthony Hopkins.............*Prime Minister Yitzhak Rabin*

Stefan Gierasch...*General Mordecai Gur*

Elizabeth Taylor................*Edra Vilnofsky*

Kirk Douglas................*Hershel Vilnofsky*

Linda Blair.........................*Chana Vilnofsky*

Helen Hayes............*Etta Grossman-Wise*

David Groh.........................*Benjamin Wise*

Helmut Berger..............*German terrorist*

Theodore Bikel..................*Yakov Shlomo*

CREDITS

Robert Guenette *(producer)*; Marvin J. Chomsky *(director)*; Ernest Kinoy *(screenplay)*; Jim Kilgore *(photography)*; Charles Fox *(music)*; Charles Rutherford *(set decorations)*; Donald Gold *(assistant director)*; Michael Gavaldon, Jim McElroy, David Saxon *(editors)*; Jack Martell *(costumes)*

RELEASE DATE: December 13, 1976

RUN TIME: 119 minutes, color

RIGHT: Elizabeth and Kirk Douglas

SUMMARY:

Based on a true story: On June 27, 1976, Palestinian terrorists hijacked Air France Flight 139, departing from Tel Aviv, Israel, headed for Paris, and rerouted its course to Entebbe airport in Uganda. Upon arrival, all non-Jewish passengers were released and the remaining 107 held hostage. Israeli intelligence, masterminded by defense minister Shimon Peres, devised a rescue mission, known as Operation Thunderbolt, that was successfully carried out on July 6, 1976. Mission commander Colonel Yonatan "Yonni" Netanyahu, the brother of Israeli leader Benjamin Netanyahu, was the only member of the rescue team to lose his life.

notes

THE STORY OF THE TERRORIST HIJACKING OF AIR FRANCE Flight 139 and the ensuing hostage rescue mission carried out by Israel Defense Forces was among the biggest news events of 1976. The operation was so well-planned and near seamlessly executed that the United States military would follow similar plans based on the Entebbe model in years to come. There was so much interest in the Entebbe tale in 1976 that it sent no less than three movies into production. *Victory at Entebbe* aired on ABC in December of that year, edging out by one month the premiere of NBC's version of the story, *Raid on Entebbe*, starring Peter Finch and Charles Bronson. Meanwhile, an Israeli feature film was also in the works and released in 1977. Both *Raid* and *Victory at Entebbe* earned numerous Emmy nominations, though more went to *Raid on Entebbe*.

The story that these three films told was close to Elizabeth's heart, and she said she participated in her small role as Edra Vilnovsky in *Victory at Entebbe* for her fellow Jewish people. She and Kirk Douglas played the Jewish parents of a sixteen-year-old girl held hostage at Entebbe. The reality of the movies was perhaps too close for comfort in some markets and not enough time had elapsed following the aftermath. Several articles reported protests and even bomb threats in reaction to screenings of the film in Germany and Italy.

A Little Night Music

**S&T-FILM BERLIN/
SASCHA-VERLEIH/
NEW WORLD PICTURES**

CAST

Elizabeth Taylor .... *Desiree Armfeldt*

Diana Rigg .... *Charlotte Mittelheim*

Len Cariou .... *Frederick Egerman*

Lesley-Anne Down .... *Anne Egerman*

Hermione Gingold ..... *Madame Armfeldt*

Laurence Guittard .... *Carl-Magnus Mittelheim*

Christopher Guard .... *Erich Egerman*

Lesley Dunlop .... *Petra*

Chloe Franks .... *Fredericka Armfeldt*

Heinz Marecek .... *Frid*

CREDITS

Elliott Kastner *(producer)*; Harold Prince *(director)*; Hugh Wheeler *(screenplay)*, based on screenplay *Smiles of a Summer Night* by Ingmar Bergman and play by Hugh Wheeler; Arthur Ibbetson *(photography)*; Paul Gemignani *(musical director)*; Stephen Sondheim *(music and lyrics)*; Patricia Birch *(choreographer)*; Herta Pisching *(art director)*; Kip Gowans *(assistant director)*; John Jympson *(editor)*; Florence Klotz *(costumes)*

RELEASE DATE: December 1977

RUN TIME: 124 minutes, color

RIGHT: With Len Cariou

SUMMARY: In turn-of-the-century Austria, three mismatched couples spend a weekend at the country estate of Madame Armfeldt. Each person present is enmeshed in romantic dramas which in some way effect all of their weekend companions, and all are decidedly uneasy and/or unhappy. Desiree, a glamorous actress, is anxious to settle down and thinks former flame Frederick may be the man for her, even though he is married (however unhappily) to young Anne Egerman. Desiree's current love, Carl-Magnus Mittelheim is present with his wife, Charlotte, who hopes to win back her husband's love by flirting with Frederick even though he is the husband of her best friend, Anne. Also adding color to the proceedings are Desiree's mother, Madame Armfeldt, and a pretty maid, Petra. A game of romantic musical chairs ensues as everyone discovers who in the immediate vicinity actually is their perfect mate.

"*A Little Night Music* is a movie musical that entertains and elevates. It is one of the few stage musicals to make a successful crossing to the more literal shores of film, keeping its reputation intact and picking up additional charm en route."

—New York *Daily News* (Rex Reed)

"As a director, Hal Prince has been responsible for some of the most inventive, stylish musicals ever to grace the Broadway stage. But in directing the movie version of *A Little Night Music*, he seems to have lost not only his inspiration but his unfailing sense of style. His direction is so overwhelmingly stodgy and ploddingly old fashioned that it detracts almost completely from Stephen Sondheim's facile, wryly humorous score which, by the way, was written almost entirely in waltz tempo. *A Little Night Music* should have been as effervescent as Dom Perignon. Instead, it seems as flat as stale beer." **—New York *Daily News* (Kathleen Carroll)**

"Harold Prince's film is richly mounted with a dazzling score by Stephen Sondheim, the most important talent now working in American musical theater. Some people may be too accustomed to naturalistic movies to respond to such a stylized musical. Prince doesn't try to hide the artifice; he calls attention to it by opening with a stage performance in a Viennese theater, then shifting to more realistic settings. . . . Elizabeth Taylor gives an affecting performance as Desiree." **—*The New York Times* (Stephen Farber)**

notes

SWEDISH FILMMAKER INGMAR BERGMAN'S FROTHY 1955 ROMANTIC comedy *Smiles of a Summer Night* is one of the most light-hearted and endearing films Bergman ever made. Though not among his most acclaimed works, its undeniable charm made it a favorite among many Bergman fans. One to whom its charm was undeniable was composer Stephen Sondheim, who teamed up with playwright Hugh Wheeler to produce a musical based on *Smiles of a Summer Night*, titled *A Little Night Music*. Under the direction of Harold Prince, the play opened on Broadway at the Shubert Theatre on February 25, 1973. It played for 601 performances, during which time it won numerous accolades, including the 1973 Tony Awards for Best Musical and Best Score.

Harold Prince continued his duties as director for the big screen adaptation, bringing with him Broadway cast members Len Cariou, Hermione Gingold, and Laurence Guittard to re-create their roles. For the female lead of Desiree Armfeldt, however, Tony-nominee Glynis Johns was replaced by Elizabeth Taylor, for whom this would be her first full-scale musical film. Another change from stage to screen was moving the setting from Sweden to Austria, which resulted in alterations to some of the characters' names.

The movie, an Ernst Lubitsch–like farce filled with complicated love entanglements, was filmed in the fall of 1976 and premiered at the Deauville Film Festival a year later. It was met with mixed reaction from the press though Stephen Sondheim's score, which included the standard "Send in the Clowns," was as melodic as ever to critics. The movie won the Oscar for Best Score and earned a nomination for Best Costume Design for Florence Klotz. The Sondheim-Wheeler musical continued to inspire revivals over the years. A made-for-TV movie premiered in 1990 starring Sally Ann Howes, and a new edition of the stage production opened on Broadway on December 13, 2009, starring Catherine Zeta-Jones and Angela Lansbury. Zeta-Jones, who made her Broadway debut in the play, won the Tony for Best Actress in a Musical for her characterization of Desiree Armfeldt.

During the time Elizabeth made *A Little Night Music* she became engaged to Republican politician John Warner. They were married on December 4, 1976. Warner had served as United States Secretary of the Navy and was on the road to becoming senator for the state of Virginia, with Elizabeth helping him along the campaign at every opportunity.

OPPOSITE, CLOCKWISE FROM TOP: A cast shot, with Len Cariou, Laurence Guittard, and Diana Rigg | With John Warner, to whom she became engaged during the making of *A Little Night Music* | With Chloe Franks, who played her daughter in the film |

Return Engagement

TV Movie

N B C

CAST

Elizabeth Taylor .... *Dr. Emily Loomis*

Joseph Bottoms .... *Stewart Anderman*

Allyn Ann McLerie .... *Florence*

Peter Donat .... *George Riley*

James Ray .... *Mr. Keith*

Susan Buckner .... *Janice*

Alston Ahern .... *Audrey*

Robin Strand .... *Victor*

CREDITS

Franklin R. Levy, Mike Wise *(producers)*; Joseph Hardy *(director)*; James Prideaux *(screenplay)*; Arthur B. Rubinstein *(music)*; Martin Allen *(choreographer)*; Phillip Seretti, Georja Skinner *(sound)*; Edith Head *(costumes)*; Sydney Guilaroff *(hairstylist)*

RELEASE DATE: November 17, 1978

RUN TIME: 74 minutes, color

RIGHT: As Dr. Emily Loomis

SUMMARY: Dr. Emily Loomis is a professor of ancient history at a California college. She rents a room in her home to the recalcitrant Stewart Anderman, one of her students at the college. Stewart prefers to spend his time watching old movies. Emily is a loner herself, in stark contrast to her past as the better half of a popular dancing partnership with her former husband. When Stewart learns of her musical past, they form a kinship that makes both begin to come out of their shells. They participate together in a hit variety show at the college. Their deep affection for each other makes both student and teacher grow wiser.

notes

REVIEW

"By now, it is merely ridiculous to point out that Miss Taylor is fat—not just plump but fat. Careful costuming and lighting, with heavy shading for the left side of her face, can only provide minimum camouflage. Below her still beautiful face, the actress teeters on the edge of being matronly. Her dancing is perfunctory, her singing worse. Yet, she is marvelously appealing. There is an admirable element of sassy determination, of what used to be called gumption, in her performance. . . . *Return Engagement* is not believable for a moment, but that flaw has rarely been fatal in televisionland."

—*The New York Times* (John J. O'Connor)

ELIZABETH STARRED AS A DANCING STAR-TURNED-COLLEGE professor in this *Hallmark Hall of Fame* television movie, part of the Thanksgiving release in the twenty-eighth season of the popular series. Elizabeth personally selected her young costar, Joseph Bottoms, for his role in *Return Engagement* after seeing his performance as a resistance fighter in the TV miniseries *Holocaust*. The twenty-four-year-old actor appreciated and admired Elizabeth, telling the New York *Post*, "She's kind and generous. Some people in this business in her position wouldn't give you the time of day. She always has time for people."

Elizabeth was married to John Warner at this time. As a politician's wife she paid far less attention to her own career than she had in the past and was admittedly becoming bored and even lethargic in the process. Elizabeth later said, "Being a senator's wife is not easy. It's very lonely. I wouldn't wish it on anyone." Her weight increased, reaching 180 pounds at her heaviest, and critics could not restrain themselves from noting it at every turn, including in reviews of *Return Engagement*.

Winter Kills

TV Movie

WINTER GOLD PRODUCTIONS/ AVCO EMBASSY

CAST

Jeff Bridges .... *Nick Kegan*
John Huston .... *Pa Kegan*
Anthony Perkins .... *John Cerruti*
Eli Wallach .... *Joe Diamond*
Sterling Hayden .... *Z. K. Dawson*
Dorothy Malone .... *Emma Kegan*
Tomas Milian .... *Frank Mayo*
Belinda Bauer .... *Yvette Malone*
Ralph Meeker .... *Gameboy Baker*
Toshirô Mifune .... *Keith*
Elizabeth Taylor .... *Lola Comante*

CREDITS

Robert Sterling, Leonard J. Goldberg (*executive producers*); Fred Caruso (*producer*); William Richert (*director, screenplay*), based on novel by Richard Condon; John Starke (*associate producer*); Vilmos Zsigmond (*photography*); Maurice Jarre (*music*); Norman Newberry (*art director*); Arthur Jeph Parker (*set decorations*); Robert Boyle (*production design*); Pete Scoppa (*assistant director*); David Bretherton (*editor*); Robert De Mora (*costumes*); Kathy Blondell (*hairstylist*); Del Acevedo (*makeup*)

RELEASE DATE: May 11, 1979
RUN TIME: 97 minutes, color

SUMMARY:

United States President Tim Kegan is assassinated. Nineteen years later, new evidence concerning a conspiracy surrounding the president's murder turns up and his younger brother, Nick Kegan, is on the trail. The wild adventures that follow lead to many strange encounters with odd characters. All the while Nick attempts to steer clear of his domineering father and keep from getting sidetracked by a growing love for his brother's former mistress.

REVIEW

"*Winter Kills*, which opens today at Cinema 2 and a number of other theaters, has been advertised with the slogan 'Something funny is happening in *Winter Kills*. Take it seriously!' You don't see desperation like this every day, nor do you happen upon movies this likable, this ridiculous, or this impossible to describe. *Winter Kills* isn't exactly a comedy, but it's funny. And it isn't exactly serious, but it takes on the serious business of the Kennedy assassination. That's why other ads for the film have been comparing it to *Dr. Strangelove* and *M*A*S*H*. They don't do the trick, either. This isn't a social satire—it's more like a movie with spring fever. It doesn't make a bit of sense, but it's fast and handsome and entertaining, bursting with a crazy vitality all its own."

—The New York Times (Vincent Canby)

notes

"SPRING SEDUCES. SUMMER THRILLS. AUTUMN STUNS. Winter kills." So ran one of many advertising lines for *Winter Kills*, a black comedy about the assassination of a U.S. president, patterned after the John F. Kennedy story. It was based on a novel by Richard Condon, author of *The Manchurian Candidate* and *Prizzi's Honor*. First-time director William Richert helmed the production. The behind-the-scenes drama concerning the making of the film included running out of funding three times and Leonard J. Goldberg, one of the marijuana-dealing co-producers of the film, being gunned down by the mafia. Many members of the *Winter Kills* cast and crew participated in another film, *The American Success Company*, just to finance the first film. All the events, rivaling anything that occurs onscreen in *Winter Kills*, were profiled in a featurette called "Who Killed *Winter Kills*?" which is included in the 2003 DVD release of the movie. Elizabeth had a cameo in the nonspeaking role of Lola Comante, a woman who keeps the president in attractive female company.

LEFT: As Lola Comante

The Mirror Crack'd

EMI FILMS/G. W. FILMS/
COLUMBIA-WARNER

CAST

Angela Lansbury .... *Miss Jane Marple*

Geraldine Chaplin .... *Ella Zielinsky*

Tony Curtis .... *Martin N. Fenn*

Edward Fox .... *Inspector Craddock*

Rock Hudson .... *Jason Rudd*

Kim Novak .... *Lola Brewster*

Elizabeth Taylor .... *Marina Rudd*

Wendy Morgan .... *Cherry*

Margaret Courtenay .... *Mrs. Bantry*

Charles Gray .... *Bates*

Maureen Bennett .... *Heather Babcock*

Carolyn Pickles .... *Miss Giles*

Pierce Brosnan ..... *actor playing "Jamie"*

CREDITS

Richard Goodwin, John Brabourne *(producers)*; Guy Hamilton *(director)*; Jonathan Hales, Barry Sandler *(screenplay)*, based on novel *The Mirror Crack'd from Side to Side* by Agatha Christie; Christopher Challis *(photography)*; John Cameron *(music)*; John Roberts *(art director)*; Michael Stringer *(production design)*; Derek Cracknell *(assistant director)*; Richard Marden *(editor)*; Phyllis Dalton *(costumes)*; Helen Lennox *(hairstylist)*; Eric Allwright, Jill Carpenter *(makeup)*

RELEASE DATE: December 19, 1980

RUN TIME: 105 minutes, color

RIGHT: On the big screen for the last time with her good friend Rock Hudson **OPPOSITE:** Signing an autograph for a fan. This situation in the film was inspired by a similar incident involving actress Gene Tierney. While pregnant, Tierney contracted German measles from a fan and it was thought to have been the cause of Tierney's daughter's mental retardation.

SUMMARY: In the quiet English village of St. Mary Mead, Marina Rudd, a Hollywood movie star past her prime, attempts to make a comeback in a large-scale production, starring as Elizabeth I. Mary, Queen of Scots, is to be portrayed by Marina's rival, Lola Brewster, who also happens to be married to the film's producer, Martin Fenn. Having her husband, Jason Rudd, as the film's director should be comforting to Marina's fragile constitution, but a series of murder attempts aimed at Marina have everyone on edge. Who could be trying to kill Marina is anyone's guess, from her screen rival to a clinging fan to the assistant suspected of being in love with Jason. Enter expert sleuth Miss Marple, with the able assistance of her legman, Inspector Craddock, to unravel the mystery.

REVIEWS

"It's jolly good fun watching Taylor and Novak go at each other like flaming fruitcakes. Liz is at her very best, parodying her own career and her vulgar taste in clothes and hairdos with a comic performance that is splendidly self-effacing. When she stares into her mirror and says: 'Bags, bags, go away—come right back on Doris Day!' you almost wonder if she didn't write the script herself."

—New York *Daily News* (Rex Reed)

"Though Angela Lansbury is top-billed in the role of Christie's famed sleuth Jane Marple the central part really is Elizabeth Taylor's. Taylor comes away with her most genuinely affecting dramatic performance in years as a film star attempting a comeback. . . . Director Guy Hamilton, not usually given a chance to direct much besides actioners recently, handles the proceedings with an indulgent but able hand. Christopher Challis' glossy lighting is a suitable recapturing of the mood of the period, as is the lush score by John Cameron."   **—*Variety* ("Mac")**

"That *The Mirror Crack'd* never builds up much momentum has less to do with Guy Hamilton's direction and the performances than with the screenplay by Jonathan Hales and Barry Sandler, which promises more sophistication than it ever delivers. Both Miss Taylor and Miss Novak, as larger-than-life silver-screen rivals of a certain age, get all wound up for some fancy, high-toned tongue-lashings, but the material isn't up to their power. It's too bad because each of them has the toughness and the wit to carry it off with some splendor."

—*The New York Times*

notes

Guy Hamilton, famed director of the James Bond movie series, guided the stars in their roles as participants in a movie being made within the movie.

AGATHA CHRISTIE'S *THE MIRROR CRACK'D FROM SIDE TO SIDE* was published in 1962 but never made it to the screen as part of the popular 1960s series produced by MGM in the U.K. starring Margaret Rutherford. Forty-five-year-old Angela Lansbury was signed to portray the famous elderly sleuth Miss Marple in *The Mirror Crack'd*. It would be the actress's only turn at Miss Marple, though she later proved herself a natural for the mystery genre as Angela Fletcher in the hit series *Murder, She Wrote*.

Like previous screen adaptations of Agatha Christie novels *Murder on the Orient Express* and *Death on the Nile*, an all-star cast of suspects was corralled for *The Mirror Crack'd*, including Elizabeth Taylor, Kim Novak, Rock Hudson, and Tony Curtis. The story was set in the 1950s, so it is rather fitting that the stars involved would have attracted audiences in droves in that decade. Guy Hamilton, famed director of the James Bond movie series, guided the stars in their roles as participants in a movie being made within the movie.

The Mirror Crack'd was filmed at Twickenham Studios in Kent, England. Elizabeth loved it because it reunited her with her dear friend and *Giant* costar, Rock Hudson, in one of his last feature films. The movie performed moderately successfully both at the box office and with critics. The story would see new life in two British TV-movie remakes in years to come: in 1992 starring Joan Hickson and in 2010, with Julia McKenzie as Miss Marple.

Elizabeth sought a new challenge following her work in *The Mirror Crack'd*. After time away from work, being Mrs. John Warner and letting her famed looks go a bit, she asked herself what was the greatest challenge she could give herself and came up with an answer: Broadway. On May 7, 1981 she opened in the Lillian Hellman play *The Little Foxes* at the Martin Beck Theatre. It was a the start of a successful four-month run in the Broadway play and she earned a Tony Award nomination as Best Actress for her work. She then continued the show in Washington, D.C. and Los Angeles in 1981 and later in London's West End in 1982.

Also making headlines between *The Mirror Crack'd* and Elizabeth's next movie was the end of her seventh marriage. In December 1981, shortly after their fifth anniversary, Elizabeth's spokeswoman Chen Sam released a statement that Elizabeth and John Warner "have agreed amicably to a legal separation." A year later their divorce was finalized.

Between Friends

TV Movie

ROBERT COOPER
PRODUCTIONS/HBO

CAST

Elizabeth Taylor .... *Deborah Shapiro*

Carol Burnett .... *Mary Catherine Castelli*

Henry Ramer .... *Sam Tucker*

Bruce Grey .... *Malcolm Hallen*

Charles Shamata .... *Dr. Seth Simpson*

Lally Cadeau... *Lolly*

Barbara Bush.................................... *Francie*

Michael J. Reynolds .... *Kevin Sullivan*

Stephen Young .... *Martin*

CREDITS

Robert Cooper, Marian Rees *(executive producers)*; Lou Antonio *(director)*; Shelley List, Jonathan Estrin *(producers/teleplay)*, based on novel *Nobody Makes Me Cry* by Shelley List; François Protat *(photography)*; James Horner *(music)*; Lindsey Goddard *(art director)*; Elinor Rose Galbraith *(set decorations)*; Martin Walters *(assistant director)*; Gary Griffen *(editor)*; Judith R. Gellman *(costumes)*

RELEASE DATE: September 11, 1983

RUN TIME: 100 minutes, color

SUMMARY: Deborah Shapiro is a devoted wife and mother of two when her world is turned upside down by her husband's decision to leave her for a younger woman. The departure of her sons to college leaves Deborah alone, turning to cocktails for comfort with increasing frequency. Mary Catherine Castelli has also recently been abandoned by her husband in favor of a younger woman, but her reaction is not to wallow in loneliness but to feel desirable again in the arms of a succession of married lovers. Deborah and Mary Catherine meet after an auto accident. They commiserate, argue, laugh, and develop a deep friendship that helps each grow and find themselves again.

RIGHT: With Carol Burnett. The two actresses became great friends during filming. Describing their instant friendship Burnett said, "There are people you know for years without feeling close and then people you meet and feel you know at once."

notes

MADE-FOR-CABLE FILMS ALWAYS HAD THE EDGE ON NETWORK television movies in terms of permissible story lines and dialogue. *Between Friends* offered juicy roles to two beloved actresses at a time when the material available to Elizabeth in the way of feature films was less than stellar. Based on the novel *Nobody Makes Me Cry* by Shelley List, the movie was an HBO original production that offered an interesting and mature look at the friendship between two middle-aged divorcées.

Cast in the lead roles was a seemingly odd pairing of comedienne extraordinaire Carol Burnett and cinema goddess Elizabeth Taylor. The two actresses complemented each other beautifully in the film. Their successful coupling was a reflection of the offscreen friendship that formed between Burnett and Elizabeth, who had never met before taking off for Toronto to make the movie. Despite just getting over a bout of bronchitis, working with Burnett made filming a pleasure for Elizabeth. When it was over, Burnett said, "I don't know what there was but I spent six weeks laughing. I felt like I was eleven years old. [Elizabeth] is a very funny person." Both Elizabeth and Burnett were nominated for CableACE Awards as Best Actress for their work. Elizabeth congratulated her costar, who took home the award.

Between Friends was made in February and March 1983. Before its HBO premiere Elizabeth would be reunited with Richard Burton on Broadway in *Private Lives*, which opened on May 8, 1983. The play, described as a tale "of two highly sexed, highly combustible, and highly sophisticated people who will love each other until hell freezes over, but cannot live with each other here on earth," seemed ideal for Taylor and Burton but while it generated enormous media interest, it was a conspicuous flop. Panned by critics, the show closed in July. Elizabeth rebounded from her professional disappointment by becoming engaged to her boyfriend, Mexican lawyer Victor Gonzalez Luna, the following month.

> ## Despite just getting over a bout of bronchitis, working with Burnett made filming a pleasure for Elizabeth.

ABOVE: With Victor Luna. The photo is from a 1987 party for her perfume, Passion, but they became engaged shortly before the premiere of *Between Friends*.

REVIEWS

"Miss Burnett demonstrates once again that, in addition to being an outstanding comedienne, she is an uncommonly sensitive serious actress. And Miss Taylor has found herself one of the best roles she has had in years. . . . Given a part that would appear to be curiously close to her own earthy personality, Miss Taylor can be quite impressive. The result, while far from a dramatic masterpiece, provides a fascinating exercise in acting, a rewarding romp in the art of performance."

—*The New York Times* (John J. O'Connor)

"*Between Friends* contains some of the frankest and most brutally honest discussions of sex I've ever heard in a television screenplay. And it provides a steak dinner for its leading ladies, who attack their roles as if they hadn't had a square meal in decades."

—New York *Post* (Rex Reed)

Malice in Wonderland

TV Movie

INCORPORATED TELEVISION COMPANY/CBS

CAST

Elizabeth Taylor .... *Louella Parsons*
Jane Alexander .... *Hedda Hopper*
Richard Dysart .... *Louis B. Mayer*
Joyce Van Patten ......*Dema Harshbarger*
Jon Cypher .... *Docky Martin*
Leslie Ackerman .... *Harriet Parsons*
Bonnie Bartlett .... *Ida Koverman*
Thomas Byrd .... *William Hopper*
Eric Purcell .... *Orson Welles*
Tim Robbins .... *Joseph Cotten*
Mark L. Taylor .... *Howard Strickling*

CREDITS

Judith A. Polone (*executive producer*); Jay Benson (*producer*); Gus Trikonis (*director*); Jacqueline Feather, David Seidler (*teleplay*), based on book *Hedda and Louella* by George Eells; Philip H. Lathrop (*photography*); Charles Bernstein (*music*); John D. Jefferies Sr. (*production design*); Keith A. Wester (*sound*); Rebecca Ross, Allan Jacobs (*editors*); Nolan Miller, Mina Mittelman (*costumes*)

RELEASE DATE: May 12, 1985
RUN TIME: 120 minutes, color

RIGHT: As Louella Parsons

SUMMARY: Amid martinis and anxious glares from the Hollywood elite, Louella Parsons and Hedda Hopper recall the highlights of their infamous blood feud. In Hollywood from the late 1920s through the early 1960s, they held the spellbound attention of the movie-going public through their gossip columns and, in effect, held Hollywood at their mercy. Louella, backed by publishing tycoon William Randolph Hearst, came to power while Hedda was struggling to make it as a character actress. After Hedda transitioned to columnist, Louella fed her tidbits of news but in time her power increased to the point of matching Louella rumor for rumor. Through spats with the likes of Louis B. Mayer, Orson Welles, and their own children, no war rivaled the one between Louella and Hedda.

notes

"*Malice in Wonderland* is two hours of delicious, back-biting entertainment, nicely recapturing the heyday of Hollywood's glamorous, bigger-than-life stars and the delightful seamy underside to it all. What fun, sweeties. . . . Elizabeth Taylor has never looked lovelier. She revels in the Parsons role. . . . And Jane, you little sneak, why didn't you tell us before that you could play something other than tired, haggard, heavy, dramatic roles about the end of the world?"

—Chicago *Sun Times* (Daniel Ruth)

"*I had a score to settle with Hedda.*"

— ELIZABETH TAYLOR

ABOVE: In period costuming, Elizabeth made an extremely glamorized version of Louella Parsons. **OPPOSITE, FROM LEFT:** At the memorial service for Richard Burton in London, 1984 | On her way to the set of *Malice in Wonderland*

MALICE IN WONDERLAND WAS AN ACCOUNT INSPIRED BY THE legendary rivalry between Hollywood gossip queens Louella Parsons and Hedda Hopper that seemed to revel in its liberties on fact in the manner of biopics of the bygone studio era. Taken as entertainment rather than gospel, it was an enjoyable romp through old Hollywood with a who's who of lookalikes including actors portraying Carole Lombard, Clark Gable, Orson Welles, Joseph Cotten, Louis B. Mayer, and Jack Warner. Perhaps the two that least resembled their real-life counterparts were leading ladies Elizabeth Taylor and Jane Alexander in the roles of the far-from-glamorous Parsons and Hopper, respectively. Elizabeth said that somewhere Louella was "laughing it up and hollering that I should have played her a year ago, when I was fat and frumpy."

In their heyday both Parsons and Hopper could be vicious, not known to be overly concerned about matters of accuracy or ethics, yet they appointed themselves moral watchdogs of the private lives of stars. For an era in Hollywood their power was such that stars and studio chiefs paid homage to these doyennes of gossip in hopes of remaining in their good graces. Elizabeth told the New York *Post* she wanted to play Parsons because "I had a score to settle with Hedda. When I confided in her as a friend she blabbed the whole story in her column about my romance with Eddie Fisher." It was not from the mouth of Elizabeth but from the typewriter of Hedda Hopper that originated an oft-quoted line supposedly on the affair: "What do you expect me to do—sleep alone?"

Also known under the title *The Rumor Mill, Malice in Wonderland* was based on *Hedda and Louella*, a 1972 dual biography by George Eells. The movie did well in its timeslot, attracting 16 million viewers. Philip H. Lathrop won an Emmy for his exquisite cinematography. Nolan Miller (designing for Elizabeth) and Mina Mittelman (designing for Jane Alexander) were acknowledged with a nomination for their period costuming, and Jane Alexander received an Emmy nomination for her performance as Hedda Hopper. Elizabeth, meanwhile, earned rave reviews.

Much had happened in Elizabeth's life between the making of *Between Friends* and *Malice in Wonderland*. She entered the Betty Ford Clinic for help in overcoming alcohol and prescription drug dependency and came out in early 1984 determined to take proper care of herself. After overcoming the affects of withdrawal she began to feel and look better than she had in years, trimming a total of forty pounds off her once portly frame. Then Elizabeth was dealt a painful personal blow by the death of Richard Burton on August 5, 1984. Fiancé Victor Luna was with her when she received the news that Burton had died in Switzerland of a cerebral hemorrhage. Luna said, "I could not get her to stop crying. She was completely hysterical. When Richard died, part of Elizabeth died. . . . I had to leave her alone with her memories of Richard, the most important man in her life." It was the beginning of the end of her relationship with Luna. Out of respect for Burton's wife, Sally Hay, Elizabeth did not attend the funeral but was present at his memorial service in England. After taking time to recover from the shock of his death, Elizabeth returned to work in *Malice in Wonderland*.

> ## "When Richard died, part of Elizabeth died. . . ."
> —VICTOR LUNA

North and South

TV Movie

DAVID L. WOLPER PRODUCTIONS/ WARNER BROS./ABC

CAST

James Read .... *George Hazard*

Patrick Swayze .... *Orry Main*

Kirstie Alley .... *Virgilia Hazard*

Leslie-Anne Down .... *Madeline Fabray LaMotte*

Wendy Kilbourne .... *Constance Flynn Hazard*

Terri Garber .... *Ashton Main Huntoon*

Genie Francis .... *Brett Main*

Philip Casnoff .... *Elkanah Bent*

David Carradine .... *Justin LaMotte*

Elizabeth Taylor .... *Madam Conti*

CREDITS

David L. Wolper, Chuck McLain *(executive producers)*; Paul Freeman *(producer)*; Richard T. Heffron *(director)*; Rob Harland *(associate producer)*; Kathleen A. Shelley, Douglas Heyes, Paul F. Edwards, Patricia Green *(teleplay)*, based on book by John Jakes; Stevan Larner *(photography)*; Bill Conti *(music)*; Archie J. Bacon *(production design)*; Richard Berger *(art director)*; Charles Korian *(set decorations)*; Skip Cosper *(assistant director)*; Michael Eliot, Scott C. Eyler *(editors)*; Vicki Sánchez *(costumes)*

RELEASE DATE: November 3–10, 1985

RUN TIME: 561 minutes, color

RIGHT: As Madam Conti

SUMMARY:
Orry Main and George Hazard meet and become best friends during military training at West Point. The Mains own a South Carolina plantation, complete with slaves, while the Hazard family of Pennsylvania has come to wealth by way of manufacturing interests. For years the men and their families interact, vacation together, find love, make enemies, and establish business partnerships. All the while, tensions between the North and South mount, leading to the outbreak of Civil War and putting the two friends on opposing sides on the battlegrounds of the war.

LEFT: With director Richard T. Heffron and the ladies of her bordello **ABOVE:** Elizabeth was one of many guest stars in this epic television production.

notes

BASED ON A TRILOGY OF BEST-SELLING NOVELS BY JOHN JAKES, the first part of *North and South* debuted as a six-episode miniseries on ABC in November 1985. The epic production, which took more than two years and a reported $25 million to mount, boasted an impressive array of guest stars, including Elizabeth Taylor, Gene Kelly, Johnny Cash, Morgan Fairchild, Robert Mitchum, and Jean Simmons. Elizabeth appeared in a glitzy role as the madam of a New Orleans bordello.

North and South was enormously successful and remains on the top-ten list of highest-rated miniseries in television history. It earned an Emmy Award for costume design and six other nominations in acknowledgment of the spectacular look of the series in terms of cinematography, music, editing, sound editing, hairstyling, and makeup. *North and South, Book II*, aired in 1986 while *Heaven & Hell: North and South, Book III*, lagged behind, not reaching the small screen until 1994. Neither sequel measured up to the critical or popular triumph of the first installment.

> North and South *was enormously successful and remains on the top-ten list of highest-rated miniseries in television history.*

There Must Be a Pony

TV Movie

R. J. PRODUCTIONS/ COLUMBIA/ABC

CAST

Elizabeth Taylor ....*Marguerite Sydney*

Robert Wagner ....*Ben Nichols*

James Coco ....*Mervin Trellis*

William Windom....................*Lee Hertzig*

Edward Winter......................*David Hollis*

Ken Olin................................*Jay Savage*

Dick O'Neill.................*Chief Investigator Roy Clymer*

Chad Lowe ....*Josh Sydney*

Richard Bright ....*the detective*

Richard Minchenberg ....*Ron Miller*

CREDITS

Robert Wagner *(executive producer)*; Howard Jeffrey *(producer)*; Joseph Sargent *(director)*; Mart Crowley *(teleplay)*, based on book by James Kirkwood, Jr.; Gayne Rescher *(photography)*; Billy Goldenberg *(music)*; James J. Agazzi *(production design)*; Ross Bellah *(art director)*; Jack Harnish *(editor)*

RELEASE DATE: October 5, 1986
RUN TIME: 95 minutes, color

SUMMARY: A lifetime in the movies has not been kind to screen queen Marguerite Sydney. She is placed in a mental institution following a nervous breakdown. Upon her release, son Josh tries to rebuild their relationship, but is inhibited by her stronger-than-ever determination to make a career comeback. Handsome real estate mogul Ben Nichols comes into their lives just as Marguerite gets a break with a starring role in a TV soap opera. Ben brings stability into their lives, but before long they find that the demands on Marguerite's time, alcohol problem, and occupational hazards do not always lead to a Hollywood ending.

RIGHT: With Robert Wagner

notes

REVIEW

"[*There Must Be a Pony*] gives Elizabeth Taylor the best TV role she's had yet—and she runs with it. . . . John Sargent's direction [is] appropriate to the storyline and Taylor, who dominates her footage, responds in triumph. . . . Chad Lowe's and Taylor's scenes together are eminently credible. Lowe's interp of the complex, lonely youth trying to handle his own difficulties as well as those of his mother, is a touching success."

—*Variety* ("Tone")

LEFT: In *There Must Be a Pony* period, arriving at the Los Angeles airport with her daughter Liza and grandson Quinn Tivey

ELIZABETH'S LONGTIME FRIEND ROBERT WAGNER BOTH produced and costarred in this screen adaptation of a semiautobiographical novel by James Kirkwood, Jr., the son of silent screen stars Lila Lee and Jack Kirkwood, Sr. Kirkwood adapted his novel into a three-act play in 1962, which starred Myrna Loy and Donald Woods, which failed to make an impact in spite of a fine cast. The film version, however, was well received. Looked at as an indictment of Hollywood, it is reminiscent of both *A Star Is Born* and *Sunset Boulevard*. Many reviewers drew comparisons to Elizabeth's own life in their reviews but her character of Marguerite Sydney had little resemblance to the life of Elizabeth herself. While as extravagant as can be, as attested by many, Elizabeth was also a very down-to-earth woman in terms of her attitude and behavior toward people she encountered, whether fellow stars, crew members, or fans.

By now Elizabeth was heavily involved in her charitable work to raise awareness and funding for AIDS research, a cause which she took up in earnest when she learned her friend Rock Hudson was suffering from the disease. The actor died in 1985, the same year Elizabeth joined forces with Mathilde Krim, a researcher at New York's Memorial Sloan-Kettering Cancer Center and other leading researchers to form the American Foundation for AIDS Research (amfAR). Krim later said, "In those days, celebrities took on safe causes. To take on AIDS was a really courageous act for a celebrity, and it took her kind of star power to draw attention."

Poker Alice

TV Movie

**HARVEY MATOFSKY
ENTERTAINMENT/
NEW WORLD TELEVISION/CBS**

CAST

Elizabeth Taylor .... *Alice Moffit*

Tom Skerritt .... *Jeremy Collins*

George Hamilton .... *John Moffit*

Richard Mulligan .... *Sears*

David Wayne .... *Amos*

Susan Tyrrell .... *Mad Mary*

Pat Corley .... *McCarthy*

Paul Drake .... *Baker*

Annabella Price .... *Miss Tuttwiler*

Merrya Small .... *Baby Doe*

CREDITS

Harvey Matofsky *(executive producer)*; Renée Valente *(producer)*; Arthur Allan Seidelman *(director)*; James Lee Barrett *(teleplay)*; Hanania Baer *(photography)*; Billy Goldenberg *(music)*; Ninkey Dalton *(production design)*; John Talbert *(set decorations)*; Donald P. H. Eaton *(assistant director)*; Millie Moore *(editor)*; Nolan Miller, Ruby Manus *(costumes)*; Cheri Montesanto *(hairstylist, makeup)*

RELEASE DATE: May 22, 1987

RUN TIME: 92 minutes, color

RIGHT: As Poker Alice

SUMMARY: Alice Moffit is a Boston-bred, Bible-toting, genuine lady in the 1870s Wild West with a serious penchant for gambling. After a lucky hand at five-card stud, Alice wins a high-class gambling hall/bordello, which she runs along with her cousin, John Moffit. While keeping her ladies of the night up on their Bible verses, Alice makes nice with bounty hunter Jeremy Collins, which threatens her relationship with John, who has always served as her faithful watchdog.

notes

POKER ALICE SEEMED TO ATTEMPT TO BE PART DESTRY RIDES
Again, part *Best Little Whorehouse in Texas*, on a much smaller scale. Filmed in
Tucson, Arizona, under the direction of Arthur Allan Seidelman, Elizabeth played
the madam of a house of ill repute, for the second time in two years.

The film served as a star vehicle for Elizabeth and her boyfriend at the time,
George Hamilton. A return of former fiancé Victor Luna and a brief relationship
with (and engagement to) Dennis Stein had ended. She had just had a face lift
and seemed to bloom on the arm of Hamilton, appearing slim, taut, and tanned.
Joan Collins observed, "When she began dating my friend George Hamilton she
was somewhat overweight, no doubt from the boredom of being a senator's wife.
George immediately took her in his capable hands and put her on a strict diet and
started telling her how to dress and style her hair."

They enjoyed their time together but her celebrity was undoubtedly a trial
for Hamilton, who said at the time, "Nobody on earth is better company than
Elizabeth Taylor, more lively, more fun, or more of a three-ring circus, despite her
desperate wishes to the contrary." It was a short-lived but memorable romance in
Elizabeth's life, commemorated by *Poker Alice*.

REVIEW

"Liz is marvelous in her new TV movie.
The New, Improved, Better-Tasting
Liz looks positively radiant. . . . *Poker
Alice* is worth seeing for Liz Taylor.
She is a star. More than that, she is a
symbol, a fixture, of American culture.
She is a legend. There aren't many
stars left from the pre-TV days. She
has a glow that not even an appear-
ance on *Hotel* can dim."   **—Newsday**

Il Giovane Toscanini
(Young Toscanini)

ITALIAN INTERNATIONAL
FILM/CARTHAGO FILMS/
CANAL +

CAST

C. Thomas Howell.........*Arturo Toscanini*

Elizabeth Taylor............*Nadina Bulichoff*

Sophie Ward.................*Sister Margherita*

Pat Heywood......................*Mother Allegri*

Jean-Pierre Cassel........*Maestro Miguez*

Nicolas Chagrin..............*Maestro Miguez*

Philippe Noiret......................*Don Pedro II*

John Rhys-Davies..............*Claudio Rossi*

Leon Lissek...*Superti*

Carlo Bergonzi................................*Bertini*

CREDITS

Carlo Lastricati, Mark Lombardo *(executive producers)*; Tarak Ben Ammar, Fulvio Lucisano *(producers)*; Franco Zeffirelli *(director)*; Pippo Pisciotto *(associate producer)*; William H. Stadiem *(screenplay)*, based on an idea by Franco Zeffirelli and Ennio De Concini; Daniele Nannuzzi *(photography)*; Roman Vlad, Giuseppe Verdi *(music)*; Gabriella Borni *(choreographer)*; Andrea Crisanti *(production design)*; Andrea Crisanti, Enrico Fiorentini, Angelo Santucci *(set decorations)*; Danilo Sterbini *(sound)*; Amedeo Giomini, Jim Clark, Bryan Oates *(editors)*; Tom Rand *(costumes)*; Cheri Ruff *(Elizabeth Taylor's hairstylist)*

RELEASE DATE: October 7, 1988 (Italy)

RUN TIME: 109 minutes, color

SUMMARY: Rejected as a cellist by the selection committee at La Scala, eighteen-year-old Arturo Toscanini's passion nevertheless makes an impression on impresario Claudio Rossi, who takes Toscanini on tour with his orchestra to South America. In Brazil, Toscanini is tasked with taming shrewish opera diva Nadina Bulichoff, who lives in a lap of luxury courtesy of her lover, Brazilian Emperor Don Pedro II. While convincing Bulichoff to rehearse, preparing for opening night, and falling in love with young missionary Sister Margherita, Toscanini also takes a firm stance against slavery in Brazil. By the time the show opens he has not only inspired Bulichoff to greatness but moves her to appeal for the abolition of slavery from the stage, as "There are things more important in life than music."

RIGHT: As opera star Nadina Bulichoff

notes

THOUGH AN ENGLISH-LANGUAGE FILM, *IL GIOVANE TOSCANINI* was an Italian-French coproduction that had no theatrical distribution in the U.S., where it eventually gained visibility on television as *Young Toscanini*. The movie reunited Elizabeth with her friend and *Taming of the Shrew* director Franco Zeffirelli and starred her opposite C. Thomas Howell (then best known for a brief performance as one of the children in *E.T.*). Zeffirelli made this biopic on acclaimed musical conductor Arturo Toscanini in lavish style, costing $14 million. It was filmed in the southern Italian port city of Bari, primarily around its grand turn-of-the-century Teatro Petruzzelli.

With *Il Giovane Toscanini* and films such as *La Traviata*, *Otello*, and *Pagliacci*, Zeffirelli brought classical music to the masses. In describing the movie to the press, star C. Thomas Howell said, "it is about this kid who never quits and puts up with a lot of pressure and succeeds, kind of like *Rocky* with music." The movie premiered at the Venice Film Festival in September 1988, where it met with derision from audiences. It was not entirely the fault of the film itself but because Zeffirelli has recently fallen out of favor with the local cabal of filmmakers and performers because of his unpopular stance against Martin Scorsese's controversial film *The Last Temptation of Christ*.

Elizabeth convincingly played an opera diva making a comeback, in a movie that was something of a comeback for her as well. It was her first feature film since *The Mirror Crack'd* in 1980 and her first work following another stay at the Betty Ford Center in Rancho Mirage, California, in 1988. After notable romances with George Hamilton and Malcolm Forbes in 1988, her interest turned to a construction worker she had met at the Betty Ford Center, the man who would be her last husband, Larry Fortensky.

REVIEWS

"A pompous comic strip rendition of the first bloomings of artistic genius amid costly overdressed sets, Liz in blackface singing *Aida*, and a Mother Cabrini nursing Brazilian slaves. Excess is the order of the day in *Young Toscanini*, and the film perversely won supporters for its very kitsch."
—*Variety* ("Yung")

"Elizabeth Taylor battles through, a star despite everything. One feels more pity for C. Thomas Howell (the boy from *E.T.*) who plays Toscanini with touching earnestness. *Young Toscanini* is a milestone in the cinema of kitsch and camp." —*The Times* (London)

ABOVE: With director Franco Zeffirelli and costar C. Thomas Howell

Sweet Bird of Youth

TV Movie

ATLANTIC/
KUSHNER-LOCKE/NBC

CAST

Elizabeth Taylor ...... *Alexandra Del Lago*
Mark Harmon .... *Chance Wayne*
Valerie Perrine .... *Miss Lucy*
Kevin Geer .... *Tom Junior*
Ronnie Claire Edwards .... *Aunt Nonnie*
Cheryl Paris .... *Heavenly Finley*
Rip Torn .... *Boss Finley*
Ruta Lee .... *Sally Powers*

CREDITS

Donald Kushner, Peter Locke, Linda Yellen, Laurence Mark *(executive producers)*; Fred Whitehead *(producer)*; Nicolas Roeg *(director)*; Gavin Lambert *(teleplay)*, based on play by Tennessee Williams; Francis Kenny *(photography)*; Ralph Burns *(music)*; Buddy Epstein *(music supervisor)*; Veronica Hadfield *(production design)*; Roger L. King *(art director)*; Marthe Pineau *(set decorations)*; Donald P. H. Eaton *(assistant director)*; Pamela Malouf-Cundy *(editor)*; Del Adey-Jones *(costumes)*

RELEASE DATE: October 1, 1989
RUN TIME: 95 minutes, color

SUMMARY: Movie star Alexandra Del Lago has fallen from glory into a despair of drug and alcohol dependency. After her latest film flops, she retreats to Palm Beach, where she meets the opportunistic Chance Wayne, who hopes to use Alexandra to suit his own ambitions of fame and fortune. They are intimately involved by the time they reach his hometown, where Chance is persona non grata because after he left town, his childhood sweetheart, Heavenly, was forced to abort his child and then required a hysterectomy. As Chance seeks to reunite with Heavenly and continues to take all he can get from Alexandra, Heavenly's brother and father are determined to run Chance out of town . . . or worse.

RIGHT: With Mark Harmon

notes

TENNESSEE WILLIAMS'S *SWEET BIRD OF YOUTH* WAS ONE
of the playwright's greatest triumphs in the 1950s. It was a hit in every form,
first appearing on Broadway in 1959, where it played at the Martin Beck Theatre
for a run of 375 performances starring Paul Newman, Geraldine Page, and Rip
Torn, who re-created their original roles in the acclaimed 1962 screen adaptation. An equally successful Broadway revival was mounted in 1975 starring
Christopher Walken and Irene Worth.

The 1989 made-for-television version of *Sweet Bird of Youth* from British
director Nicolas Roeg met with considerably less enthusiasm than past adaptations. It was a promising return to Tennessee Williams for Elizabeth, though she
might have fared better if the teleplay had remained truer to Williams. Her costar
was Mark Harmon, *People* magazine's Sexiest Man Alive in 1986 and a respected
actor as well. A member of the original stage and screen productions, Rip Torn
made a return, though now playing Boss Finley instead of Tom Junior. Elizabeth's
favorite cast member, however, was her son, Michael Wilding, Jr., who played the
small role of a film producer. When he told his mother that he had landed the part,
Michael said, "She was delighted. She thought it was a hoot."

Playing an aging star involved with a much younger man, critics could not
help but draw comparisons to Elizabeth's own life. She had recently met Larry
Fortensky, a man twenty years her junior, during a stay at the Betty Ford Center
and they would be married on October 6, 1991, amid a media circus hovering
above the storied setting for the wedding ceremony: Neverland Ranch, the home
of Elizabeth's good friend Michael Jackson.

LEFT: Alexandra Del Lago tries to hang on to
her beauty in *Sweet Bird of Youth.*

The Flintstones

UNIVERSAL PICTURES/ AMBLIN/HANNA-BARBERA

CAST

John Goodman .... *Fred Flintstone*
Elizabeth Perkins .... *Wilma Flintstone*
Rick Moranis .... *Barney Rubble*
Rosie O'Donnell .... *Betty Rubble*
Kyle MacLachlan .... *Cliff Vandercave*
Halle Berry .... *Sharon Stone*
Elizabeth Taylor .... *Pearl Slaghoople*
Dann Florek .... *Mr. Slate*
Richard Moll .... *Hoagie*
Irwin Keyes .... *Joe Rockhead*

CREDITS

Steven Spielberg, Joseph Barbera, William Hanna (*executive producers*); Bruce Cohen (*producer*); Brian Levant (*director*); Tom S. Parker, Steven E. de Souza, Jim Jennewein (*screenplay*); Dean Cundey (*photography*); David Newman (*music*); William Sandell (*production design*); Christopher Burian-Mohr, Nancy Patton, William James Teegarden (*art directors*); Rosemary Brandenburg (*set decorations*); Kent Beyda (*editor*); Rosanna Norton (*costumes*)

RELEASE DATE: May 27, 1994
RUN TIME: 91 minutes, color

ABOVE: As a Stone Age mother-in-law, with John Goodman and Elizabeth Perkins

SUMMARY:

Fred, Wilma, Pebbles, and Dino, make up the "modern stone-age family," with best friends Barney and Betty Rubble in on all of their adventures. Fred loans Barney money so that he and Betty can adopt a baby boy, Bamm-Bamm. To repay his friend, Barney switches their results on an intelligence exam they are given at work to prevent Fred from failing. As a result, Barney finds himself out of a job while Fred is moved from digging in the quarry to an executive berth at Slate & Company. Unbeknownst to Fred, his boss, Cliff Vandercave and sexy secretary Sharon Stone are in cahoots to implicate Fred in an embezzlement scheme to benefit Vandercave. But all ends well for Fred and company in Bedrock.

REVIEWS

"If you're looking for a yabba-dabba-doo time, it's possible to get it from *The Flintstones*—but it helps to be under 12 or a die-hard fan of the early '60s TV series. Otherwise, you will have to be content with the numerous visual distractions that are both the movie's chief asset and liability."
—**New York** *Daily News* (Jami Bernard)

"With all manner of friendly beasts, a super energetic John Goodman and a colorful supporting cast inhabiting a Bedrock that resembles a Stone Age version of Steven Spielberg suburbia, this live-action translation of the perennial cartoon favorite is a fine popcorn picture for the small fry, and perfectly inoffensive for adults. . . . Given that it requires her almost exclusively to complain about Fred, the mother role brings out Taylor's coarse side, although she looks beauteous."
—*Variety* (Todd McCarthy)

"All the characters remain faithful to the '60s series, right down to their voices, costumes and roles in life. As Fred's neighbor, best friend and co-worker at the quarry, Rick Moranis has that Barney Rubble smirk and second-banana attitude. Elizabeth Perkins as Wilma and Rosie O'Donnell as Betty are stay-at-home wives and mothers, and the actresses even have the characters' unmistakable giggles down cold. Elizabeth Taylor offers a refreshing contemporary touch as Wilma's social-climbing mother, Pearl Slaghoople. Miss Taylor looks as if she has just stepped out of one of her own perfume ads. In the middle of so much déjà vu, she works effectively against the grain, although she plays the classic complaining sitcom mother-in-law. 'You could have married Eliot Firestone,' she snaps at Wilma, 'the man who invented the wheel.'"
—*The New York Times* (Caryn James)

notes

THE FLINTSTONES MOVIE, BASED ON THE BELOVED ANIMATED
series of the 1960s, was a pet project of filmmaker Steven Spielberg for years.
The production, directed by Brian Levant, mixed live action with computer ani-
mation and was a box-office smash. For the leg-
endary role of Fred Flintstone, Spielberg looked
no further than John Goodman, and in the other
lead roles cast Elizabeth Perkins, Rick Moranis,
and Rosie O'Donnell, who nailed the spirit of
their animated counterparts.

Elizabeth, who had not made a movie for five
years, said she participated as Wilma Flintstone's
nagging stepmother in the family-friendly picture for her grandchildren. She was
also coaxed back to acting duties by a guarantee that the film's U.S. premiere
would be a benefit for her eponymous AIDS foundation that she founded in 1991.
That year Elizabeth also launched her first, hugely successful perfume, White
Diamonds. As an inside joke, when she is seated at a makeup table in the movie,
a stone bottle engraved "White Diamonds" is visible.

Director Brian Levant found her a pleasure to work with: "She was such
a pro. She considered herself a working actress. There was no star behavior.
[Actors like her] who literally grew up on studio lots can just walk in and they
own the place. She did her own makeup. The crew was just enraptured. The
first day everyone wore a tie." Elizabeth put everyone at ease by kidding with
them. One day during shooting Levant accidentally stepped on her foot. She
later came to the set on crutches. As Levant apologized profusely Elizabeth
giggled. It was a joke. She made sure everyone knew that "ET" or "Elizabeth,"
as she asked them to call her (not "Liz" or "Miss Taylor"), was not an untouch-
able movie goddess but one of them—even if the friends she brought to the set
included Michael Jackson.

> *"She was such a pro. She considered
> herself a working actress. There was
> no star behavior."*
> —BRIAN LEVANT

ABOVE: Though it was unexpected for Elizabeth to turn up in *The Flinstones*, she was as
glamorous as ever.

These Old Broads

TV Movie

COLUMBIA TRISTAR/ABC

CAST

Shirley MacLaine......... *Kate Westbourne*

Debbie Reynolds................ *Piper Grayson*

Joan Collins .... *Addie Holden*

Elizabeth Taylor .... *Beryl Mason*

Jonathan Silverman .... *Wesley Westbourne*

Nestor Carbonell................................ *Gavin*

Peter Graves... *Bill*

Carlos Jacott .... *Tom*

Pat Crawford Brown .... *Miriam Hodges*

Suzanne Carney .... *Connie*

CREDITS

Carrie Fisher, Elaine Pope, Laurence Mark *(executive producers)*; Lewis Abel *(producer)*; Matthew Diamond *(director)*; Carrie Fisher, Elaine Pope *(screenplay)*; Eric Van Haren Noman *(photography)*; Steve Tyrell, Guy Moon *(music)*; Alfred Sole *(production design)*; Jack D. L. Ballance *(art director)*; Don Diers *(set decorations)*; Casey O. Rohrs *(editor)*; Richard P. Schroer *(assistant director)*; Nolan Miller *(costumes)*; José Eber *(Elizabeth Taylor's hairstylist)*; Christina Smith *(makeup)*

RELEASE DATE: February 12, 2001

RUN TIME: 89 minutes, color

ABOVE: In good company in her last movie, with Debbie Reynolds, Shirley MacLaine, and Joan Collins

SUMMARY: Kate Westbourne, Piper Grayson, and Addie Holden were once the queens of Hollywood, and are presently enjoying a revival, thanks to the success of the re-release of a film they made together thirty years prior. Gavin, a TV executive is determined to produce a television special starring the three women, but it is no easy task bringing their larger-than-life tempers and egos together. Trying to talk "these old broads" into doing the show is Kate's estranged son, Wesley, with able assistance from their dizzy, high-powered agent, Beryl Mason. The three aging divas agree, but before the show reaches screens they rehash past feuds, argue over billing, fight over men, exhaust their creaking joints, and threaten to quit at every turn. Still, the show must go on!

REVIEWS

"There are plenty of zings and zippy one-liners, the stars' ability to make fun of just about everything they've gone through in life is a hoot. (Reynolds and Taylor's husband-stealing conversation will make Eddie Fisher very proud.) . . . All four thesps are game for anything, so there's no shortage of wig-pulling knockdowns or bitchy standoffs."

—*Variety* (Michael Speier)

"Don't watch *These Old Broads* expecting sense or modern sensibility. You'll only be disappointed. Watch for the sheer outrageousness of everything—their plots, the women, their cattiness, their sex obsession. . . . Amid the ribald repartee there's slapstick and there's sentiment. Reynolds is amazing with the body language. MacLaine acts up a storm in acting up, and *Dynasty* diva Joan Collins looks fabulous. Taylor shows up a few times, briefly—which is all we require, isn't it?"

—*Newsday* (Diane Werts)

notes

THE GENESIS OF *THESE OLD BROADS* WAS A CONVERSATION about how there were no good roles in movies for older women between Elizabeth, Lauren Bacall, Shirley MacLaine, Debbie Reynolds, and Reynolds's celebrated actress-screenwriter daughter, Carrie Fisher. Fisher got to work on a screenplay for them with writing partner Elaine Pope, but they could not interest any major studio in financing a theatrical release in spite of a stellar cast that included Elizabeth and Reynolds of the unforgettable Liz-Eddie-Debbie Scandal. According to Fisher, "All the studios said no even though they've made films with older men." (*Space Cowboys* being a recent hit for Warner Bros.) So she took her script and her leading ladies to television.

ABOVE: Elizabeth holds a bottle of Passion, one among her successful line of perfumes.

> "*All the studios said no even though they've made films with older men.*"
>
> —CARRIE FISHER

Lauren Bacall was unavailable at the time of filming and was replaced by Joan Collins. Elizabeth agreed to do it as a favor to Fisher. Reynolds said, "Liz has health problems and was in a lot of pain, but she was a great sport. She said, 'I'm doing this for you and Carrie, who I love as my own child. I did not do right by you in real life, so I'm doing this for you now.'" An appreciative Fisher promised Elizabeth that all of her scenes would be staged sitting in bed or in a chair.

The women all had a ball making *These Old Broads*, which ceaselessly poked fun at their well-known real lives. Each of the stars encouraged Fisher to put more of their own stories into the script for laughs. MacLaine, a well-known believer in reincarnation, asked her to play up the bits about her past lives. Elizabeth and Reynolds had long since patched up their friendship and Elizabeth insisted on going all the way in a scene in which their characters discuss how she had stolen Reynold's husband decades ago. Reynolds recalled, "Liz told Carrie to write that scene because she said I deserved to have that after all these years. She kept saying, 'Have her really tell me off and make it meaner—it's not funny enough.'"

Surrounded by close friends, Elizabeth enjoyed making *These Old Broads*, but it would be her final film. There was by no means any letup in terms of her work in the ten years that followed before her death, at age seventy-nine, on March 23, 2011. A best-selling line of fragrances, including White Diamonds, Passion, Black Pearls, and Violet Eyes would be her biggest money-making venture. The House of Taylor, a jewelry line and culmination of a lifetime passion for precious gems, was launched in 2007. Most of all, though, Elizabeth devoted her time, money, fame, and all the energy her increasingly weakening body could muster to the cause closest to her heart: AIDS. Elizabeth truly wanted to make a difference and "change the course of the disease," beyond just lending her name. Already heavily involved in the cause as a founding member of amfAR, Elizabeth went further by founding the Elizabeth Taylor AIDS Foundation. Over the years her work raised an estimated half billion dollars for research. As in all areas of her life, whatever Elizabeth did, she did it big.

> *The women all had a ball making* These Old Broads, *which ceaselessly poked fun at their well-known real lives.*

ABOVE FROM LEFT: At the GLAAD Media Awards in 2000 with Carrie Fisher, the co-producer of *These Old Broads* | At a 1991 event in which she auctioned off jewelry with proceeds going to amfAR. It was a benefit for one of the great passions of Elizabeth's life.

acknowledgments

THIS BOOK CAME TOGETHER THROUGH THE ASSISTANCE AND support of many. First, as always, my mother and father, who encouraged my every writing endeavor from day one. Joseph Cruz: You were a real partner in this book. Thank you for your trust in me and your expertise. Your vast collection of Elizabeth Taylor photos made this book. Thanks to Lou Valentino for introducing us and for his own contribution to the imagery.

At Running Press: Chris Navratil, our Publisher—how lucky I am that you love classic Hollywood too. Greg Jones, I would never be in the happy position I am without you. My editor, Jennifer Kasius, thank you for your invaluable guidance. The design expertise of Susan Van Horn made this a beautiful tribute. Stacy Schuck oversaw the book from the production end.

Others whose love, friendship, patience, and support help me in a myriad of ways: For starters my "sisters" who inspired the dedication to this book include Jenny, Marissa, Jordana, Cara, Betsy, Melissa G., Melissa R., Danielle, Naomi, Gavy, Beata, Karen, and Darina. Trisha, Manny, Jess, my amazing siblings. My dear Frankie, your handiwork gave this book a stunning cover and your talent is inspiring. Markus and Indrani, thank you for the endless motivation in the past year to go above and beyond. I also find inspiration from my grandmothers, little Tristan and Michael, and the newest addition to my family: Ava.

This book would not be possible without the comprehensive archives and knowledgeable staffs of the Academy of Motion Picture Arts and Sciences, the New York Public Library, the American Film Institute, the UCLA Arts Library, the USC Cinematic Arts Library, and the Free Library of Philadelphia.

And to Elizabeth: Writing about a legend can be intimidating, but delving into such a rich, full, and purposeful life inspired me from start to finish, and always will.

index

Heyes, Herbert, 75

Heyman, John, 220

Heywood, Pat, 282

Hickman, Darryl, *39*

Hickson, Joan, 270

Hill, Arthur, 189

Hilton, Nicky, 12, 13, *85*, 87, 88, 93, 97

Hird, Thora, 68

Hitchcock, Alfred, 33, 47, 102

Hold High the Torch, 44

Holden, Fay, 72

Holmes, Phillips, 78

Holmes, Taylor, 82

Holocaust, 266

Hopalong Cassidy, 94

Hopkins, Anthony, 262

Hopper, Dennis, 124, 130

Hopper, Hedda, 274, 275

Hordern, Michael, 192, 226

How Green Was My Valley, 30

Howell, C. Thomas, 282, 283

Howell, George, 218

Howes, Sally Ann, 264

HUAC, 97

Hudson, Rock, 10, 124, *125*, *127*, *128*, 129–131, 268, 270, 279

Hunter, Tab, 216

Hussein, Waris, 240

Huston, John, 17, 202, 204, 267

Hutchinson, Josephine, 95

Hutton, Brian G., 230, 232, 242, 245

Hyde-White, Wilfred, 68

I

I Remember Mama, 81

I Want to Live!, 145

Identikit (The Driver's Seat), 10, 253–256

Il Giovane Toscanini (Young Toscanini), 282–283

In Which We Serve, 102

Indiscreet, 74

Indrisano, Johnny, 94

Inescort, Frieda, 75, *76*

International Hotel, 172

Irish, Tom, 89

Ivan, Rosalind, 111

Ivanhoe, 13, 98, 99–102, 105

Ives, Burl, 139, *140*, 142

J

Jackson, Michael, 9, 21, 285, 287

Jacott, Carlos, 288

Jak, Lisa, 236

Jakes, John, 277

Jameson, Pauline, 242

Jane Eyre, 32–33, 122

Jarman, Claude, Jr., *53*

Jarrott, Charles, 226

Jenkins, Jackie, 36, *37*

John and Mary, 222

Johns, Glynis, 234, 264

Johns, Shirley, *45*

Johnson, Michael, 226

Johnson, Van, 34, 72, 74, 120, 123

Jolson, Al, 97

Jolson Story, The, 97

Jones, James Earl, 22, 206, 209

Jones, Jennifer, 64

Jourdan, Louis, 170, 173

Judd, Ashley, 145

Julia Misbehaves, 58–61

K

Kanin, Fay, 109

Kanin, Michael, 109

Karl, Harry, 178

Kasznar, Kurt, 120

Kaufman, Millard, 136

Kazan, Elia, 142

Keel, Howard, 94

Keith, Brian, 202, *204*

Kelly, Dan, 28

Kelly, Gene, *66*, 97, 252, 277

Kelly, Grace, 129, 255

Kennedy, Douglas, 94

Kennedy, Edgar, 26

Kennedy, John F., 267

Kensit, Patsy, 257

Kerr, Deborah, 88, 102

Keyes, Irwin, 286

Kibbee, Guy, 26

Kilbourne, Wendy, 276

Killing of Sister George, The, 232

King Solomon's Mines, 113

Kirkwood, Jack, 279

Kirkwood, James, Jr., 279

Kiss Me Kate, 195

Klansman, The, 228

Klotz, Florence, 264

Knight, Eric, 30

Kohlmar, Fred, 225

Krasna, Norman, 72, 74

Krim, Mathilde, 279

L

La Traviata, 283

Ladd, Alan, 129

Lady in Waiting, 60

Laffan, Patricia, 88

Lamarr, Hedy, 31

Lamas, Fernando, 103, 105, 106

Lancaster, Burt, 262

Lanchester, Elsa, 29

Landau, Martin, 160

Landor, Rosalyn, 240

Lang, Robert, 242

Lange, Jessica, 145

Lansbury, Angela, 36, 264, 268, 270

Larkin, Mary, 230

Lassie Come Home, 29–31

Last Temptation of Christ, The, 283

Last Time I Saw Paris, The, 120–123

Lathrop, Philip H., 275

Lawford, Peter, 34, 35, 57, 58, 59, 61, 62, 66, 100, 252, 256

Lawrence of Arabia, 173

Lee, Lila, 279

Lee, Ruta, 284

Lehman, Ernest, 189, 191

Leigh, Janet, 62, 64, 65

Leigh, Vivien, 112, 166, 173

Leighton, Margaret, 230, 232, 233

Leonard, Robert Z., 49, 50, 52

LeRoy, Mervyn, 62, 66, 88

Levant, Brian, 286, 287

Levine, James, 22

Lewis, Edward, 259

Lewis, Jarma, 132

Lewis, Mitchell, 42

Life with Father, 46–48, 50

Lindsay, Howard, 47

Lissek, Leon, 282

List, Shelley, 271

Little Caesar, 227

Little Foxes, The, 19, 270

Little Night Music, A, 263–265

Little Princess, The, 27

Little Women, 62–67

"Lochinvar," 101

Lockhart, Gene, 49, 72

Lockhart, June, 35

Lockridge, Ross, Jr., 136

L'oiseau Blue, 259

Lombard, Carole, 274

Lookinland, Todd, 257

Loren, Sophia, 195, 256

Lorre, Peter, 154

Losey, Joseph, 212, 214, 215, 216, 218, 220

Lost Weekend, The, 74

Louis, Jean, 153

Love Is Better Than Ever, 95–98

Lovsky, Celia, 107, 120

Lowe, Chad, 278

Loy, Myrna, 279

Lubitsch, Ernst, 264

Lucas, Alex, 238

Lukas, Paul, 154

Luna, Victor Gonzalez, 20, 272, 275, 281

Lunt, Alfred, 195

Lupino, Richard, 107

Lydon, Jimmy, 46, 47, 49, 50, 61

Lynch, Alfred, 192

Lynn, Jeffrey, 155

M

Macbeth, 195

MacDonald, Jeanette, 56

MacDonald, Richard, 217

MacKay, Angus, 218

MacLachlan, Kyle, 286

MacLaine, Shirley, 225, 260, 288, 289, 290

MacMurray, Fred, 94

Maeterlinck, Maurice, 259

Magnificent Ambersons, The, 33

Mailfort, Maxence, 253, 254

Malice in Wonderland (TV), 273–275

Malone, Dorothy, 267

Mamoulian, Rouben, 166, 251

"Man Bring This Up the Road!," 216

Man or Mouse, 28

Manchurian Candidate, The, 267

Mandel, Johnny, 183

Mankiewicz, Joseph L., 137, 146, 150, 151, 160, 164, 166, 167, 168, 169, 251

Mann, Daniel, 155, 158

Mannari, Guido, 253

Mansfield, Jayne, 9

Mansfield, Richard, 118

Marecek, Heinz, 263

Marlowe, Christopher, 199, 201

Marmont, Patricia, 146

Marshal, Alan, 34

Marter, Ian, 198

Martinelli, Elsa, 170, 256

Marvin, Lee, 132, 136, 204

Marx, Sam, 30

Masalila, Abrose, 18

Masé, Marino, 253

Mason, Morgan, 176, 179

Mastroianni, Marcello, 195

Mather, Aubrey, 32

Maurice Guest, 109

Mayer, Louis B., 12, 35, 40–41, 56, 85, 110, 274

McCambridge, Mercedes, 124, 128, 131, 146

McCann, Doreen, 95

McCullers, Carson, 204

McDowall, Roddy, 12, 29–31, 34–35, 55, 57, 66, 160, 164

McGuire, Dorothy, 94

McIntosh, David, 198

McKenzie, Julia, 270

McKern, Leo, 154

McLeod, Catherine Frances, 42

McLerie, Allyn Ann, 266

McWhorter, Richard, 199

Medford, Kay, 155

Meeker, Ralph, 267

Meet Me in St. Louis, 48

Mele, Dino, 246

Melvazzi, Gino, 230

Merchant, Vivien, 234

Merrill, Dina, 155, 158

Mifune, Toshirô, 267

Milian, Tomas, 267

Milk Train Doesn't Stop Here Anymore, The, 216

Miller, Alice Duer, 35

Miller, Deborah, 139